AF822001

ABOUT THIS PLAYBOOK

The *Canva Coach Playbook* is your go-to visual guide for mastering popular tasks in Canva®. With clear, step-by-step instructions, you can follow along effortlessly and start creating with confidence.

This comprehensive playbook covers everything you need to know about using Canva on desktop (Mac and Windows) and phones/small tablets (iPad and Android), making it easy to design wherever you go. You can also follow along if you are using the Canva app from your standard-sized Android or Apple tablet (more on that on page 80).

If you have any questions about using the playbook, please email me at hello@jennifermaker.com.

For more Canva ideas and inspiration, join me at jennifermaker.com.

Happy making,

Jennifer

Key to Playbook Pages:

- Desktop pages are outlined in purple
- Mobile pages are outlined in blue
- Steps are in blue
- Tips are in yellow
- Notes are in purple
- Warnings are in pink

PLAYBOOK PAGES

WHAT EXACTLY IS CANVA?

Creativity thrives when given the right tools, and Canva is one of the most accessible and versatile design platforms available. Whether you're new to digital design or looking for a simple way to bring your ideas to life, Canva provides an intuitive and user-friendly experience that makes designing truly effortless and enjoyable.

Unlike traditional design software, Canva requires no formal training—just a willingness to explore and create. Its drag-and-drop interface allows users to design everything from custom craft labels and project templates to printable designs, business cards, and even videos. If you can move elements around on a screen, you can design with Canva.

Another advantage of Canva is its seamless cross-device functionality. You can start a project on your computer, refine it on a tablet, and review the final details on your phone, making it easy to work anytime, anywhere.

Whether you're crafting for fun, designing a special project, or creating something personal, Canva simplifies the process and enhances the experience.

In the following pages, we'll explore how to make the most of this powerful tool and unlock your creative potential.

WHAT CAN YOU DO WITH CANVA?

If you're wondering what you can create with Canva, the possibilities are endless. Whether you're designing for yourself, your family, your business, or your community, this versatile tool makes it easier than ever to bring your ideas to life. Think of Canva as your personal design assistant—always ready to help you create with ease and confidence.

Here are just a few ways you can use it:

- **Personalized Gifts and Keepsakes:** Design custom cards, calendars, or scrapbook pages with a unique, handmade touch.
- **Craft Materials:** Create labels, tags, and packaging to give your handmade products a polished look.
- **Project Templates:** From printable patterns to reusable templates, Canva can help streamline your creative process.
- **Business and Marketing Materials:** Easily put together business cards, social media posts, and promotional designs tailored to your brand.

Canva also makes collaboration simple, whether you're planning a group project, organizing a craft fair, or working on a shared design. Instead of juggling multiple files and messages, everything stays in one place, making teamwork more seamless.

As your projects and needs evolve, Canva can adapt along with them, offering a flexible way to design and create.

CANVA FREE VS. PRO

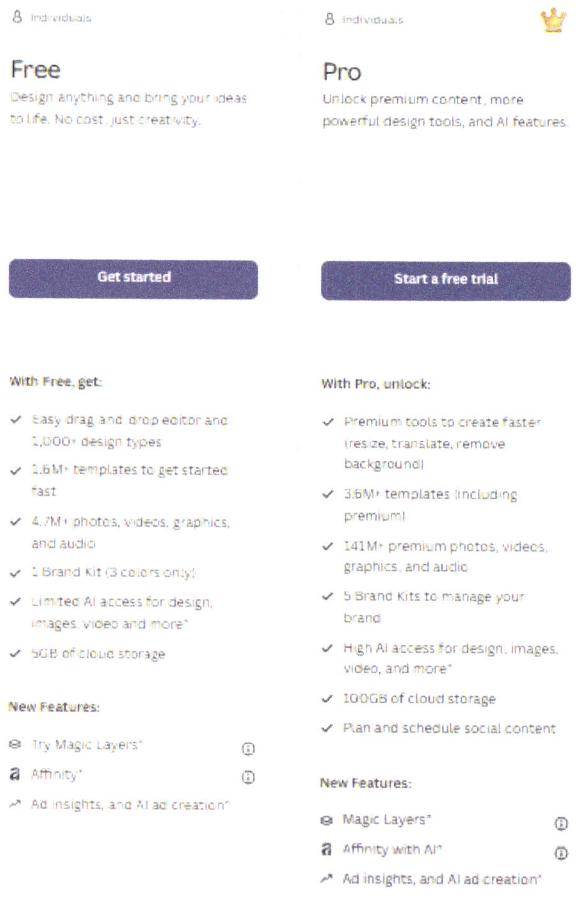
Individuals
Free
Design anything and bring your ideas to life. No cost, just creativity.
Get started
With Free, get:
Easy drag and drop editor and 1,000+ design types
1.6M+ templates to get started fast
4.7M+ photos, videos, graphics, and audio
1 Brand Kit (3 colors only)
Limited AI access for design, images, video and more*
5GB of cloud storage
New Features:
Try Magic Layers*
Affinity*
Ad insights, and AI ad creation*
Individuals
Pro
Unlock premium content, more powerful design tools, and AI features.
Start a free trial
With Pro, unlock:
Premium tools to create faster (resize, translate, remove background)
3.6M+ templates (including premium)
141M+ premium photos, videos, graphics, and audio
5 Brand Kits to manage your brand
High AI access for design, images, video, and more*
100GB of cloud storage
Plan and schedule social content
New Features:
Magic Layers*
Affinity with AI*
Ad insights, and AI ad creation*

A common question that comes up is whether to use Canva Free or Canva Pro. Both versions offer plenty of useful tools, and the best choice depends on how you plan to use Canva.

Canva Free is a great starting point, providing access to a large selection of templates, fonts, and design tools. **It's well-suited for personal projects, occasional crafting, or basic designs.** You can create and download designs in formats like PNG, JPG, and PDF, making it a solid option for everyday use without any cost.

Canva Pro offers additional features that may be useful if you're using Canva **more frequently or for professional purposes.**

Some of these include:

- A larger selection of premium templates, stock photos, and videos.
- The ability to save designs with transparent backgrounds.
- Advanced tools like animated graphics, social media scheduling, and expanded storage.
- Collaboration features that make it easier to share and edit designs with others.

Ultimately, whether you stick with the free version or upgrade, **the key is finding what works best for your needs.** Both options provide useful design tools that can help bring your ideas to life.

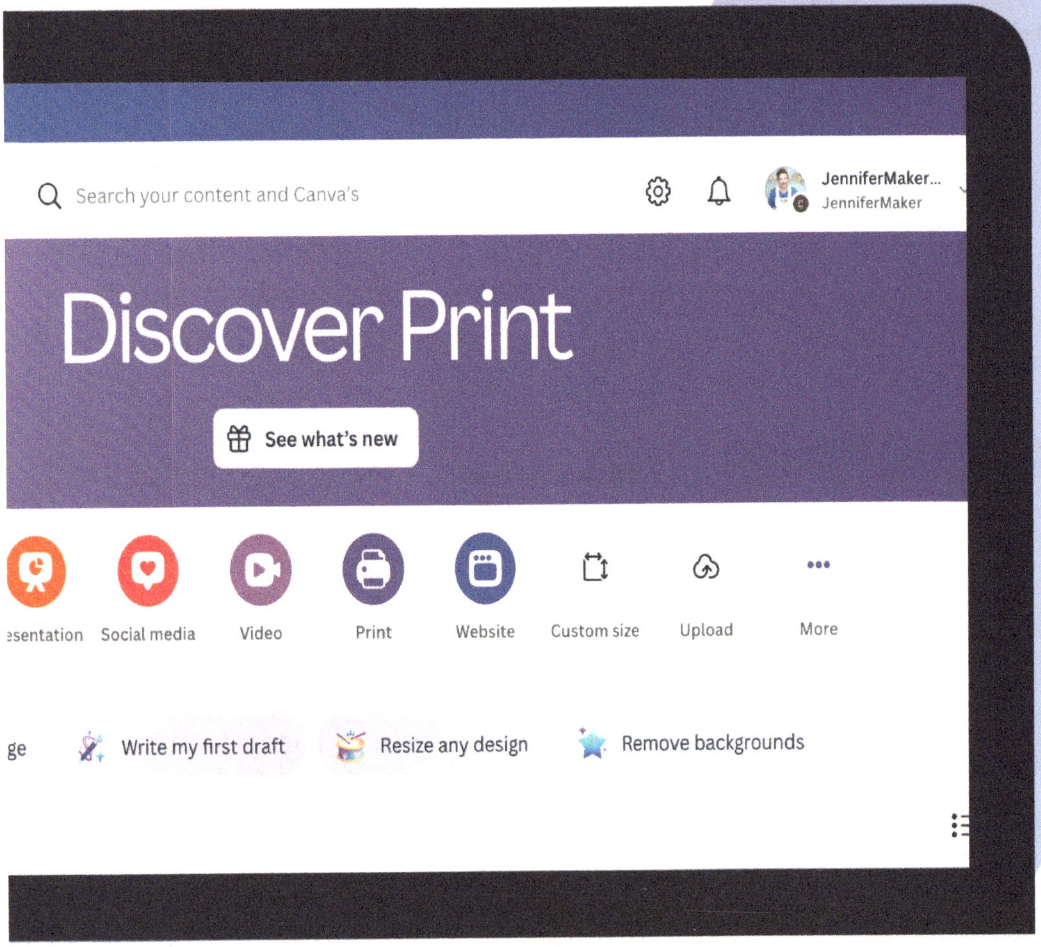

HOW TO:

DESKTOP: GETTING STARTED WITH CANVA

- ✔ OPEN CANVA IN A BROWSER
- ✔ INSTALL AND OPEN THE CANVA APP ON MAC
- ✔ INSTALL AND OPEN THE CANVA APP ON WINDOWS
- ✔ FIND WHAT YOU NEED ON THE HOMEPAGE

DESKTOP

HOW TO OPEN CANVA IN A WEB BROWSER

You can use Canva right in your web browser, making it easy and fast to get started anytime. Here's how to navigate to the Canva website.

Step 1: Open your web browser. Type **Canva.com** into the address bar and press the **Enter/Return key** on your keyboard to navigate to the website.

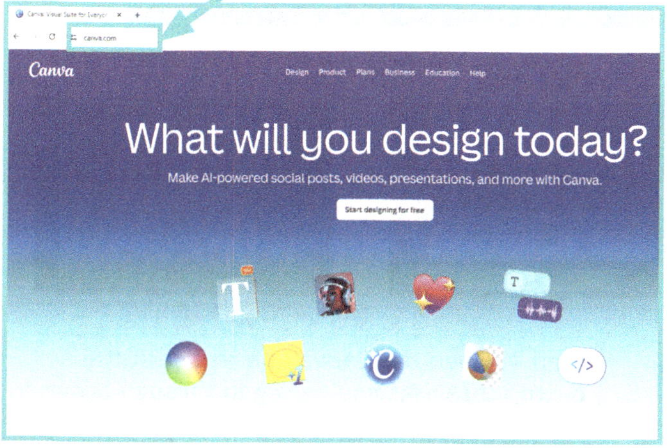

Step 2: Click either the **Log in** or **Sign up** button in the top right corner of the screen.

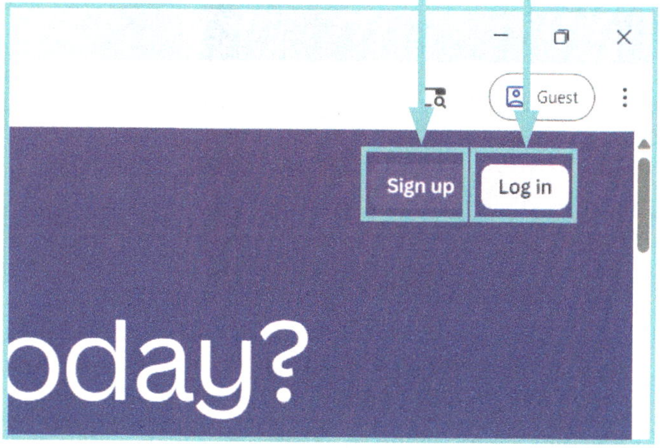

Step 3: Follow the steps in the pop-up screen to create a new account or log into your existing Canva account.

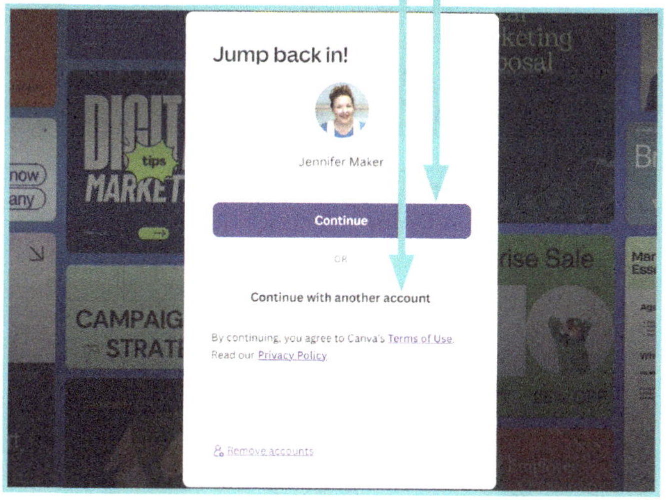

Step 4: Once you are logged in, your profile photo (if you have one) or default profile image will appear in the bottom left corner of the screen.

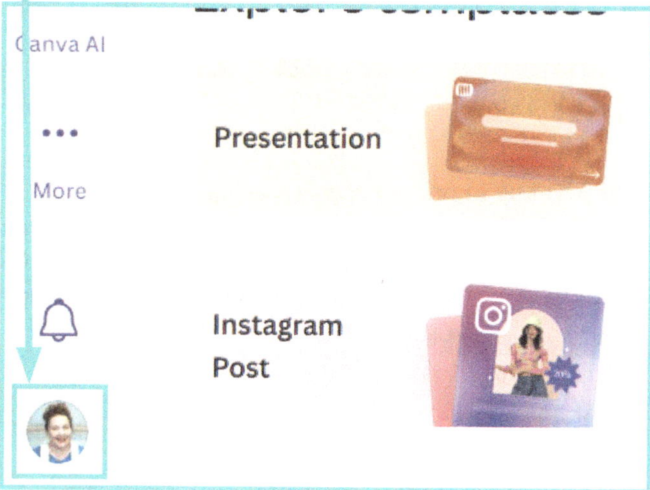

HOW TO INSTALL AND OPEN THE CANVA APP ON MAC

You can use Canva in your web browser, but you can also download the desktop app on a computer. Follow these steps to install the Canva app on your Mac:

Step 1: Search for the App Store in your Finder.

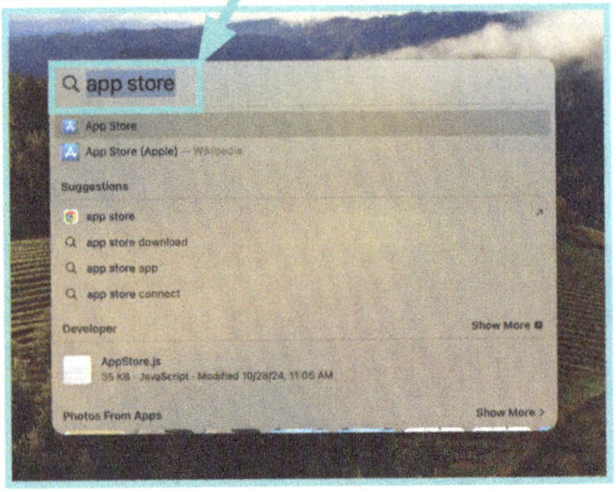

Step 2: Search for Canva in the App Store and click the **Get** button to start downloading the app.

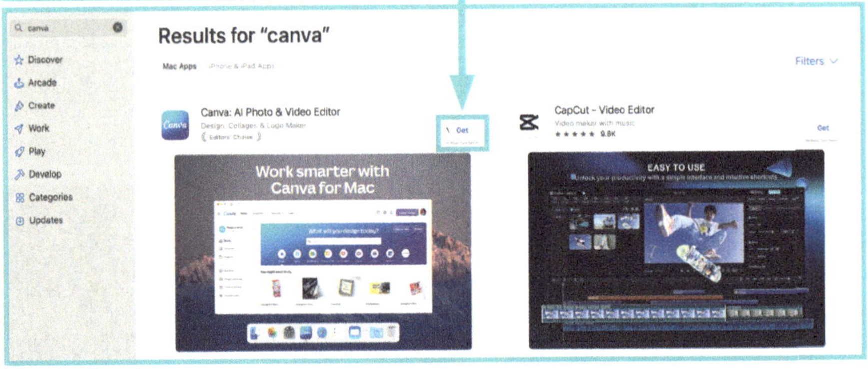

Step 3: Once the download is finished, you will find the Canva app in your Applications tab in your Finder.

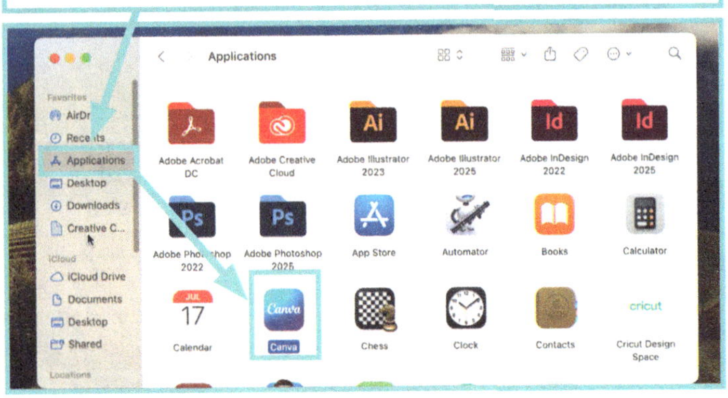

Step 4: Open the Canva app and click the button that asks you to **Log in through browser.**

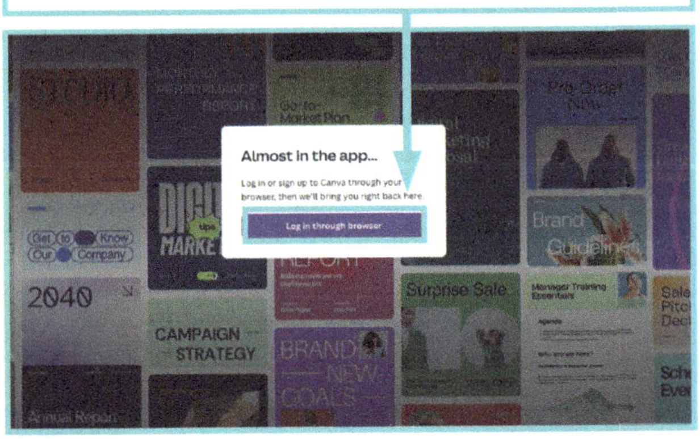

Step 5: Log in or sign up using any of the methods listed.

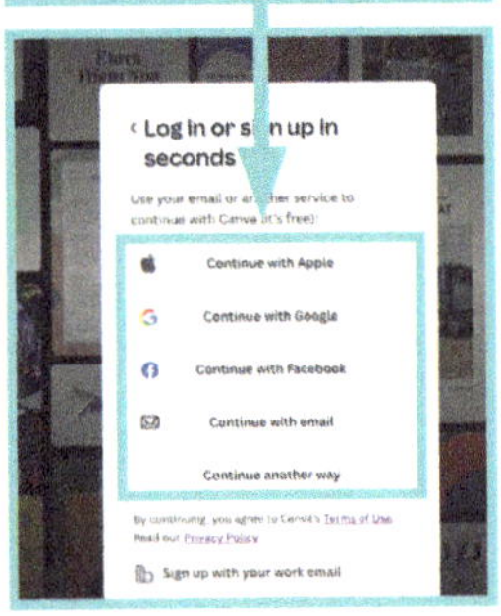

TIP: After signing in to your Canva account, check the box to **Always allow Canva.com** to open links of this type in the app. Click **Open Canva** after checking the box.

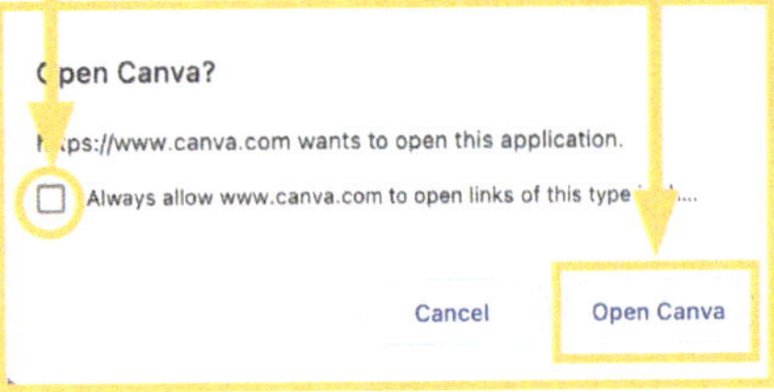

NOTE: Your dashboard may look different than mine after opening the app.

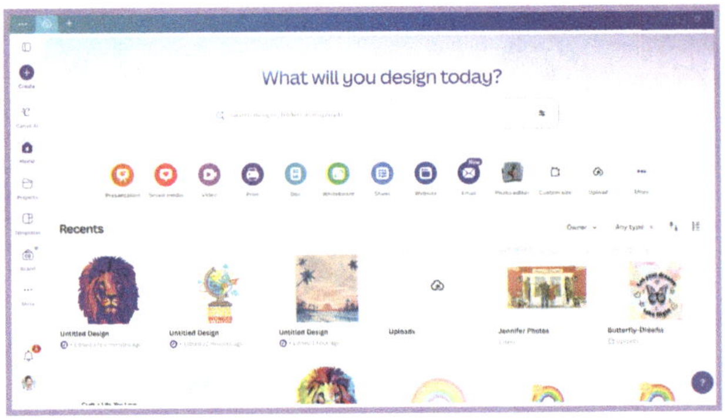

HOW TO INSTALL AND OPEN THE CANVA APP ON WINDOWS

You can use Canva in your web browser, but you can also download the desktop app for Windows. Follow these steps to install the Canva app on your Windows PC:

Step 1: Open your web browser and type in **Canva.com/download/windows** in the address bar. Press the Enter/Return key. Click **Download Canva for Windows** to start the download.

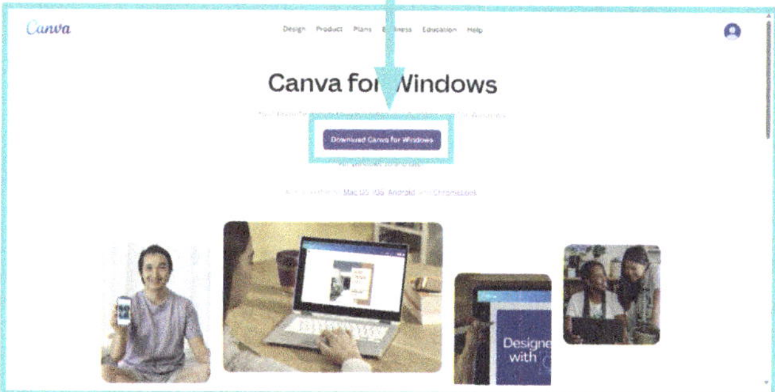

Step 2: Click the **Download** icon in the top right corner of the screen, then click on **Canva Setup**. The download and installation will start automatically.

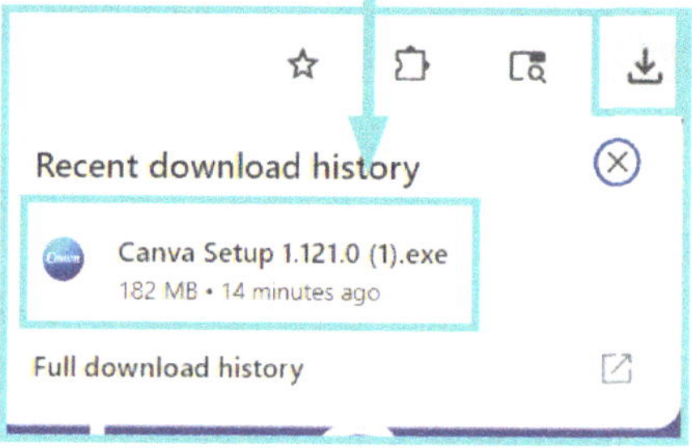

Step 3: The Canva app will open automatically. Click the **Log in through browser** button.

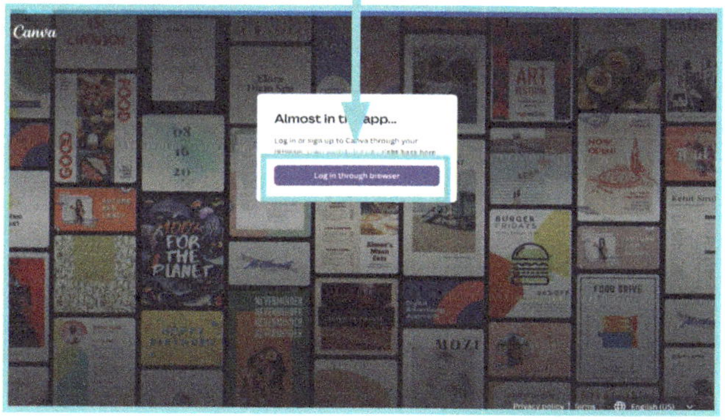

Step 4: Log in or sign up using any of the methods listed.

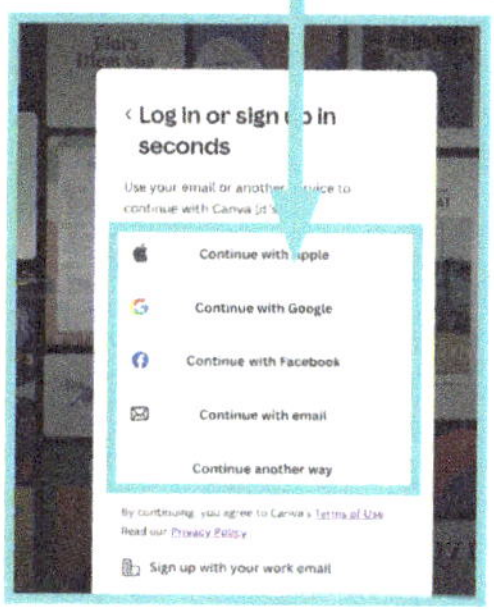

TIP: After signing in to your Canva account, check the box to **Always allow Canva.com** to open links of this type in the app. Click **Open Canva** after checking the box.

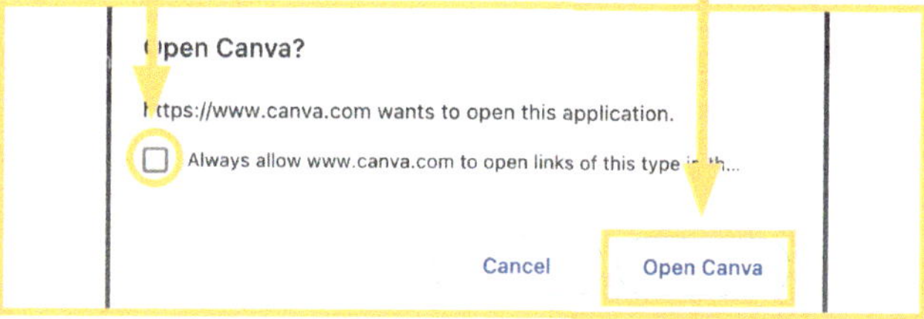

NOTE: Your dashboard may look different than mine after opening the app.

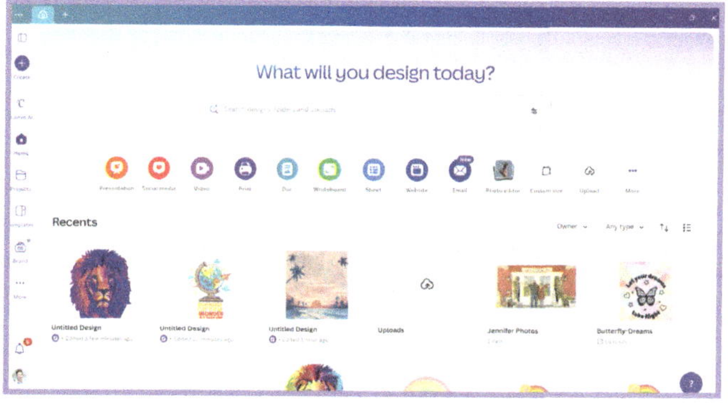

HOW TO FIND WHAT YOU NEED ON THE HOME PAGE

The home page can be overwhelming, so this page will help you find and learn about the basics – everything you need to know to get started.

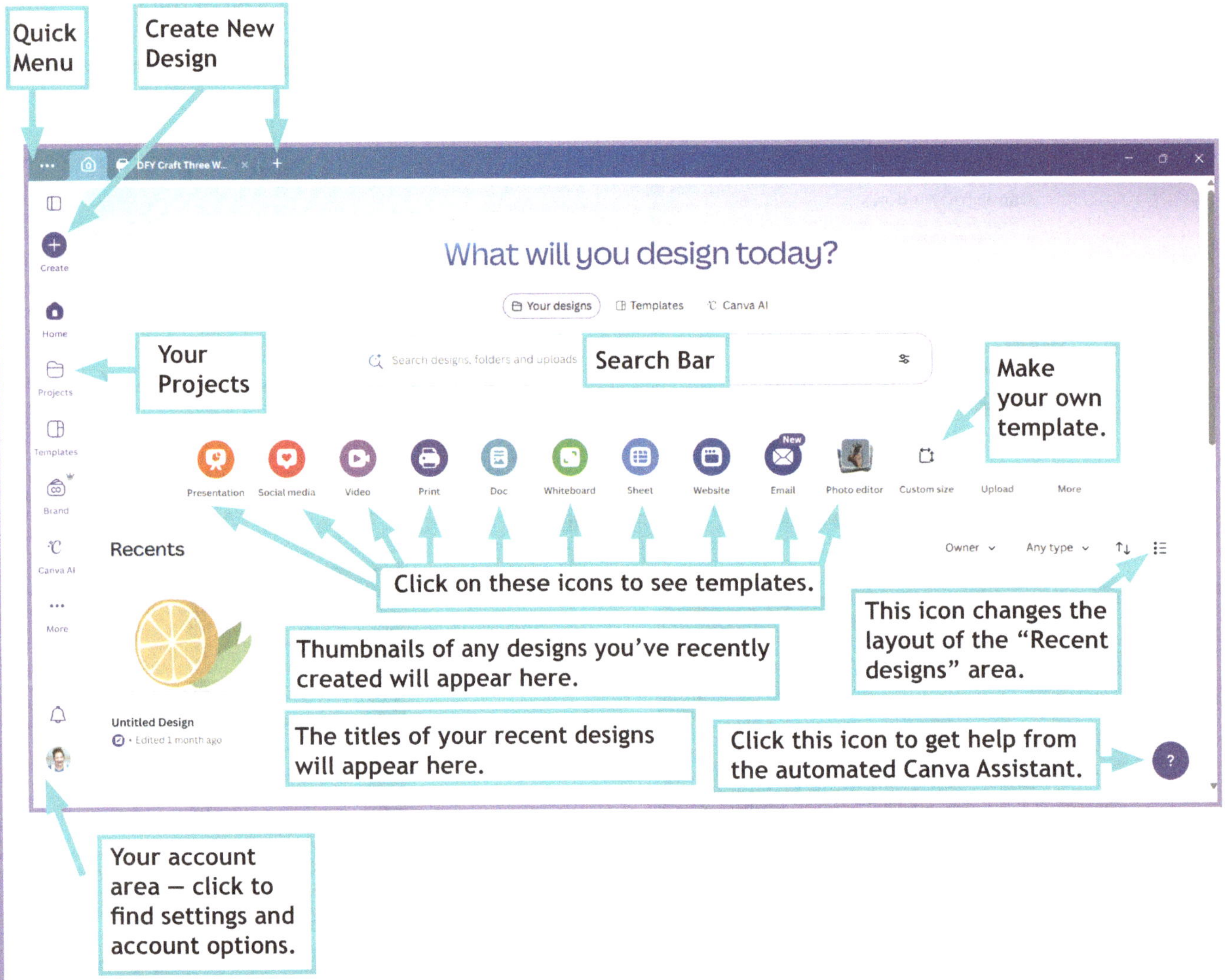

NOTE: Your dashboard may look slightly different than mine after opening the app.

TIP: Take some time to familiarize yourself with the home page. You will find there is more than one way to open and use templates. Once you are comfortable with Canva basics, have fun identifying what works best for you.

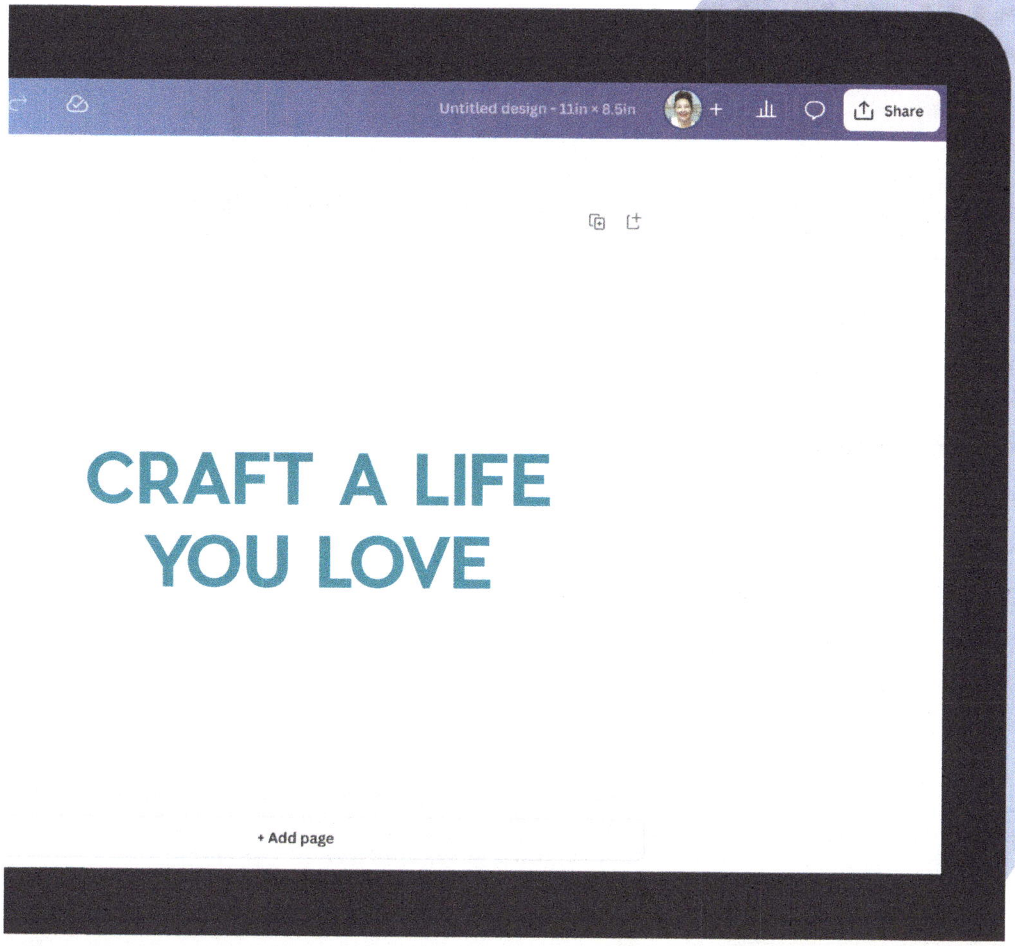

HOW TO:

DESKTOP: NAVIGATING THE CANVA WORKSPACE

- ✔ START A NEW DESIGN FROM A TEMPLATE
- ✔ NAME YOUR PROJECTS
- ✔ FIND YOUR TOOLS ON THE DESIGN PAGE
- ✔ USE THE DESIGN TOOLBAR
- ✔ KEEP YOUR DESIGN ALIGNED WITH RULERS & GUIDES
- ✔ ALIGN ELEMENTS FOR A CLEAN LAYOUT
- ✔ STACK AND ARRANGE LAYERS

DESKTOP

HOW TO START A NEW DESIGN FROM A TEMPLATE

Canva has a huge number of templates that you can use to create your designs instead of starting from scratch. These templates are a great time-saver!

Step 1: Click the **Create** button in the menu on the left side of the window.

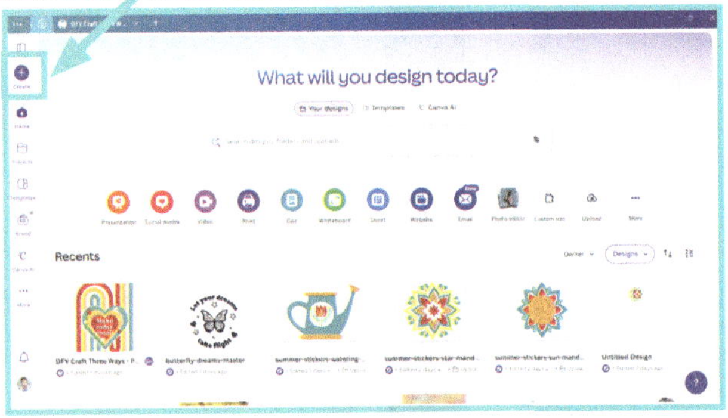

Step 2: Look at the menu on the pop-up and click on the **template category** you want.

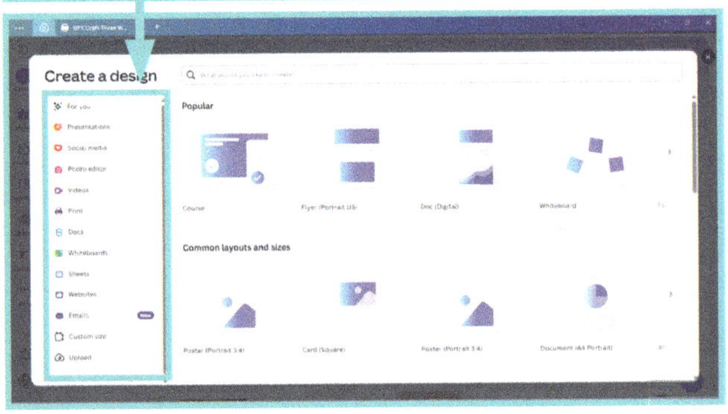

Step 3: Look through the templates in the category to find what you need.

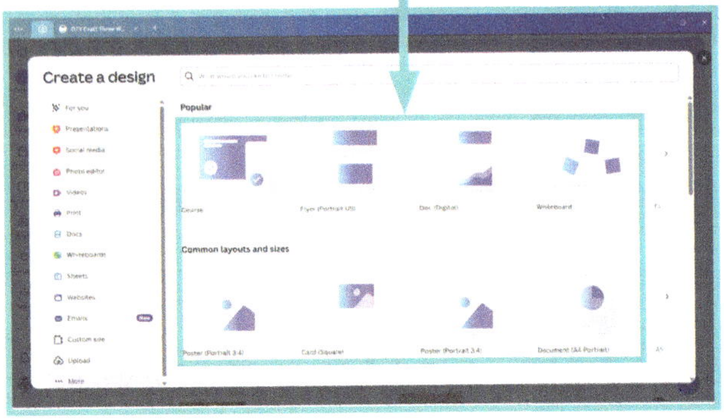

Step 4: To see more template categories, click **More** at the bottom of the menu.

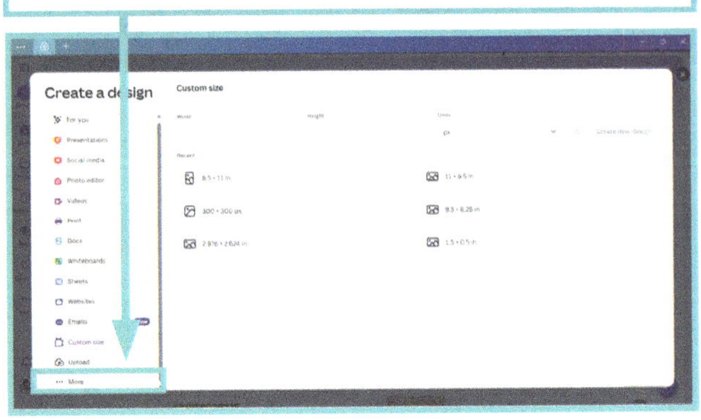

Step 5: Click on the **template** you want to use. A new tab with the template will open.

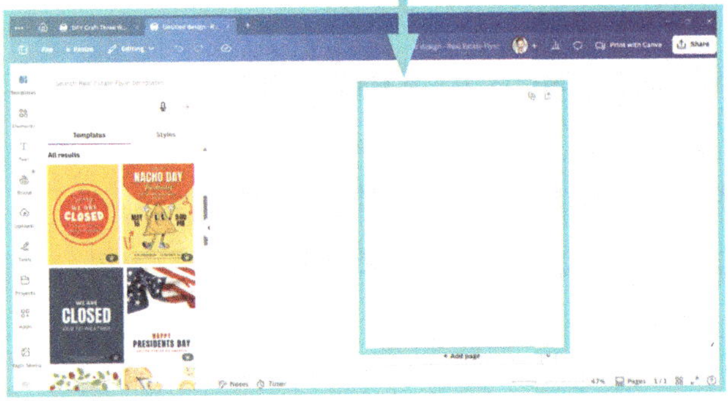

TIP: If you can't find a template that works for you, you can create a custom template. Look for "How to Make a Custom Size Template" on page 22.

DESKTOP

HOW TO
NAME YOUR PROJECTS

You should name your projects when you first start them. It's very easy to name a project. Follow the steps below to learn how.

Step 1: Click on "**Untitled design**" in the menu bar at the top of the page.

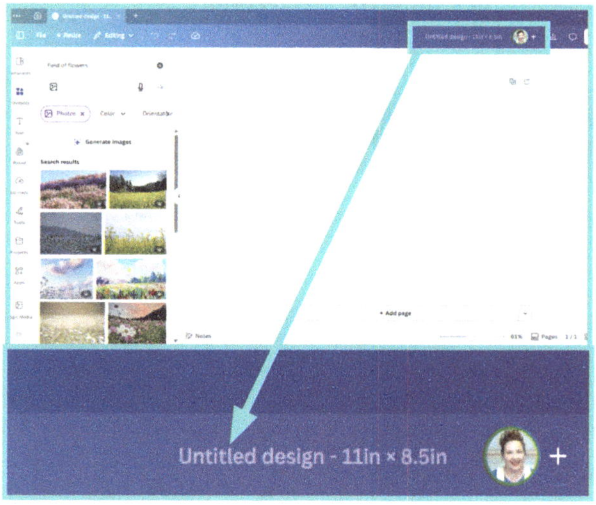

Step 2: Type in a name for your project, then press Enter. I'll name mine "Project 1."

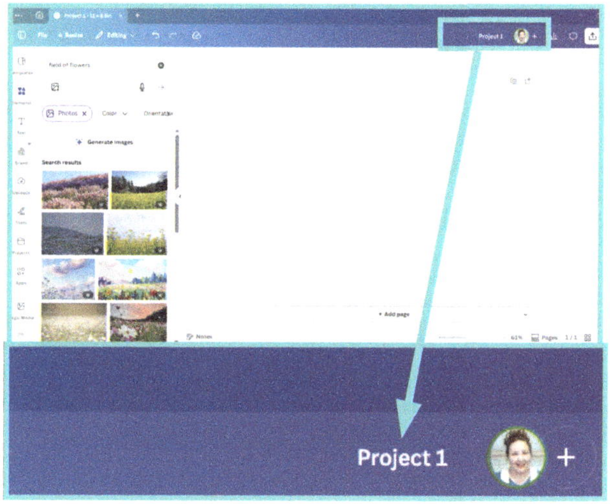

Step 3: When you need to find your project again, click on **Projects**, then find yours.

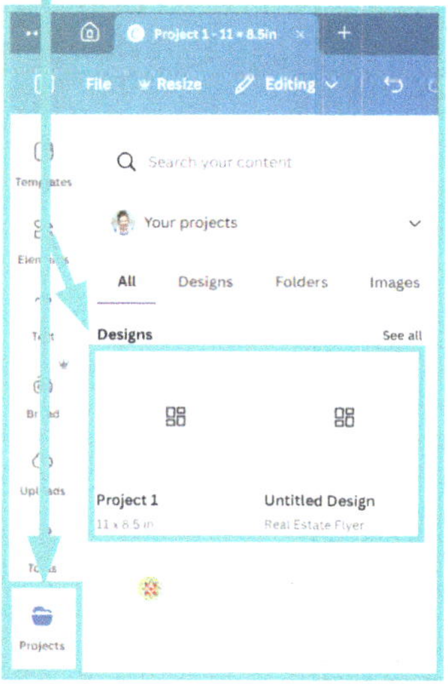

Step 4: When you open your project again, the tab at the top will have the project name.

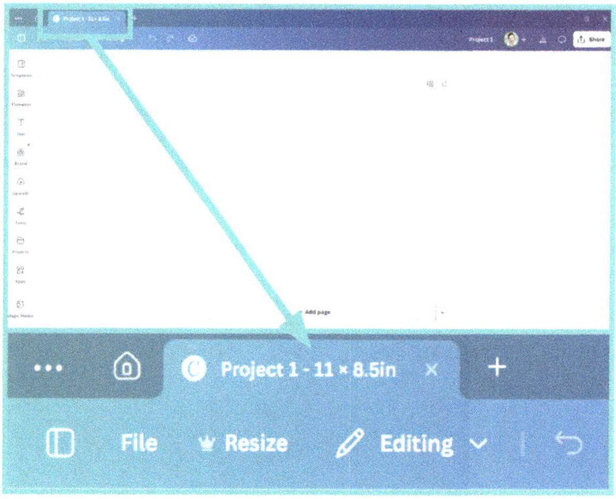

NOTE: You do not have to give your project a name — it will still save automatically and just remain named as the default "Untitled design" followed by the canvas dimensions. But it's a good idea to always give your projects a name so that they are easier to find later.

HOW TO FIND YOUR TOOLS ON THE DESIGN PAGE

The design page looks complicated at first glance, but once you know where all of the tools and functions are, you'll be ready to create!

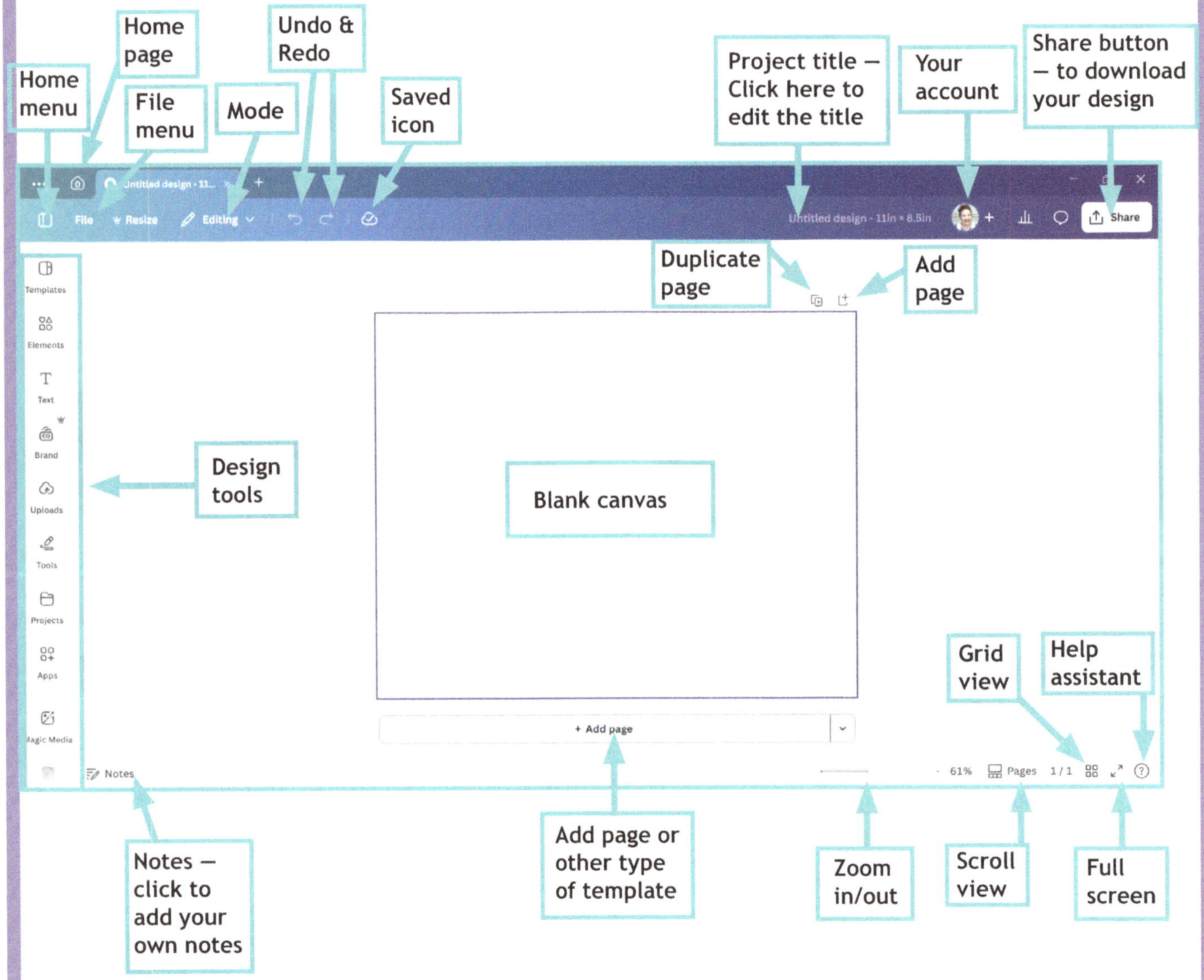

TIP: Take time to familiarize yourself with everything on the design page before you begin creating. It will make your experience much easier and more enjoyable.

DESKTOP

HOW TO USE
THE DESIGN TOOLBAR

The design toolbar contains tabs that have everything you need to create your projects. Each tab opens a wide selection of design tools.

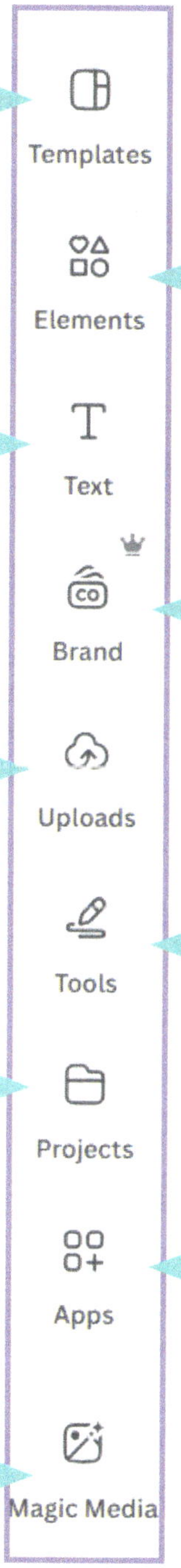

Templates: This tab is where you can find layout templates that fit your canvas, as well as curated color palettes, font sets, and recent design styles.

Elements: This tab is where you will spend a lot of time. You can find a vast array of images, audio and video clips, and more to add to your designs.

Text: Add text boxes, use an AI text generator, set text styles, choose fonts and font combinations, and more.

Brand: This feature is for Canva Pro members only. Set up your brand logo, palette, and images for quick use. (Note the crown icon that indicates a Pro feature.)

Uploads: Upload any image, audio, or video file from your computer to the Canva platform. You can also record your own audio and video.

Tools: Add building blocks like text, tables, sticky notes, lines, shapes, and drawings. These elements help you structure and customize your design layout.

Projects: Find all of your past projects and uploaded elements here.

Apps: Search for and access helpful design apps within Canva's platform.

Magic Media: This feature is Canva's AI art generator. Use the generator to create unique elements for your projects.

HOW TO KEEP YOUR DESIGN ALIGNED WITH RULERS & GUIDES

Guides in Canva are visual lines that help you align and position elements precisely on your canvas. They are especially useful for creating professional layouts, balanced designs, and consistent spacing.

Step 1: On your design canvas, click **File** in the top-left menu. Click **Settings** and select **Show rulers and guides** to enable them.

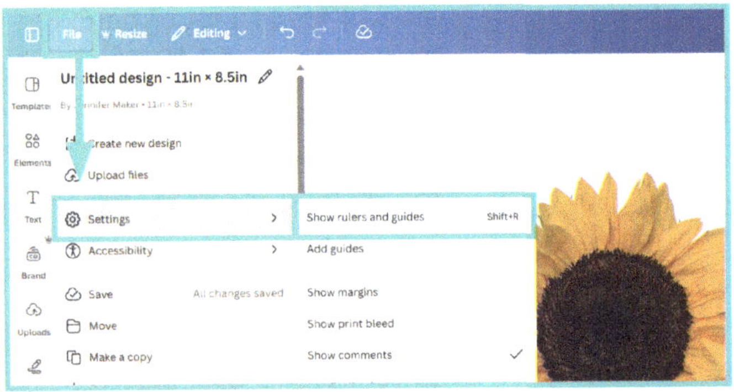

Step 2: Click on the **ruler** (top or left) and **drag your mouse** onto the canvas to create a guide. Drop the guide in your desired position.

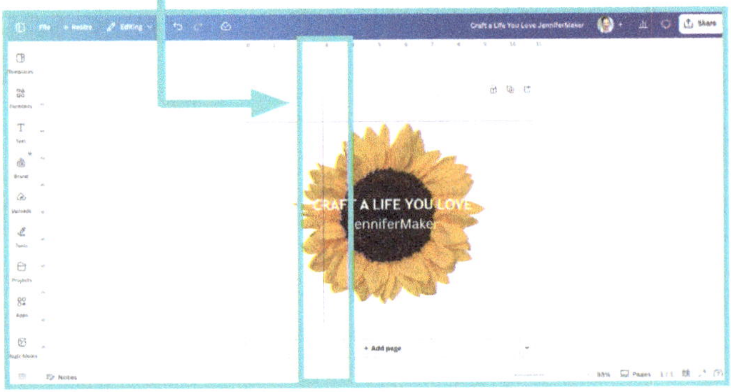

Step 3 (Optional): Click and drag an existing **guide** to reposition it. To remove a guide, drag it back to the ruler or off the canvas.

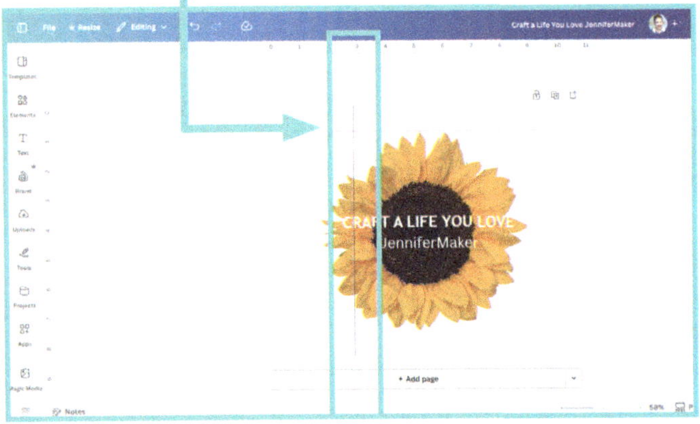

Step 4: Canva's Snap to Guides feature automatically aligns elements with nearby guides. Position your elements until they "snap" into place for precise alignment.

NOTES:

- Guides are only visible during editing and will not appear in your exported design.
- To hide guides, go to **File** > **Settings** > **click Show rulers and guides**.

HOW TO ALIGN ELEMENTS FOR A CLEAN LAYOUT

Aligning elements to the page in Canva ensures precise placement, creating clean and professional designs. This feature allows you to center, justify, or position elements relative to the entire canvas.

Step 1: Click on the element you want to align. To select multiple elements, hold Shift and click on each element.

Step 2: In the top toolbar, click Position to access alignment options.

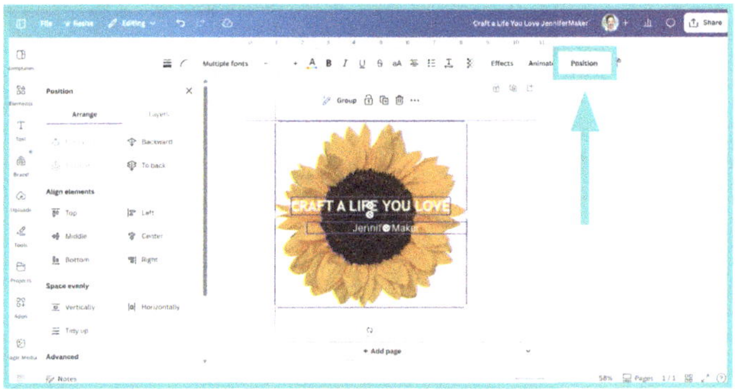

Step 3: Choose an Alignment Option

Vertical Alignment:

- Top: Aligns the element to the top edge of the page.
- Middle: Centers the element vertically on the page.
- Bottom: Aligns the element to the bottom edge of the page.

Horizontal Alignment:

- Left: Aligns the element to the left edge of the page.
- Center: Centers the element horizontally on the page.
- Right: Aligns the element to the right edge of the page.

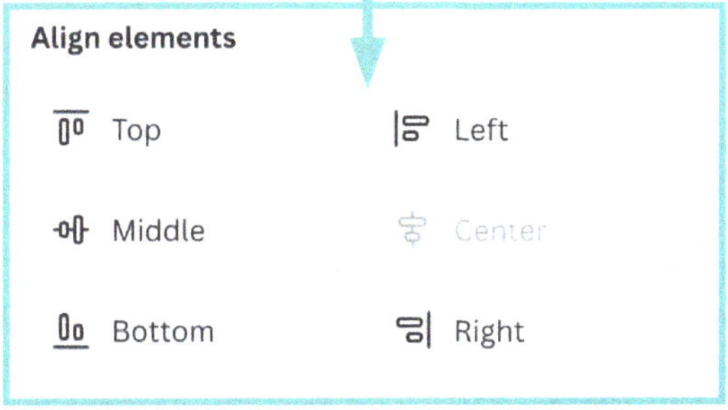

Step 4 (Optional): If multiple elements are selected, use the Tidy up option under Position to evenly distribute them.

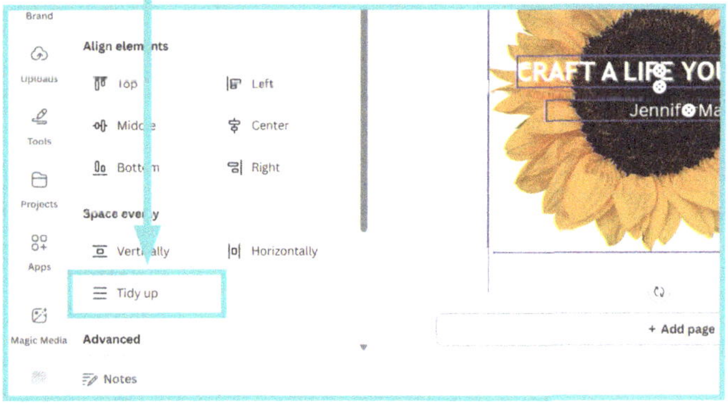

TIPS:

- Combine the alignment tool with Guides (File > Settings > Show rulers and guides) for precise placement.
- Group elements after aligning to keep them locked in place while editing other parts of your design.

HOW TO STACK AND ARRANGE LAYERS

Layering in Canva helps you organize overlapping design elements. By changing layers, you can move items forward or backward to create depth, emphasize certain elements, or fix layout issues.

Step 1: Click on the design element (e.g., text, image, shape) that you want to adjust.

Step 2: In the top toolbar, click **Position** to access layer controls.

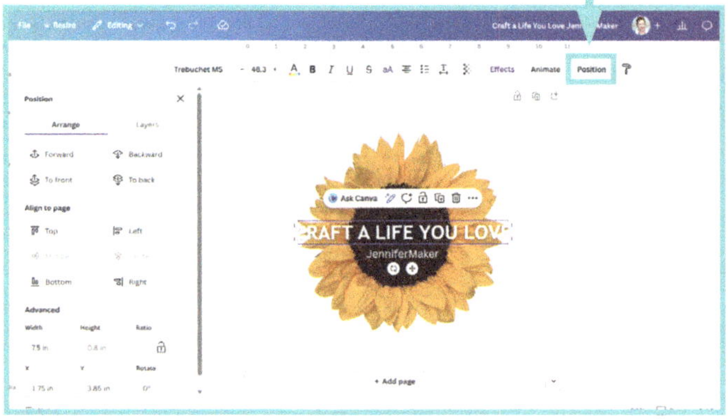

Step 3: Choose one of the following options:

Forward: Moves the element one layer closer to the front.

To Front: Brings the element to the very front.

Backward: Moves the element one layer closer to the back.

To Back: Sends the element to the very back.

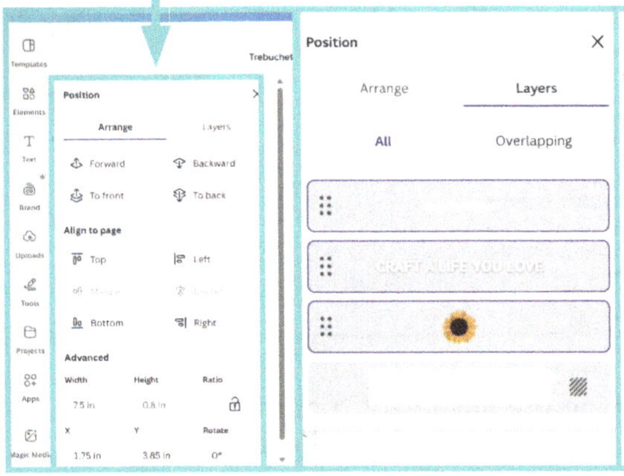

You can also change layers by opening the **Layers** panel under Position.

Step 4 (Optional): Right-click on the element and select **Bring Forward**, **Send Backward**, **Bring to Front**, or **Send to Back** for quick adjustments.

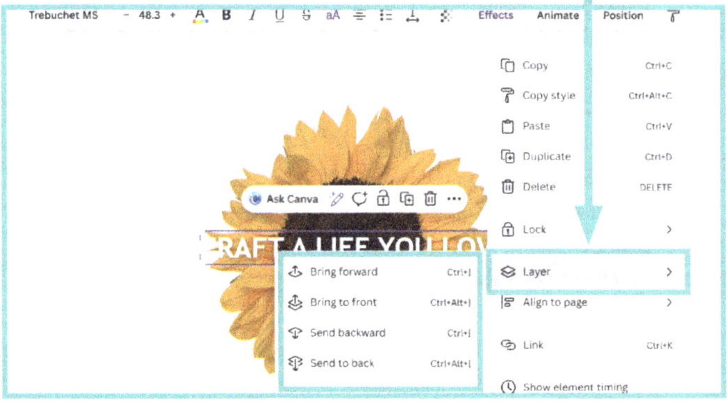

WARNING: Be cautious when sending elements to the back, as they may become hidden behind background layers or locked items.

TIPS:

- Use **Transparency** (checkerboard icon in the top toolbar) to make overlapping layers blend more naturally.
- **Group** related elements after layering to keep them aligned while editing.
- Elements at the top of the **Layers** panel list are in front of the design, while elements at the bottom of the **Layers** panel list are at back of the design. Click and drag an element in the list to change its position.

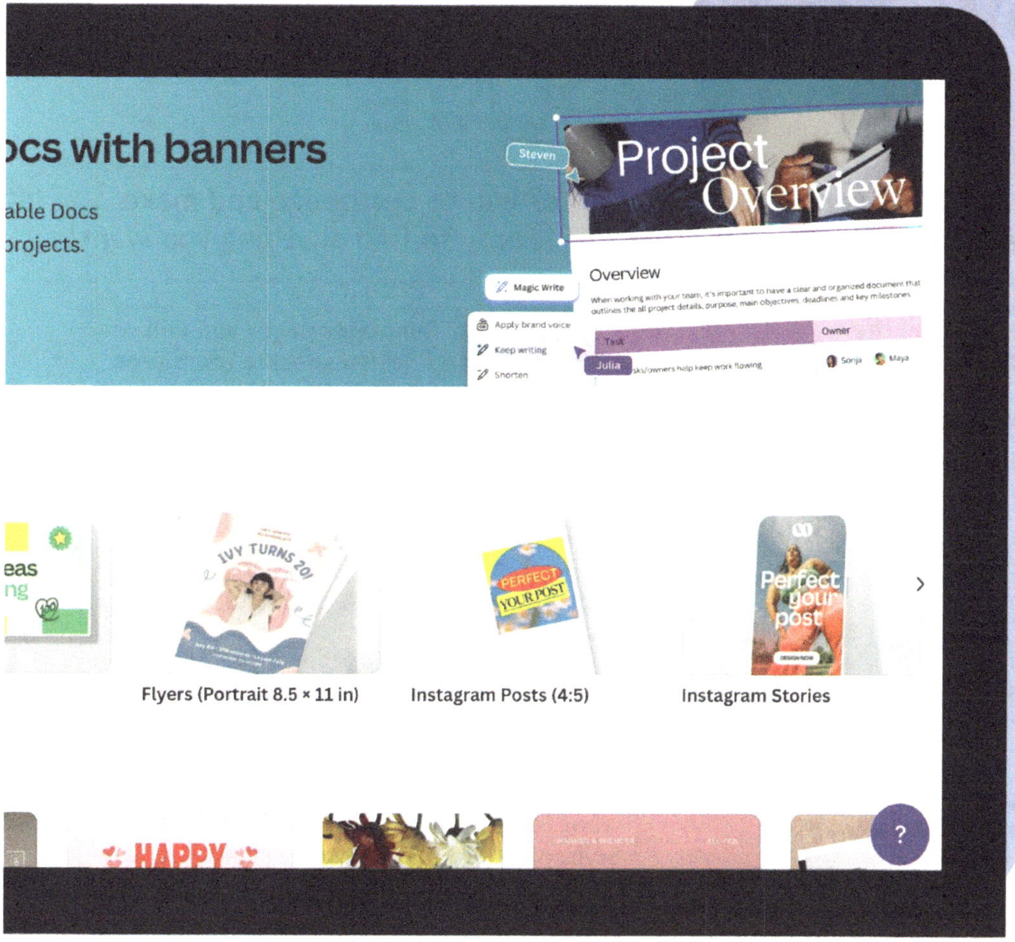

HOW TO:

DESKTOP: WORKING WITH TEMPLATES

- ✔ SEARCH FOR ANY TEMPLATE
- ✔ FIND THE MOST POPULAR TEMPLATES
- ✔ MAKE A CUSTOM SIZE TEMPLATE
- ✔ APPLY A PRE-MADE DESIGN TEMPLATE
- ✔ RESIZE YOUR DESIGN IF YOU NEED A DIFFERENT SIZE

DESKTOP

HOW TO SEARCH FOR ANY TEMPLATE

Canva has millions of pre-made templates available for you to customize and make your own. The new Template Search function makes it easy to find anything you want!

Step 1: On the homepage, click on the Templates icon in the left toolbar.

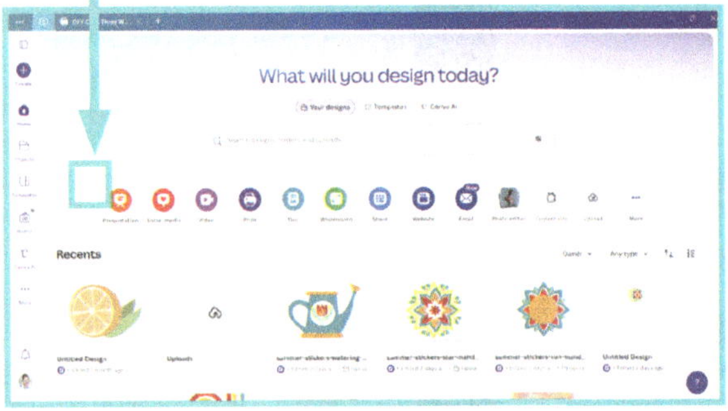

Step 2: On the Templates page, you will see a search bar and design specific templates.

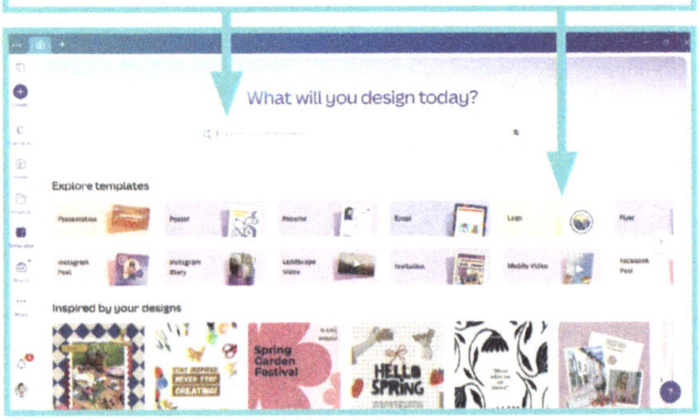

Step 3: To look for a template for a specific design type, look under explore templates and click the arrow to view more.

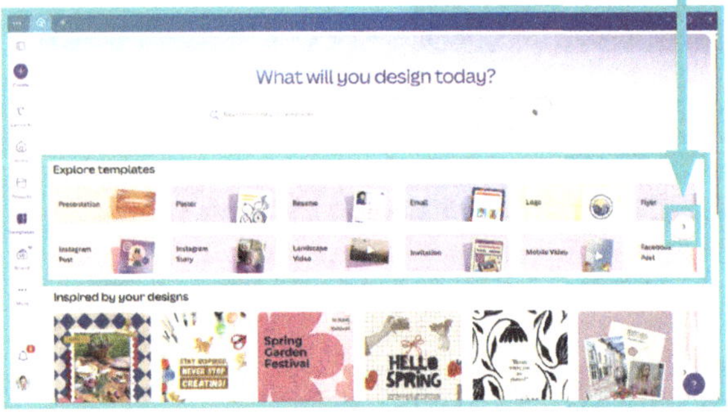

Step 4: Type in what kind of template you want to search for and press Enter. Use Style filters to narrow your results.

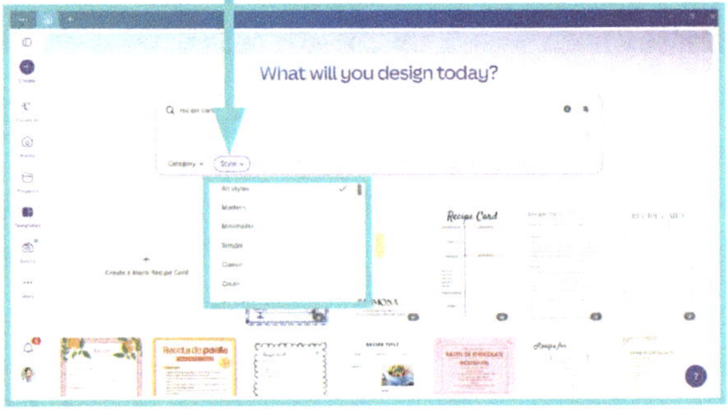

Step 5: Scroll down to look through the templates available.

Step 6: Click on a template. Then click Customize this template to make changes.

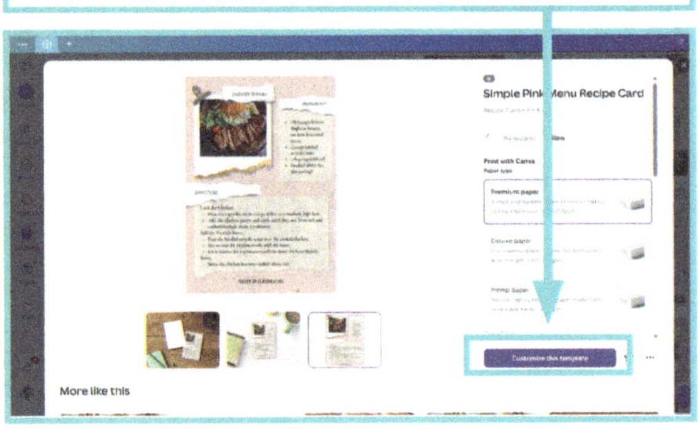

DESKTOP

HOW TO FIND THE MOST POPULAR TEMPLATES

Canva has many popular pre-made templates for a variety of needs. You can start with one of the most popular templates and then edit it to make it your own.

Step 1: On the home page, click on the **Create** button.

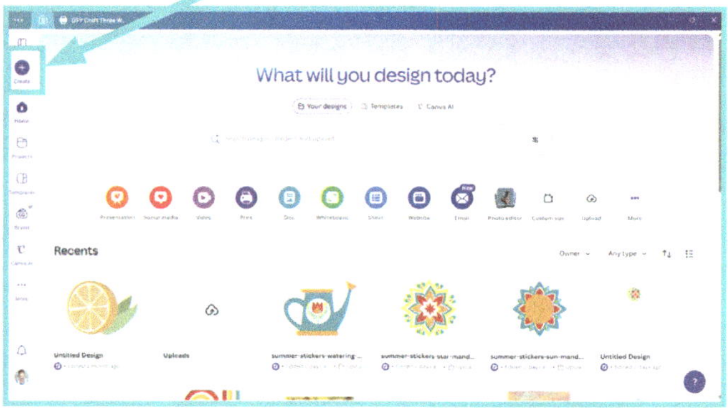

Step 2: Click on one of the template categories: **Presentations**, **Social Media**, **Photo Editor**, **Videos**, **Print**, **Docs**, **Whiteboard**, **Sheets**, **Websites**, or **Emails**. Click **See all** to view all templates in that category.

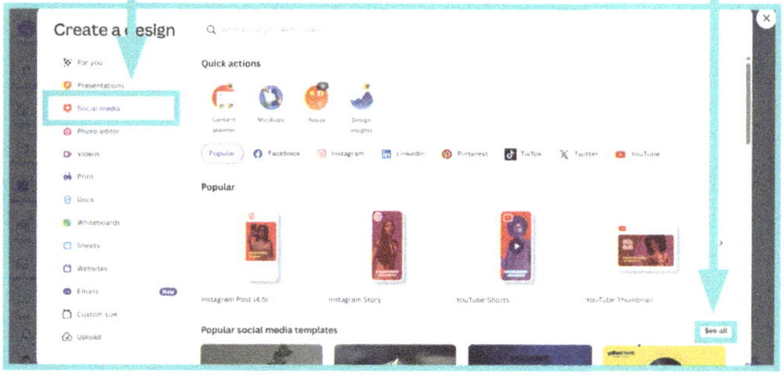

Step 3: Scroll through the available options to find a template that you want to use. Click **Browse by category** to narrow your results. You can filter further using the **Filter** buttons.

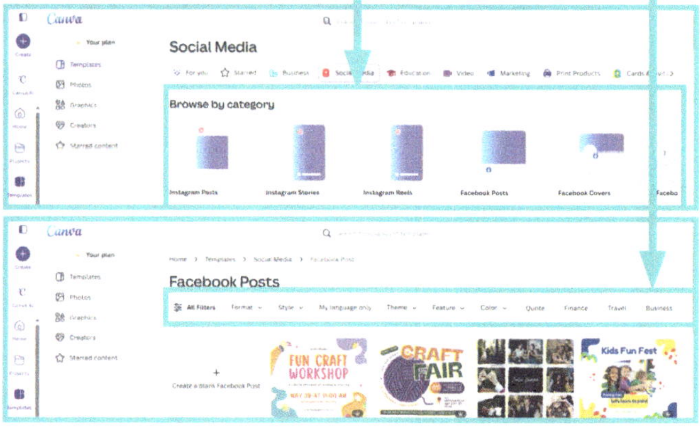

Step 4: Click on the template you want to use, then click **Customize this template**. The template will open in a new tab.

NOTE: Social Media, Video, Print Product templates are divided into categories, so just click on a specific category to see just templates that fit your needs.

TIP: Make sure you choose the category that has templates to fit your purpose:

- **Sheets:** Record data in an organized format.
- **Docs:** Create posters, menus, flyers, and more.
- **Whiteboards:** Map out ideas, plans, and other related works.
- **Presentations:** Create a high-quality multi-slide presentation.
- **Social Media:** Curate styled posts for your social media presence.
- **Videos:** Put together well-designed videos.
- **Print Products:** Create and order physical products, such as business cards, invitations, cards, and marketing materials.

DESKTOP

HOW TO MAKE A CUSTOM SIZE TEMPLATE

If there are not any pre-made templates that will work for your design, you can make your own custom template in the exact size you need.

Step 1: On the Home page, click the **Custom Size** icon.

Custom size

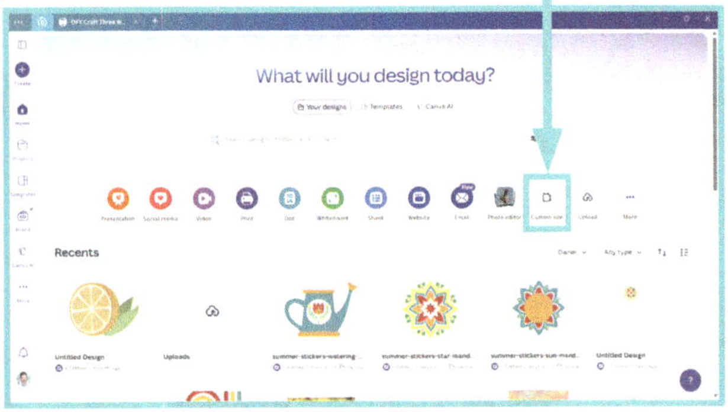

Step 2: Click on the drop-down box under **Units** and click on your unit of choice.

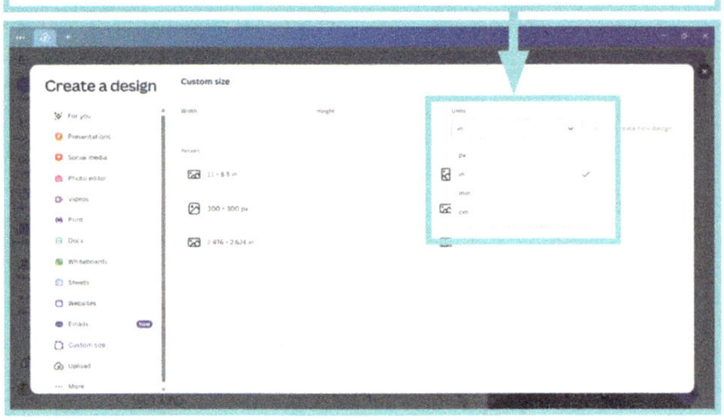

Step 3: Type in your desired **Width** and **Height** dimensions in the boxes.

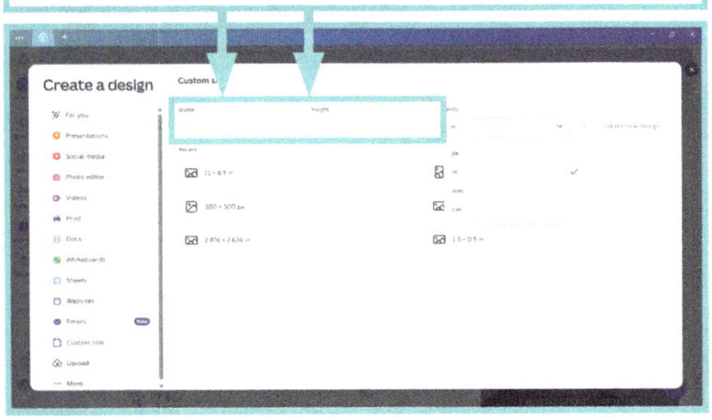

Step 4: Click the **Create new design** button. A new tab with your template will appear.

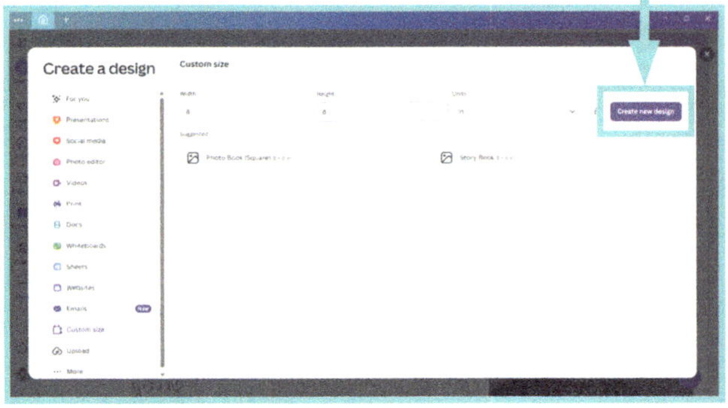

WARNING: You MUST create your new design at the size you want if you're using the Free version of Canva because you cannot resize it later. You can only resize your designs if you are a Pro member.

HOW TO APPLY A PRE-MADE DESIGN TEMPLATE

Templates are an excellent resource for when you don't want to start a project from scratch. There are a wide variety of templates to suit your needs.

Step 1: Click on **Templates**.

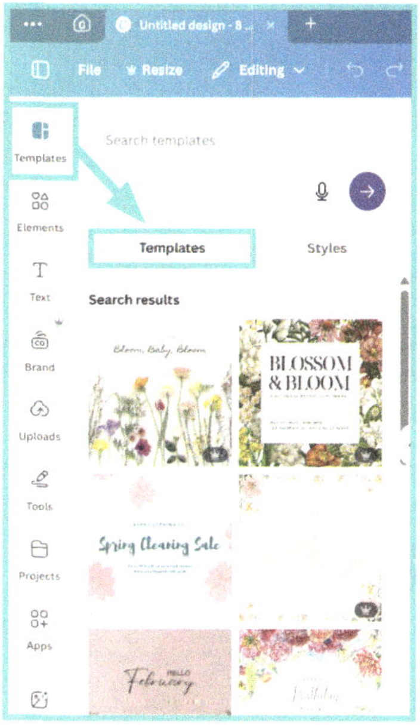

Step 2: Type descriptive words into the search bar to help find templates.

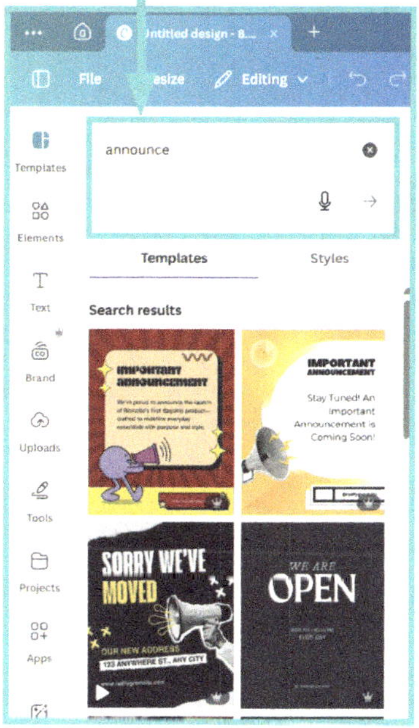

Step 3: Scroll through the results to find the template you want to use.

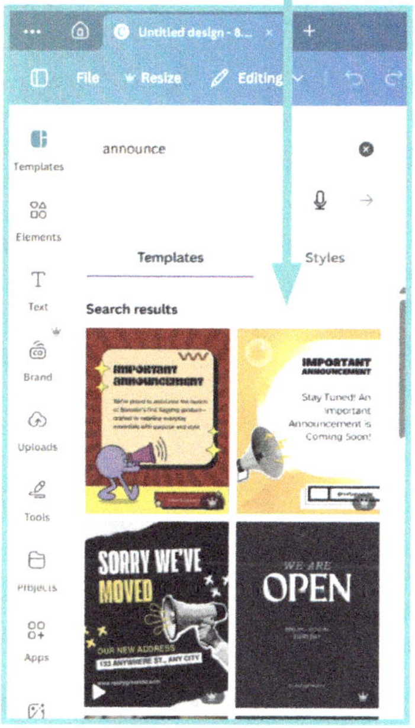

Step 4: Click on the template you want to use to add it to your canvas.

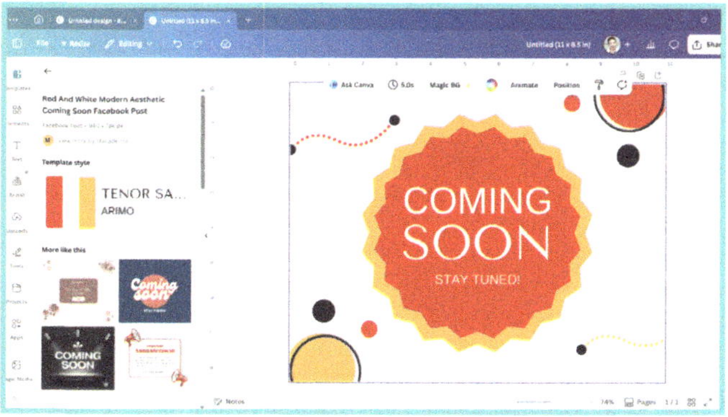

Step 5: To edit the template, click on an area. Then change the **text**, **color**, **image**, **background**, and more.

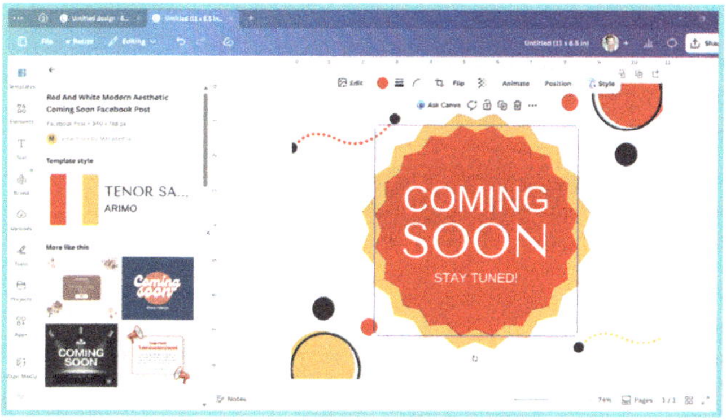

HOW TO RESIZE YOUR DESIGN IF YOU NEED A DIFFERENT SIZE

For Pro members only, Canva has a "Resize" feature that allows you to change the size of your canvas after you've already started creating.

Step 1: On the design you want to resize, click the "Resize" icon in the top left side of the top menu bar.

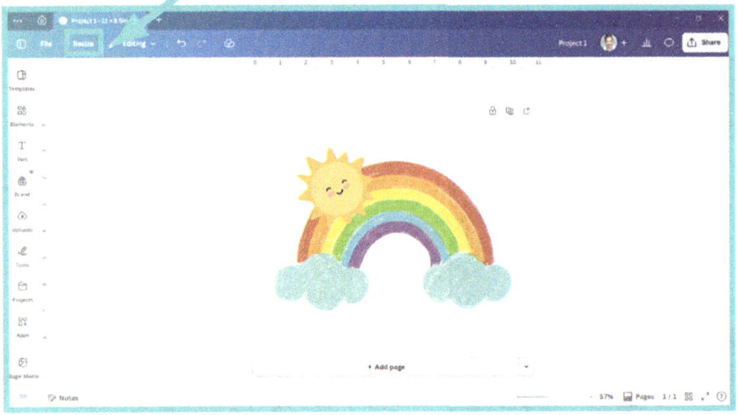

Step 2: Choose a new size from the pop-up menu, then click either "Copy & resize" to make a copy of the project in the new size, or "Resize this design."

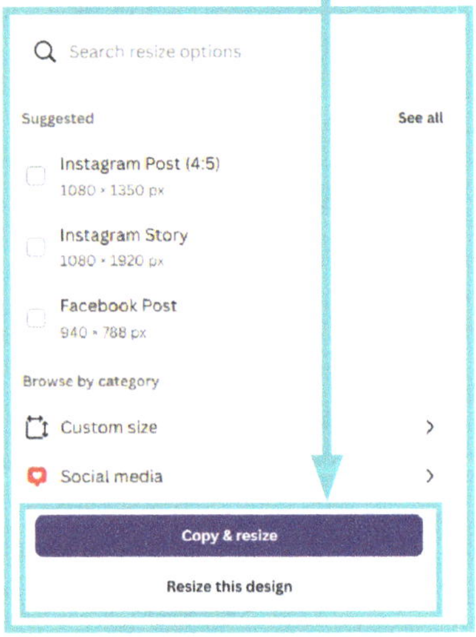

Step 3: If you clicked "Copy & resize," you will see the image and new size. Click “Open (new size)” to view it on your canvas. If you clicked "Resize this design," The new size will automatically appear in your project.

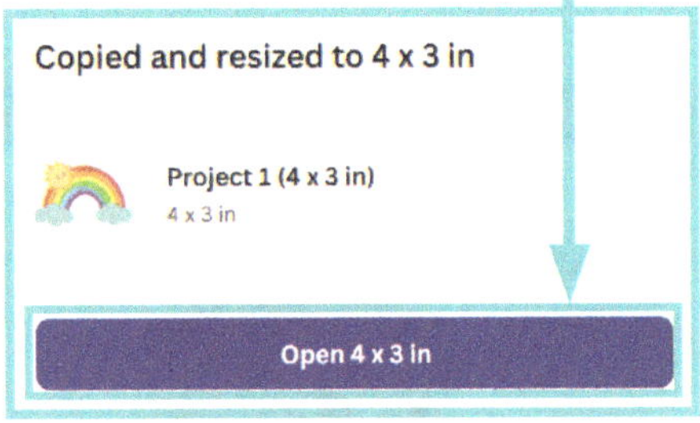

Step 4: Your resized design will appear.

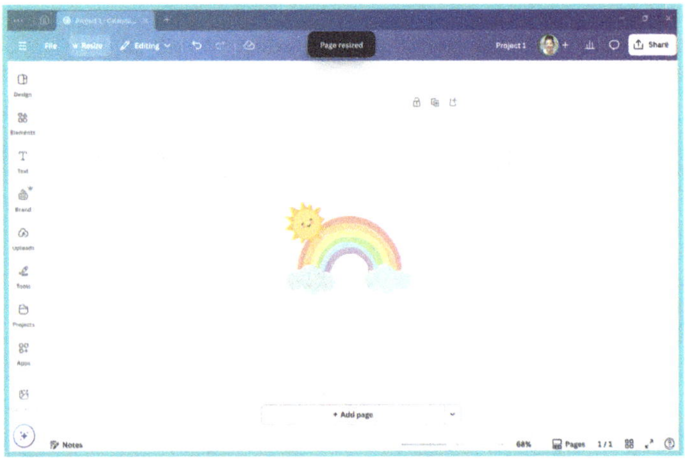

WARNING: You MUST create your new design at the size you want if you're using the Free version because you cannot resize it later.

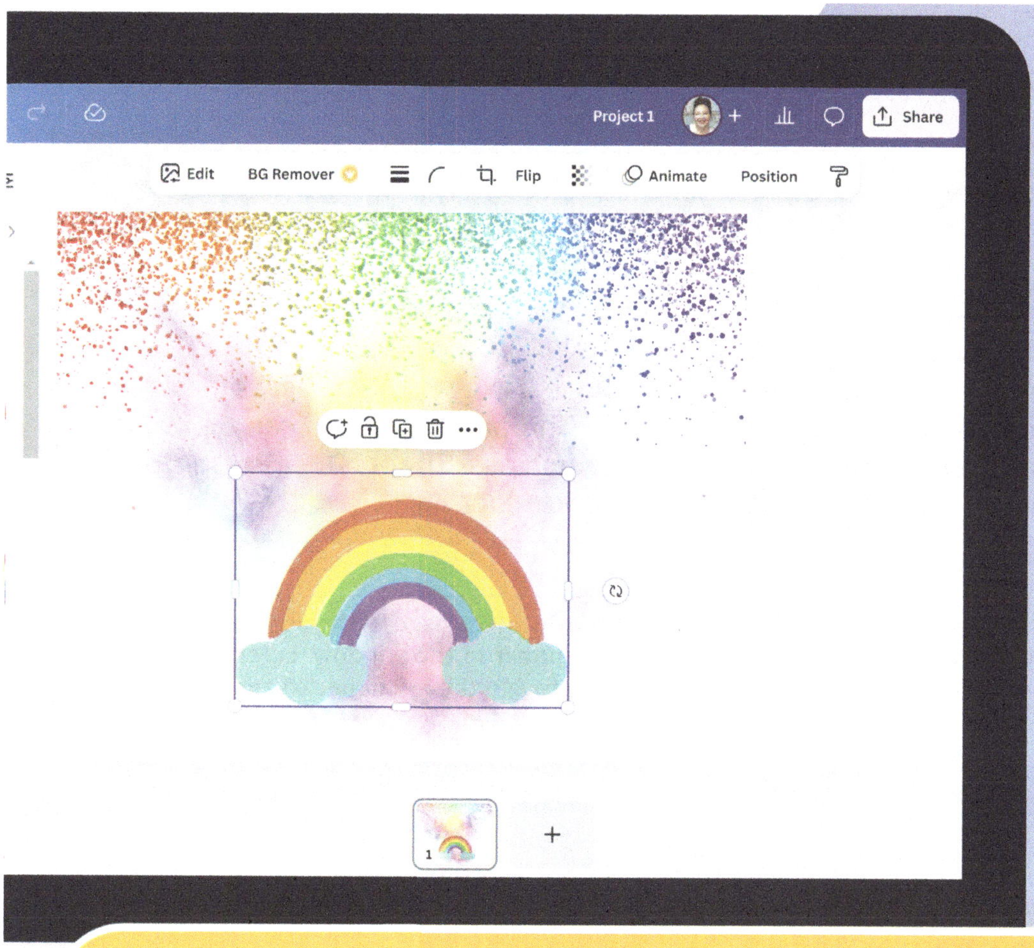

DESKTOP: DESIGNING WITH ELEMENTS

HOW TO:

- ✔ ADD AND DUPLICATE PAGES IN YOUR DESIGN
- ✔ QUICKLY CHANGE THE LOOK OF YOUR DESIGN
- ✔ MATCH COLORS AND FONTS WITH CANVA STYLES
- ✔ APPLY A BACKGROUND TO YOUR CANVAS
- ✔ FIND AND USE DESIGN ELEMENTS
- ✔ SEARCH SMARTER FOR GRAPHICS AND IMAGES
- ✔ SHAPE YOUR IMAGES WITH FRAMES
- ✔ ADD EYE-CATCHING GRAPHICS TO YOUR DESIGN
- ✔ CHOOSE THE RIGHT PHOTOS FOR YOUR DESIGN
- ✔ EDIT PHOTOS
- ✔ USE SHAPES TO ENHANCE YOUR LAYOUTS
- ✔ FIND AND USE VIDEOS
- ✔ EDIT AND ENHANCE VIDEOS
- ✔ ADD AUDIO TO YOUR PROJECTS
- ✔ MAKE YOUR DESIGNS LOOK REAL WITH MOCKUPS
- ✔ CREATE CHARTS TO VISUALIZE DATA
- ✔ ARRANGE PHOTOS AND ELEMENTS WITH GRIDS
- ✔ FIND CURATED ELEMENT COLLECTIONS
- ✔ ADD STICKERS FOR FUN DESIGNS

HOW TO ADD AND DUPLICATE PAGES IN YOUR DESIGN

You can add multiple pages of the same size to your existing project, as well as duplicate a page to create a second identical page. The pages you add can be of the same type, or you can add a different type of file, such as a Sheet, Doc, Presentation, Whiteboard, Social Media template, Video, or Print Product.

Add a Page

Step 1: Option A: Click on the icon that looks like a rectangle with a plus sign. Option B: Click on the +Add page bar. Option C: Click on the arrow by the +Add page bar to see other types of templates.

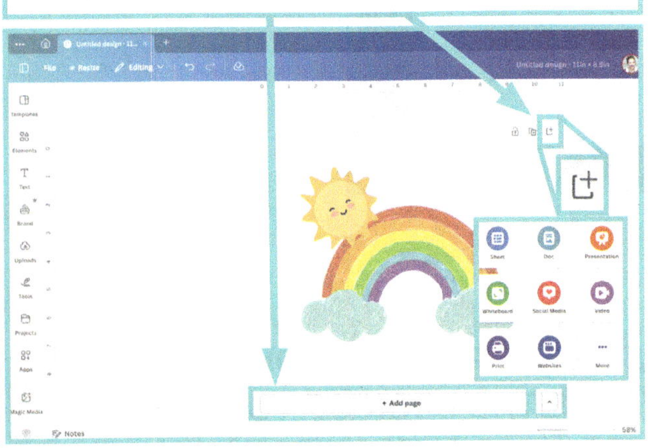

A new project page with your custom template will appear in the window. Scroll down to see it, or toggle the zoom bar to zoom out to see multiple pages at once.

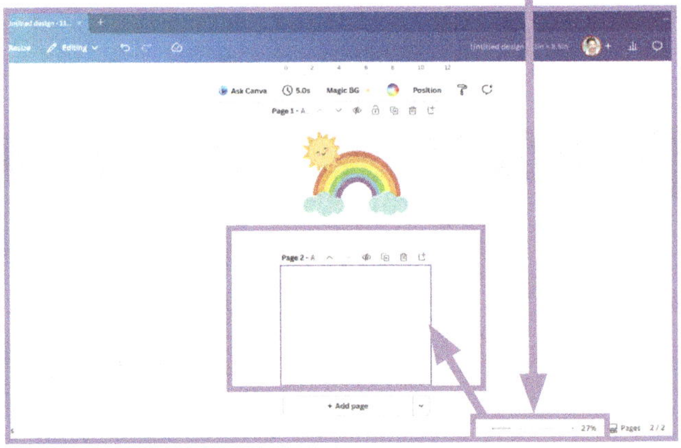

Duplicate a Page

Step 1: On the page you want to duplicate, click on the icon that looks like two vertical rectangles, with a plus sign on the front rectangle.

An identical project page will appear in the window. Scroll down to see it, or zoom out to see multiple pages at once.

NOTE: Adding new pages to a design is a good way to keep all designs — even those of a different format — for a single project in one place. This is ideal for projects with multiple designs, such as a sublimated blanket, or a project that has a presentation that accompanies it.

DESKTOP

HOW TO QUICKLY CHANGE THE LOOK OF YOUR DESIGN

The Templates tab is where you can find layout templates that fit your canvas, as well as curated color palettes, font sets, and recent design styles.

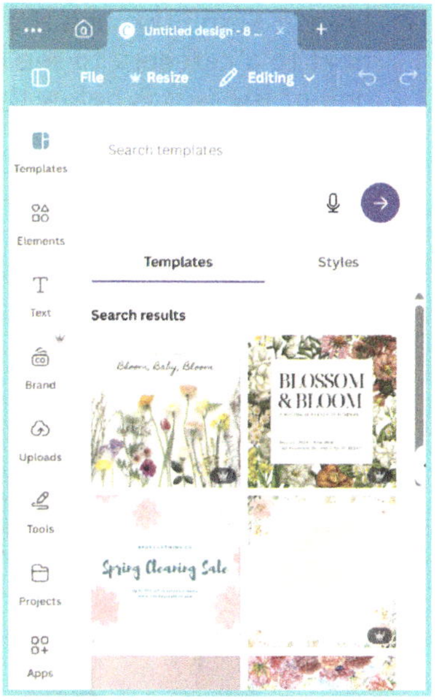

Type in your search term in the search box and press the **Enter/ Return** key to bring up results.

TIP: Templates and Styles are useful when you have an idea in mind and want to find something that matches. They are also good to look through if you need design inspiration.

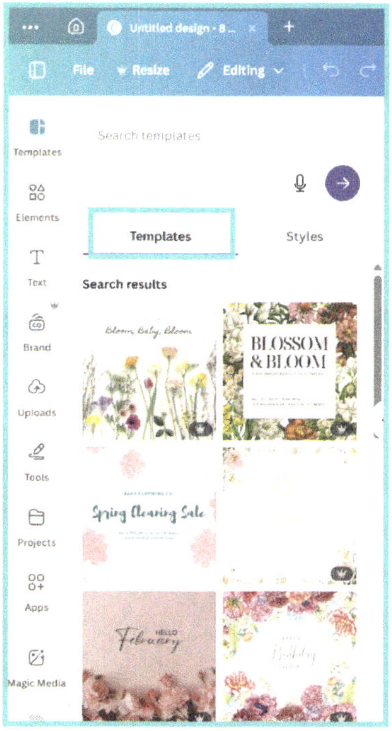

Templates: Click on **Templates** below the search bar to access all templates that fit your canvas size and shape.

Styles: Click on **Styles** below the search bar to find preset color palettes, font combinations, and color/font combinations.

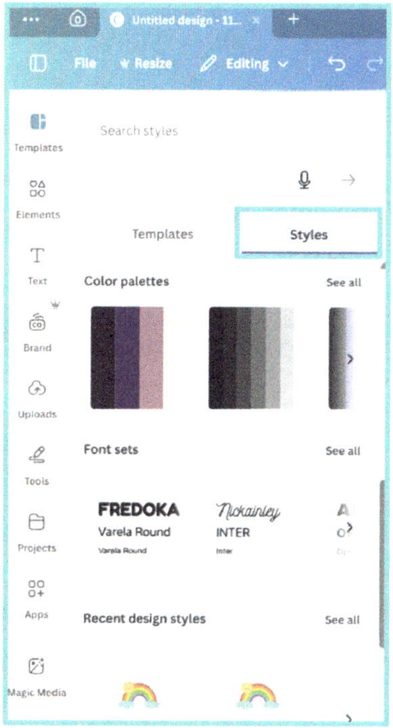

HOW TO MATCH COLORS AND FONTS WITH CANVA STYLES

Use the Styles section to search through and choose from curated collections of color palettes and font sets.

Step 1: Click on the Templates tab, then click Styles. Optionally, type a word or two into the search box if you have a style in mind.

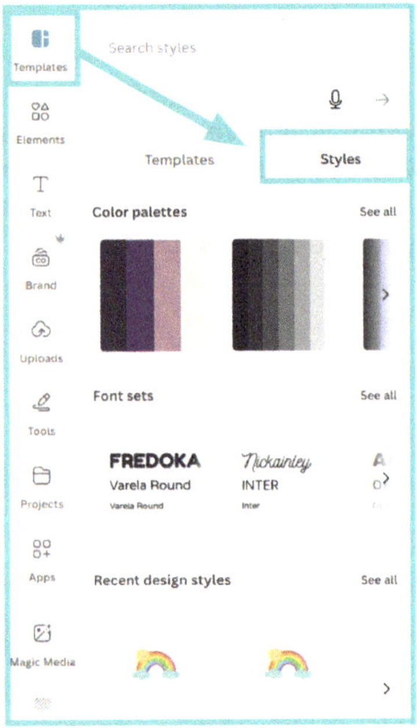

Step 2: Scroll through the results. Click See all next to a category to see more results. Click on one of the words below the search box to narrow the results.

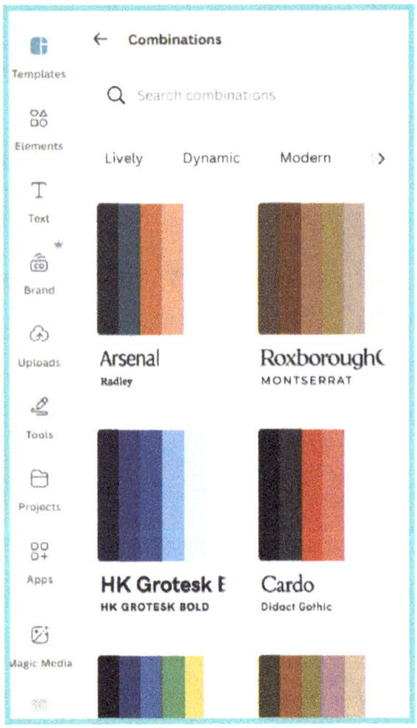

EXAMPLES:

- Vibrant
- Bright
- Strong
- Lively
- Loud

Step 3: Click on a style to add it to your canvas. One of the color options will appear, along with the font styles.

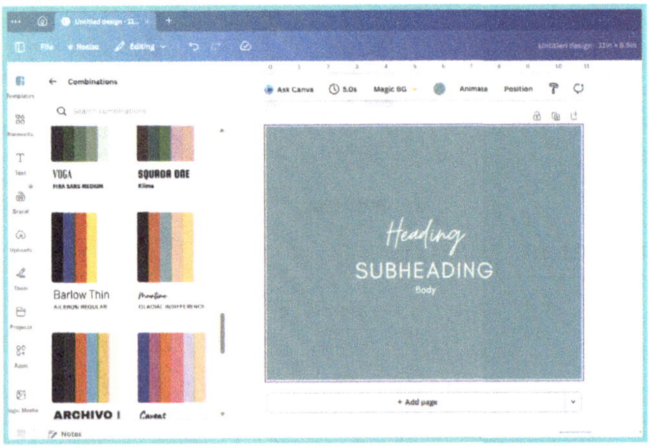

Step 4: Click on the same style again to try one of the other colors in the style collection. Click again to change the colors once more.

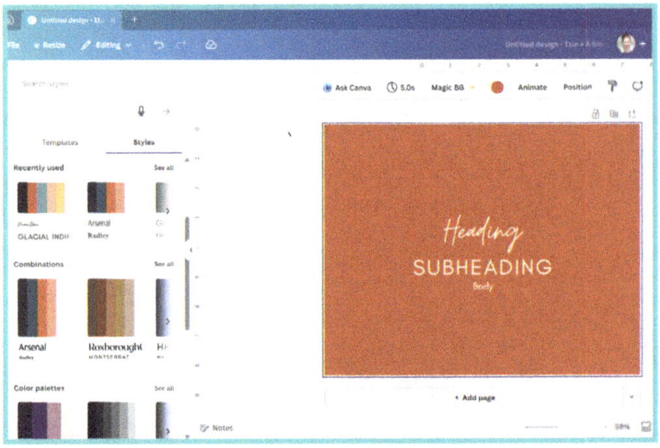

DESKTOP

HOW TO APPLY A BACKGROUND TO YOUR CANVAS

The Background tab is a quick way to add a full-coverage background to your canvas. Canva has a large library of ready-to-use backgrounds.

Step 1: Click on the **Background** tab in the vertical menu. You many need to scroll down to find it.

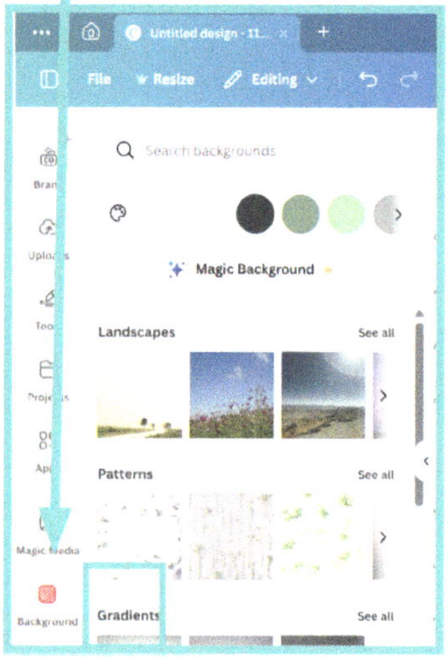

Step 2: Optionally, click the palette to narrow your search to a specific color.

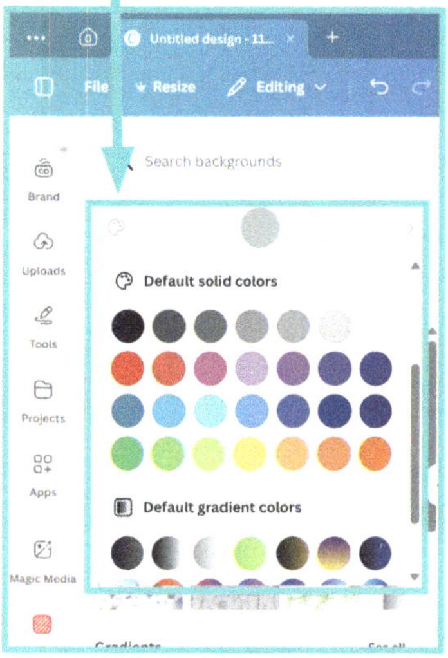

Step 3: Look through the categories and click **See all** on one you want to look at.

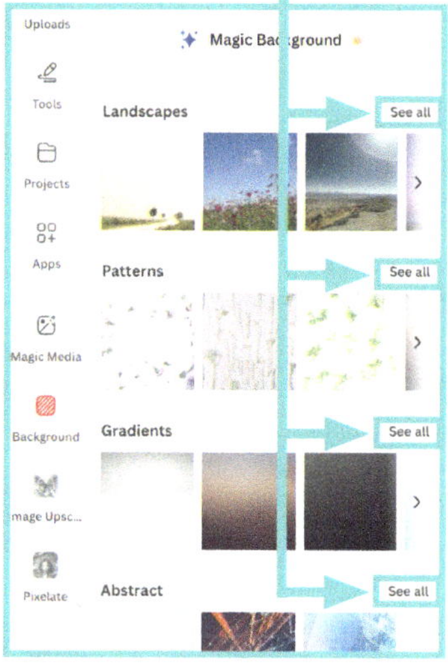

NOTE: You can use other elements as backgrounds. You will just have to resize and position them for yourself.

NOTE: Like other elements, you can change the transparency, which may be necessary to make the other elements on your canvas more visible.

Step 4: Look through the background options in the category.

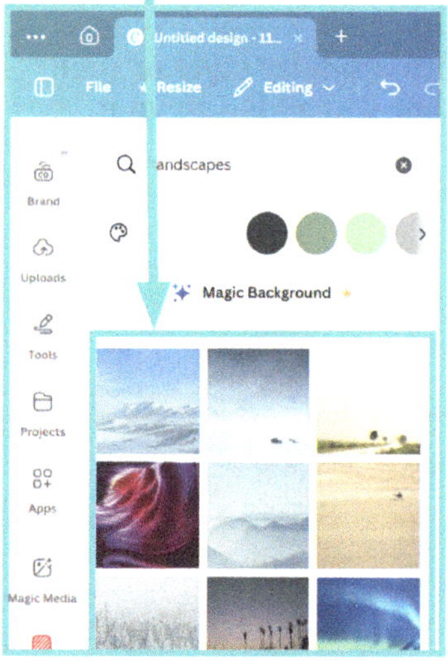

Step 5: Click on a background to add it to your canvas. It will cover the entire canvas.

Step 6 (Optional): Click **Magic Background** then type in keywords for the background that you want. Then click **Generate Background**. Refine your search by updating your description and clicking **Generate again.**

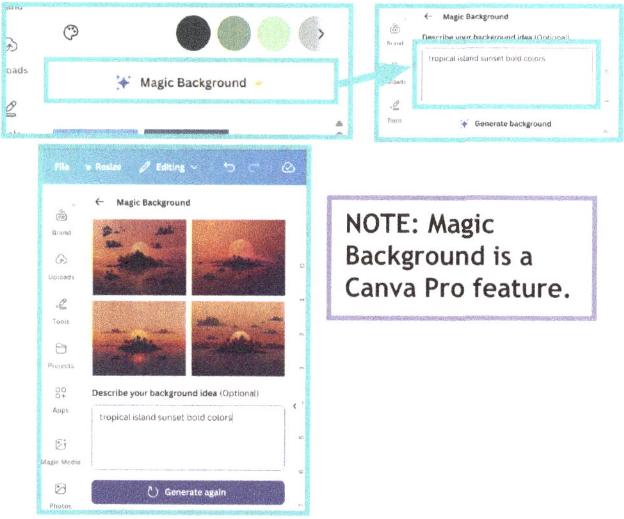

NOTE: Magic Background is a Canva Pro feature.

DESKTOP

HOW TO FIND AND USE DESIGN ELEMENTS

The Elements tab is where you'll find most of the resources you'll need for your projects: frames, graphics, photos, shapes, audio, video, mockups, charts, and more.

Step 1: Click on the **Elements** tab. Type in a word or short phrase into the search bar.

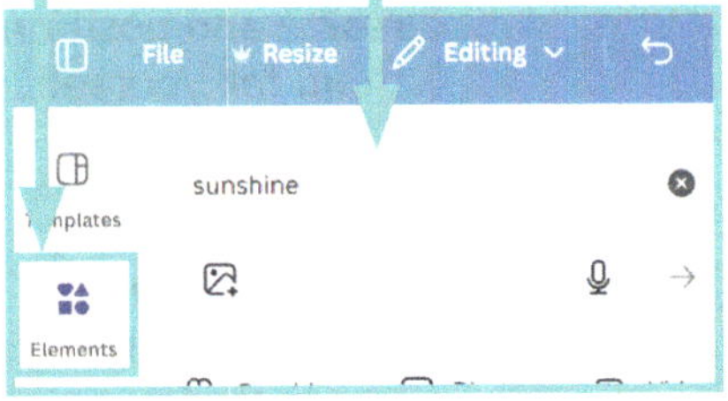

Step 2: Click **See all** to see more results in any category.

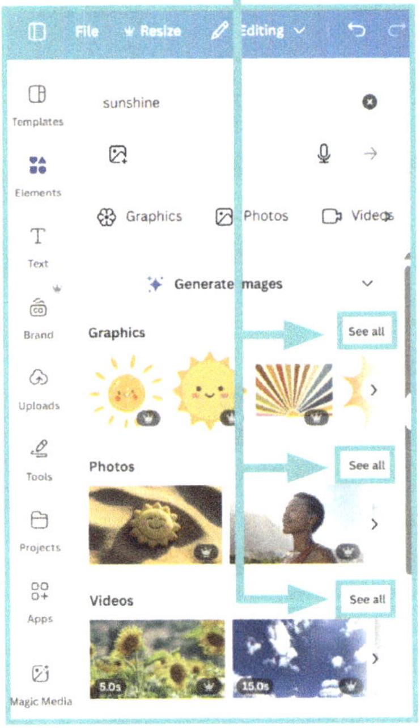

Step 3: Scroll through the results to find the element you'd like to use.

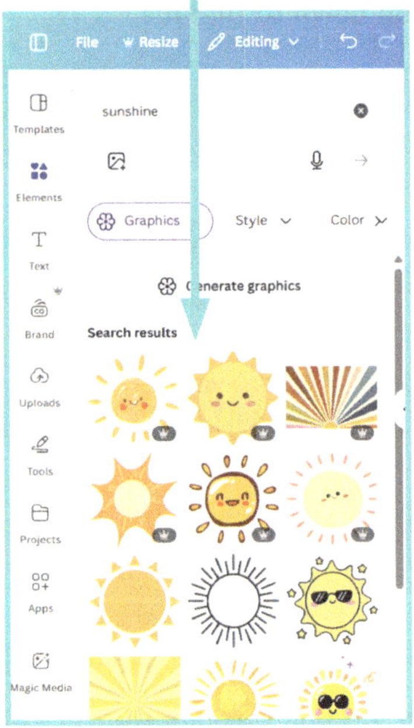

Step 4: Refine your search by clicking on **Style**, **Color**, **Orientation**, **Animation**, or **Price**.

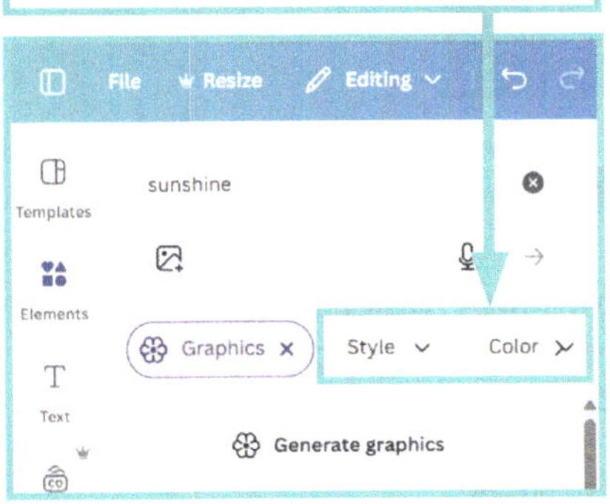

Step 5: Click on an **element** to add it to your canvas. You can add more than one element.

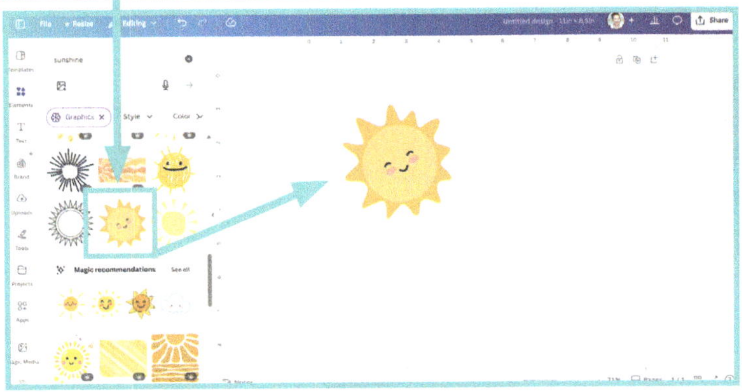

TIP: If you see a "Magic Recommendations" box within the search results, click **See all** to see elements with a similar style or feel to the element you added to your canvas.

DESKTOP

HOW TO SEARCH SMARTER FOR GRAPHICS AND IMAGES

After searching, Canva may show related searches and filters that help refine your results.

Option 1: Click **See all** next to a category to view more graphics options.

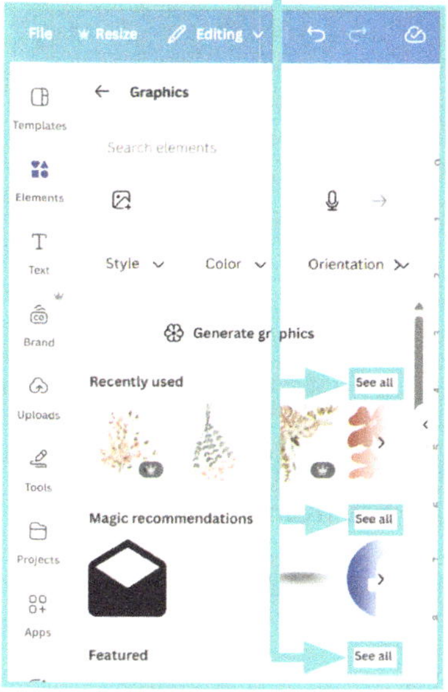

Option 2: Search on a specific term, then scroll down to see **Related searches** within the results.

Option 3: Search a specific term, click on a graphic, then look at **Magic recommendations**.

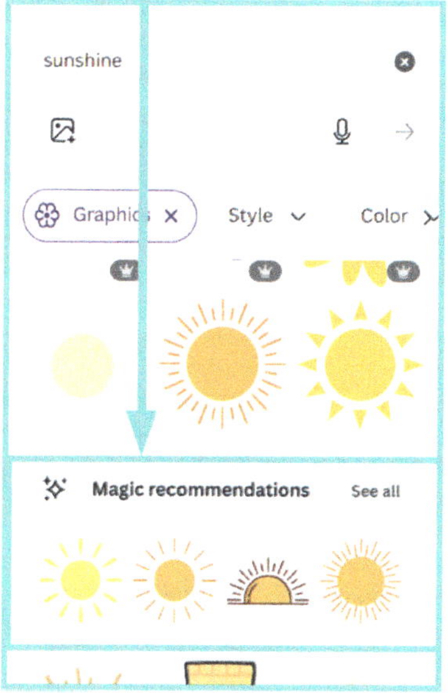

Option 4: Search a specific term, then click **Generate graphics**.

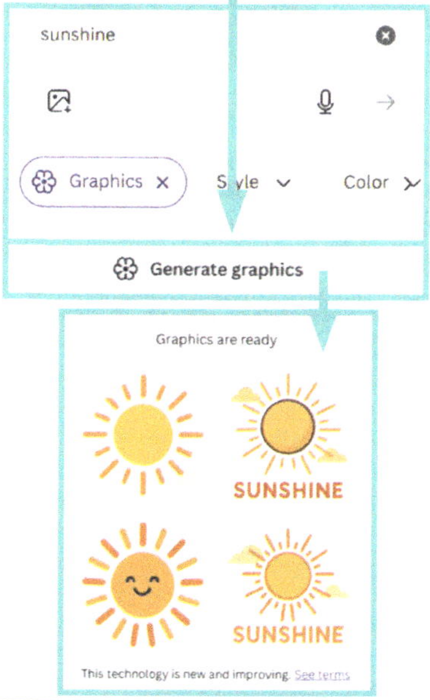

Once you find the element you need, click it to add it to the canvas.

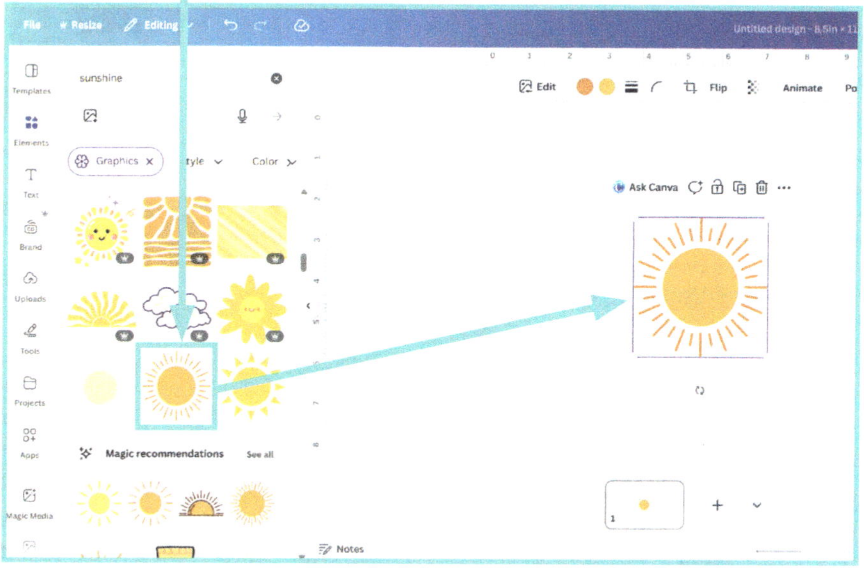

HOW TO SHAPE YOUR IMAGES WITH FRAMES

Frames are very useful elements that allow you to add any image inside. There are many shapes and styles of frames available within the Elements tab.

Step 1: Click on the Elements tab, scroll to find **Frames**, and add one to your canvas.

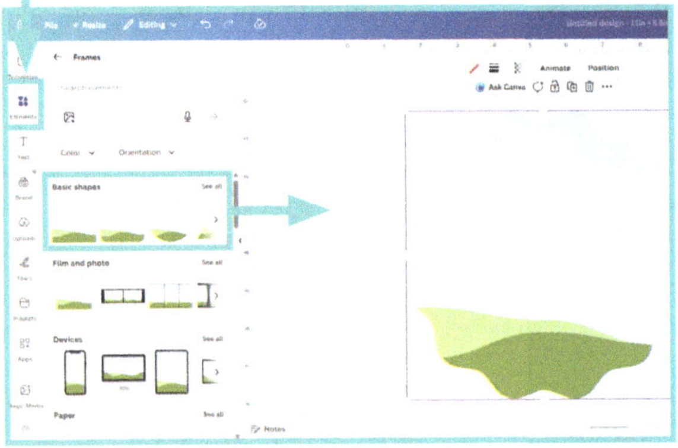

Step 2: Click on the **Elements** tab again and search for an image to add to the frame.

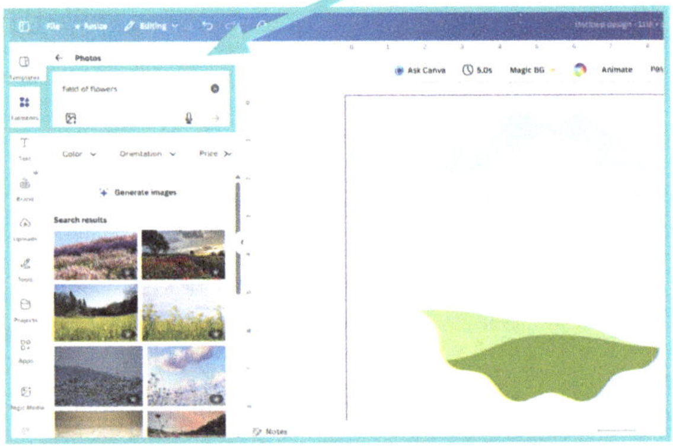

Step 3: Click on the **frame** on your canvas so that it is selected.

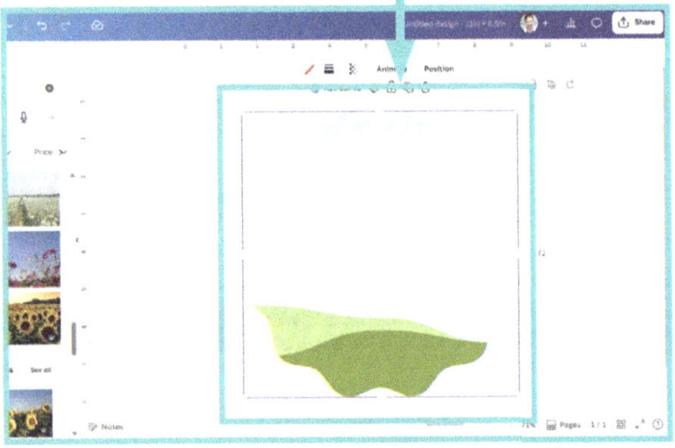

Step 4: Click and drag the image from the Elements area onto the frame.

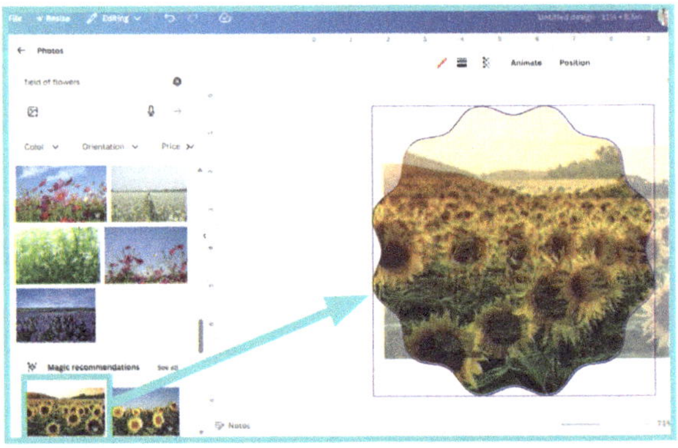

Step 5: Click on the image within the frame to crop, move, resize, and rotate it as needed.

The image is fit inside the frame. You can also do this with an uploaded image.

DESKTOP

HOW TO ADD EYE-CATCHING GRAPHICS TO YOUR DESIGN

Graphics can be used in almost any project, whether you plan to print it or share it digitally. Canva includes a huge library of graphics to choose from.

Step 1: Click on the **Elements** tab. Type in your search term(s) in the search bar and press Enter.

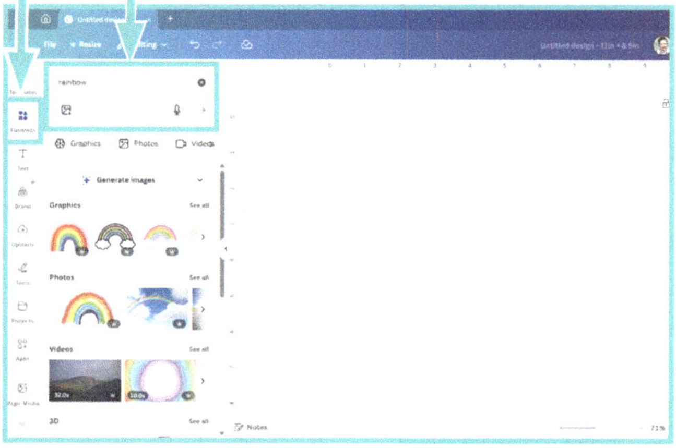

Step 2: Click on **See all** next to **Graphics** to see all search results.

See all

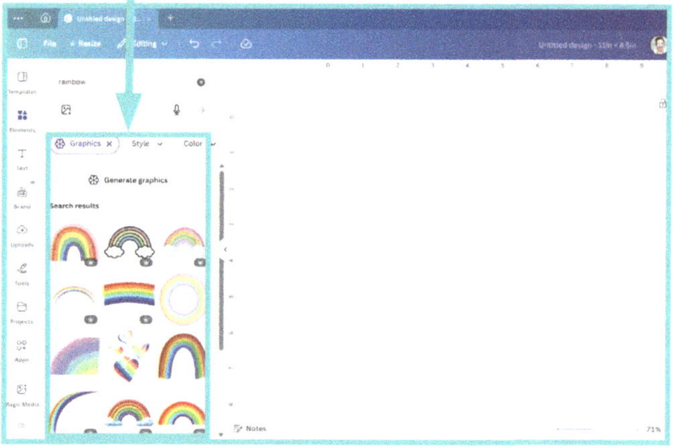

Step 3: Scroll through the results to find a graphic you want. Click on it to add it to the canvas.

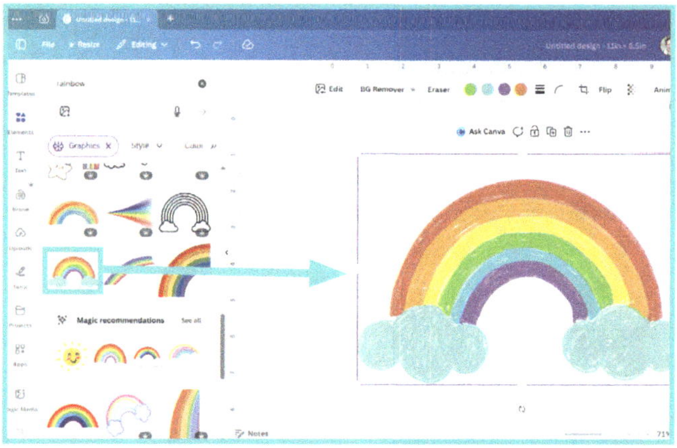

Step 4: Add additional graphics as desired.

TIP: You can add additional photos and other elements that are outside of your original search results. Just click on the **Elements** tab again, type in a new search term, click on **See all** next to the category you want to look under, and click on the next element you want to add to your canvas. You can repeat this process as many times as desired.

Note: Graphics with a crown icon are only available to Canva Pro members.

DESKTOP

HOW TO CHOOSE THE RIGHT PHOTOS FOR YOUR DESIGN

Photos can be used in almost any project, whether you plan to print it or share it digitally. Canva includes a huge library of photos to choose from.

Step 1: Click on the **Elements** tab. Type in your search term(s) in the search bar and press **Enter**.

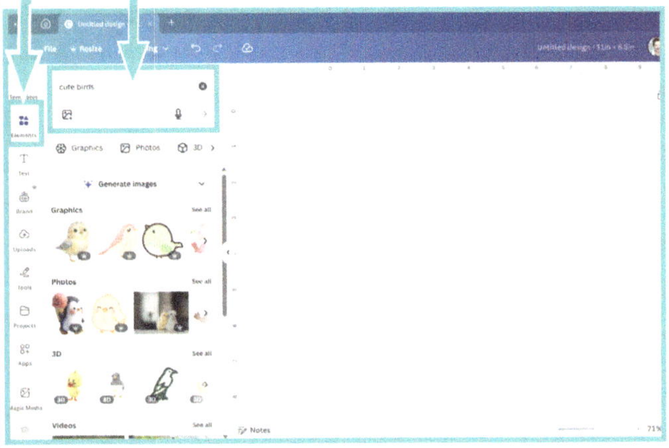

Step 2: Click on **See all** next to **Photos** to see all search results.

See all

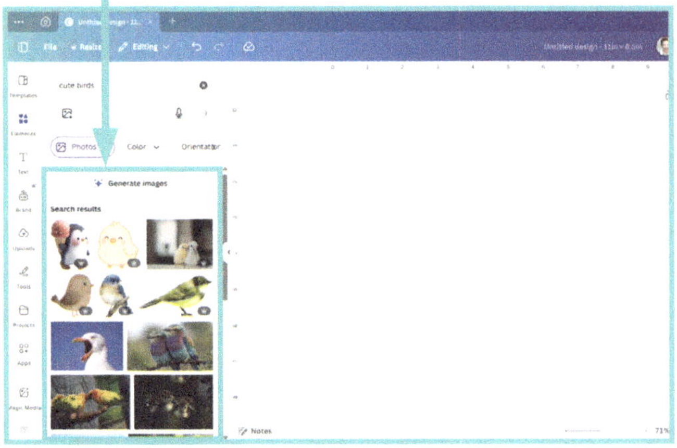

Step 3: Scroll through the results to find a photo you want. Click on it to add it to the canvas.

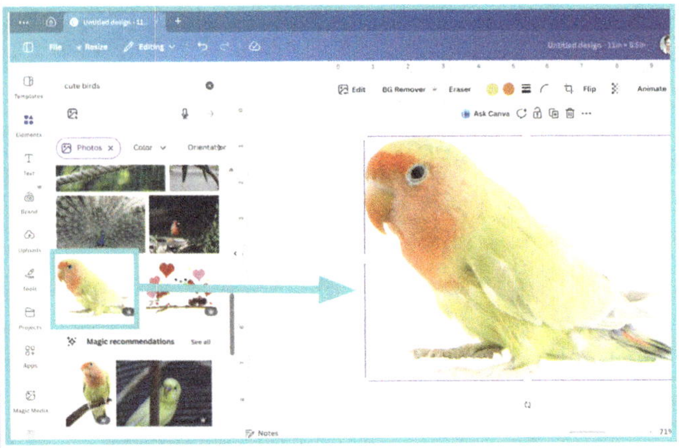

Step 4: Add additional photos as desired.

TIP: You can add additional photos and other elements that are outside of your original search results. Just click on the **Elements** tab again, type in a new search term, click on **See all** next to the category you want to look under, and click on the next element you want to add to your canvas. You can repeat this process as many times as desired.

Note: Graphics with a crown icon 👑 are only available to Canva Pro members.

DESKTOP

HOW TO EDIT PHOTOS

Canva's Photo Editor is part of its new Visual Suite 2.0 and allows you to customize your uploaded photos before opening or creating a new project.

Step 1: On the homepage, click on the **Photo Editor** icon below the big search bar.

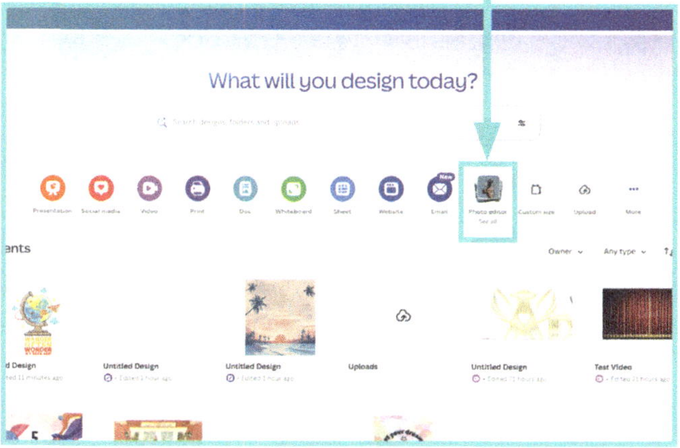

Step 2: In the pop-up menu, click on the photo you want to edit or upload a new photo.

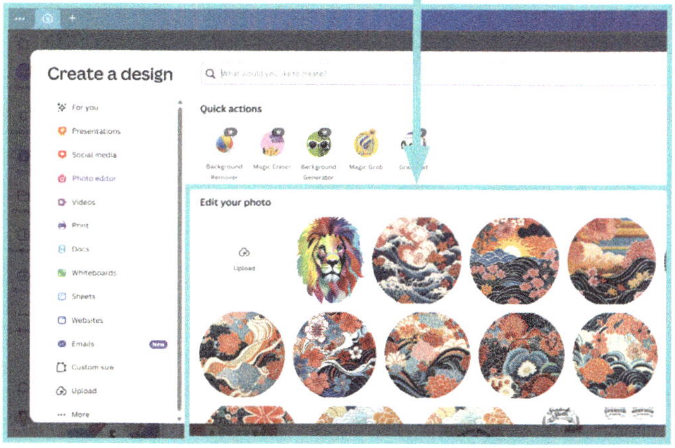

Step 3: Edit your photo using the **Crop**, **Adjust**, **Pixel Eraser**, **Magic Studio**, **Filters**, and **Effects** functions.

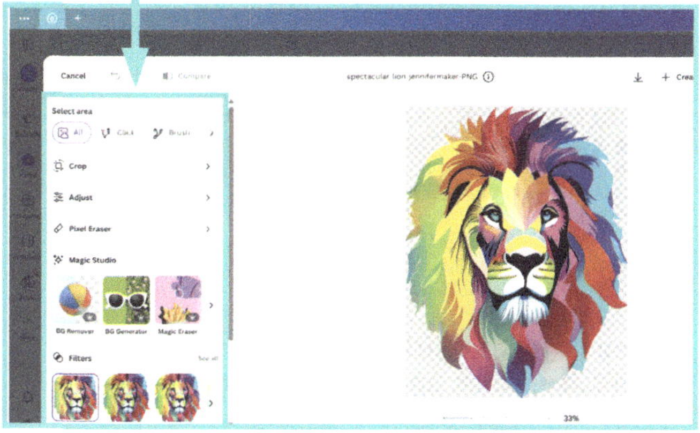

Step 4: Click **Save** to save the image or **+Create design** to open the image as part of a new project.

NOTE: You can also edit photos while you're working on a design. Just click on your photo, then click **Edit** in the menu bar that appears above the canvas, then use the tools that appear on the left side of the screen.

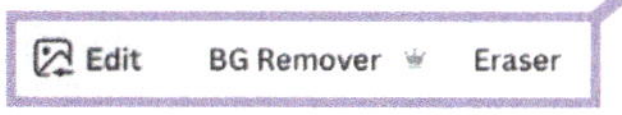

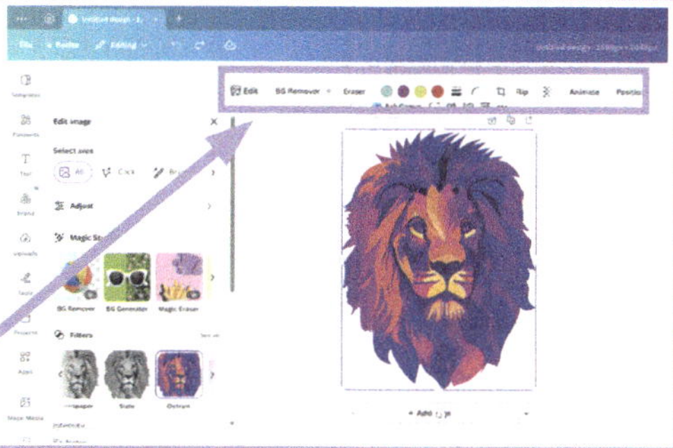

DESKTOP

HOW TO USE SHAPES TO ENHANCE YOUR LAYOUTS

Shapes are a very versatile element available in the Canva library. They have a variety of purposes that you'll find useful in your projects.

Step 1: Click on the **Elements** tab. Click **Shapes**.

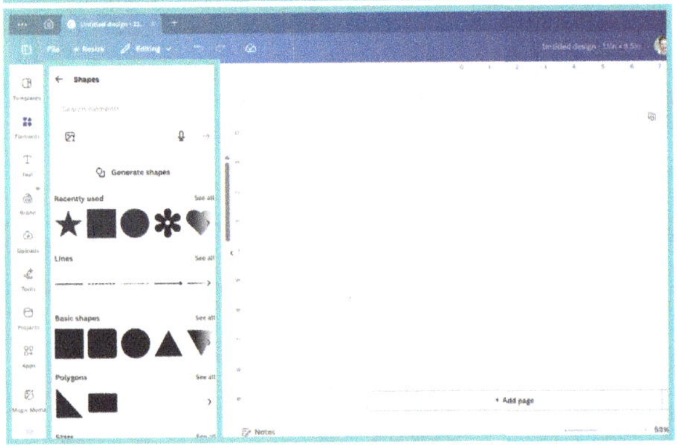

Step 2: Click on a **shape** element to add it to your canvas.

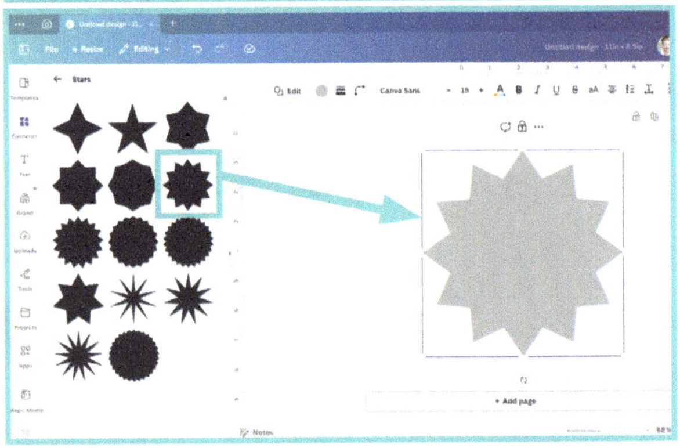

Step 3: Color – Click on the **shape**, click the **Color Picker**, then choose a **color**.

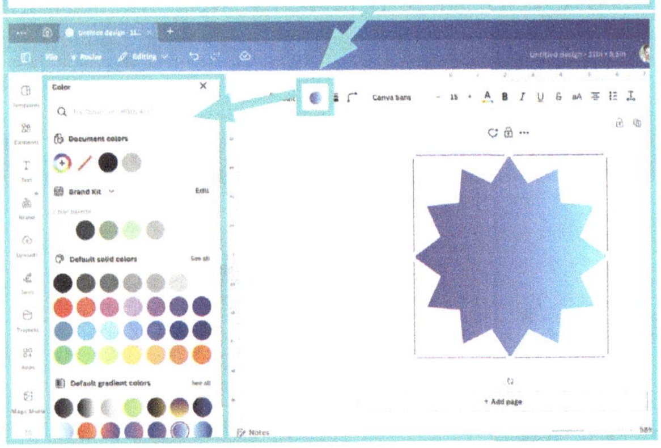

Step 4: Border – Click the **shape**, click the **stacked lines**, choose a **border** and **weight**.

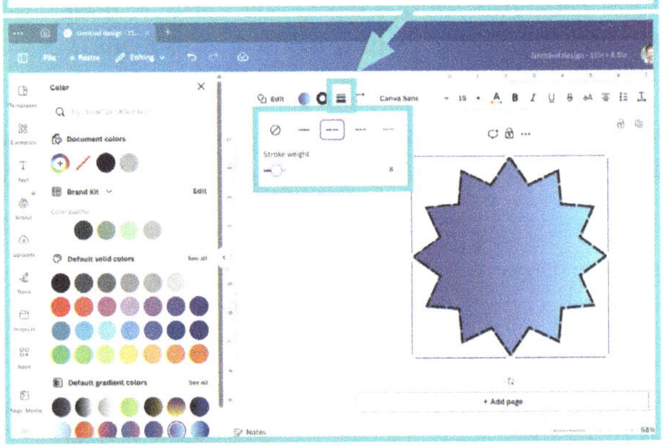

Step 5: Rounding – Click the **shape**, click the **curved line**, and change **corner rounding**.

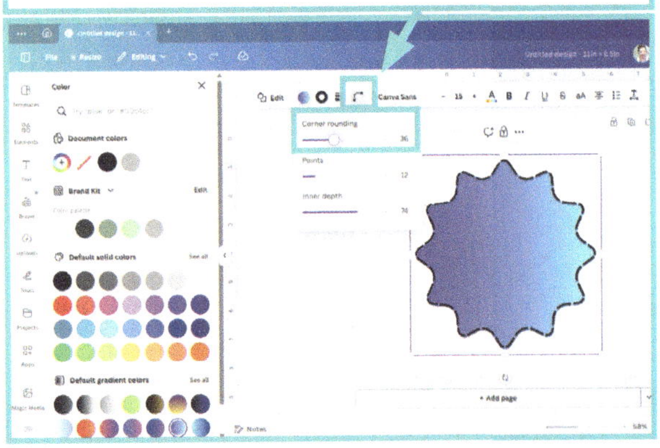

Step 6: Text – Click the **shape**, then choose **font size**, **color**, and **style** in the menu.

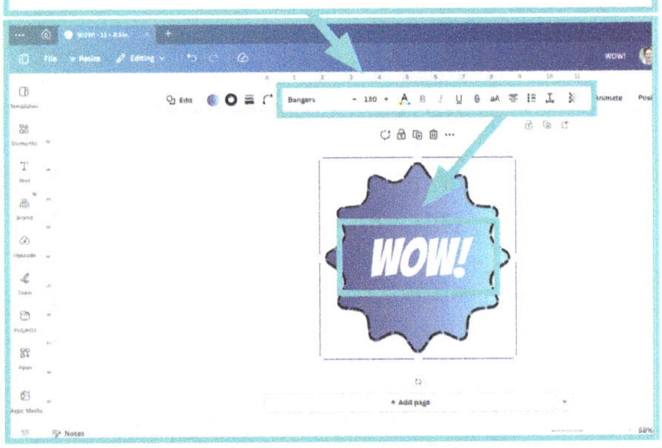

DESKTOP

HOW TO
FIND AND USE VIDEOS

Videos can be great additions to any project you plan to view, send, or present in digital format. Canva has a large library of videos to choose from.

Step 1: Click on the **Elements** tab. Type in your search term(s) and press **Enter**.

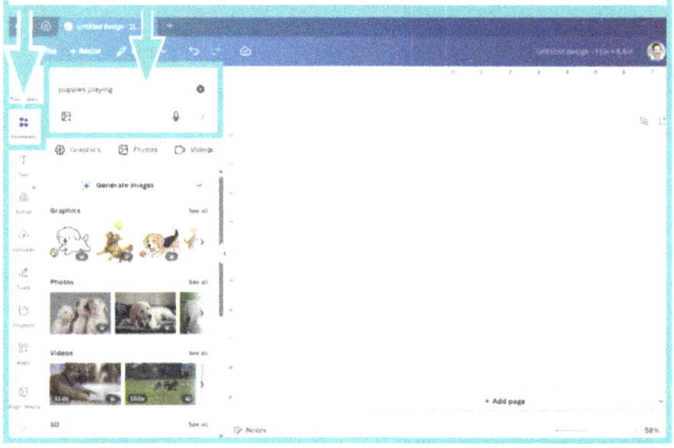

Step 2: Click on **See all** next to **Videos** to see all search results.

See all

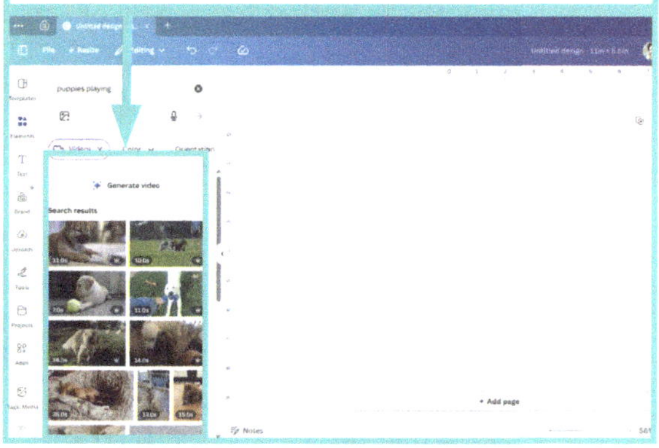

Step 3: Scroll through the results to find a video, then click it to add it to the canvas.

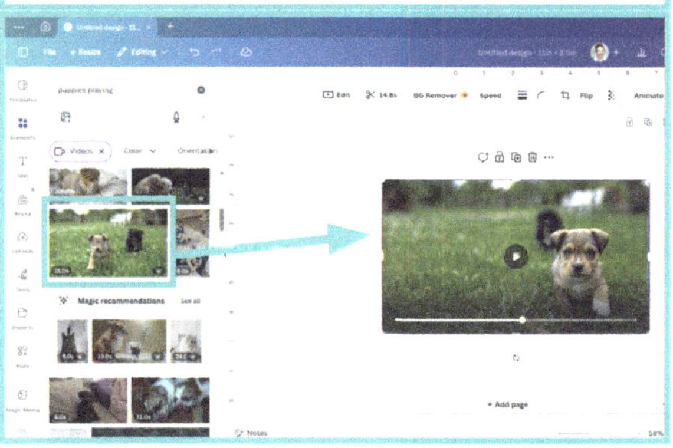

Step 4: The video will start playing automatically.

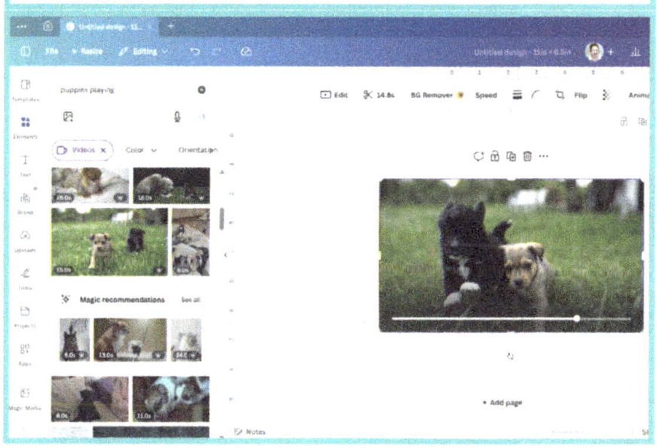

Step 5: To see video options, click on the video on your canvas.

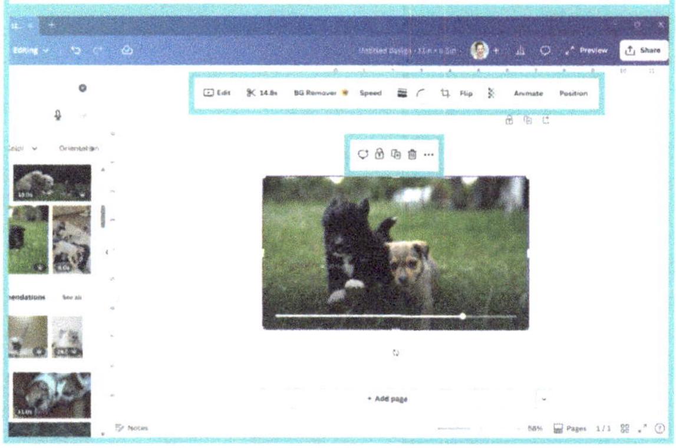

NOTE: You can see the length of each video in the bottom left corner of each thumbnail. The videos lengths are listed in minutes and seconds. For example, the videos to the right are 19.0 seconds, 19.0 seconds, and 11.0 seconds, from top to bottom.

HOW TO
EDIT AND ENHANCE VIDEOS

You can make some changes to video clips in the Canva library through the **Edit** button and by trimming the video clip down in length.

Click on the video clip on your canvas. To edit the video, click the **Edit** button. To trim the clip length, click the **icon** that has a pair of scissors.

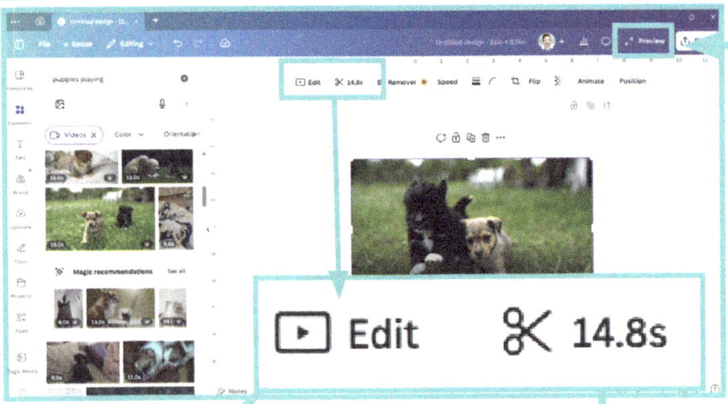

Click here to preview the full slide.

NOTE: Videos are only for digital finished projects.

Use Magic Studio (Pro members only) to remove the background. For all users, apply a **filter**, **adjust the volume**, **playback speed**, **looping**, **white balance**, **light balance**, **color**, and **texture** of the video.

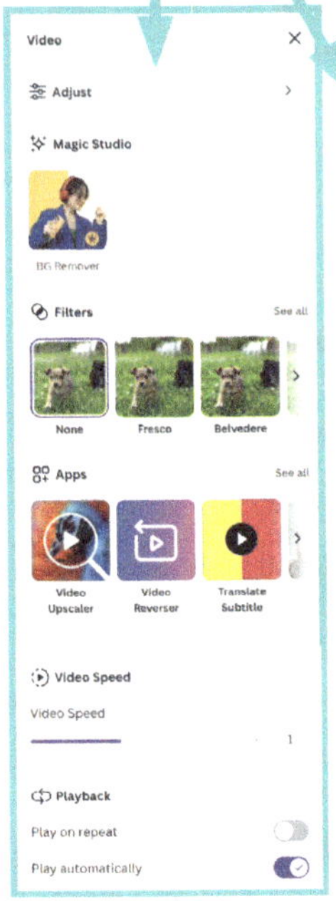

Use your mouse to click and drag the purple areas of the video bar to shorten the video. The length of the clip will appear to the left of the video bar.

NOTE: Some features are available only to Canva Pro members. For example, **Auto-trim** can automatically shorten a video clip by detecting and removing pauses or unnecessary sections, helping you quickly focus on the most important parts of the footage.

Auto-trim

HOW TO ADD AUDIO TO YOUR PROJECTS

Audio clips can be great additions to any projects you plan to view, send, or present in digital format. Canva has a large library of audio clips to choose from.

Step 1: Click on the **Elements** tab, then type in your search term into the search bar.

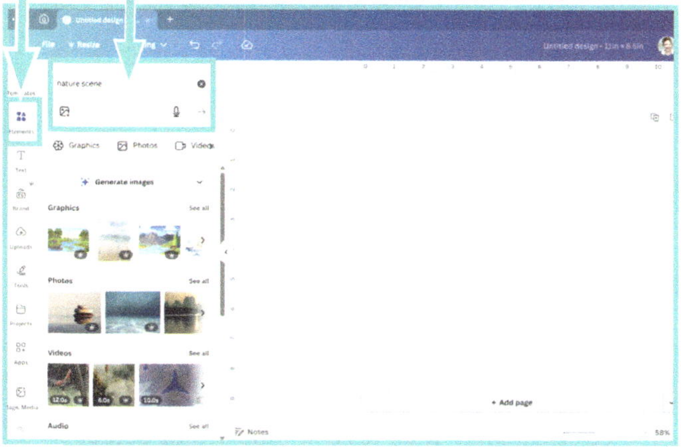

Step 2: Click on **See all** next to the Audio category to see all search results.

See all

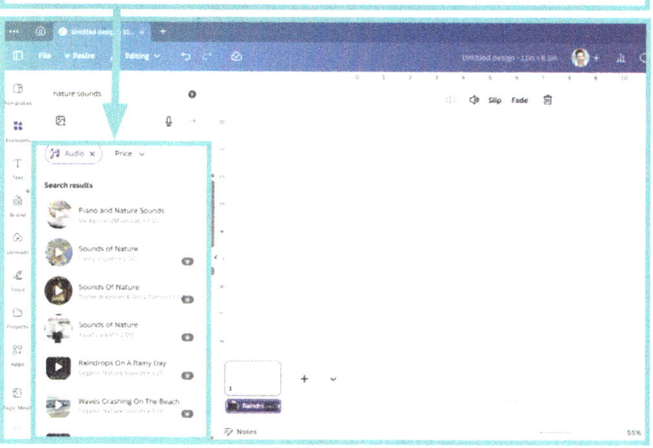

Step 3: Click on the **play icon** to the left of the audio clip to hear it. Click on the title to add it to your canvas.

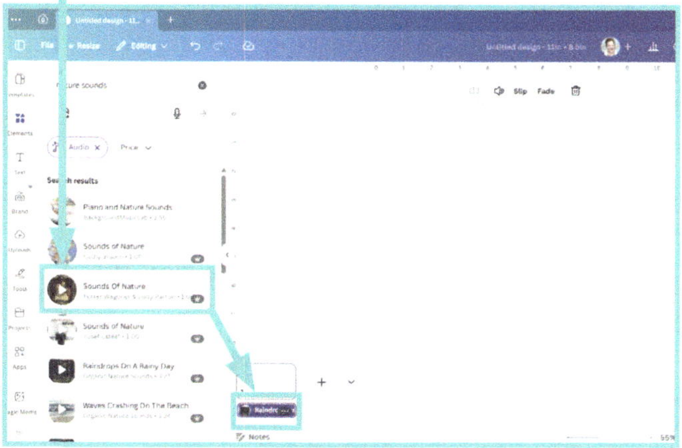

NOTE: Audio is only for digital finished projects.

Step 4: Edit the audio clip by adjusting volume, fading it in or out, and selecting a section by clicking on the audio clip.

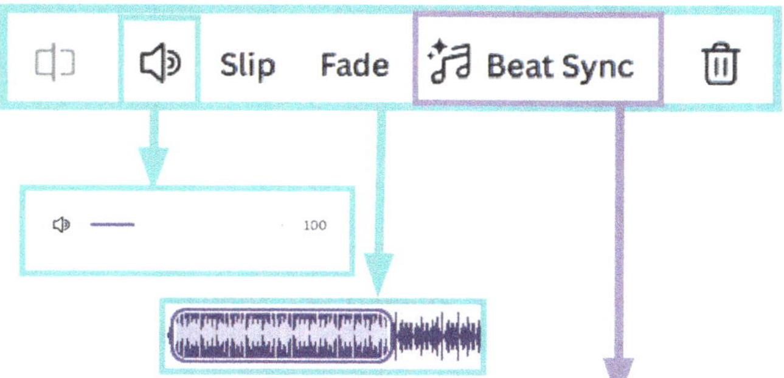

NOTE: The "Beat Sync" feature for Pro members will automatically time your project pages and elements to the music.

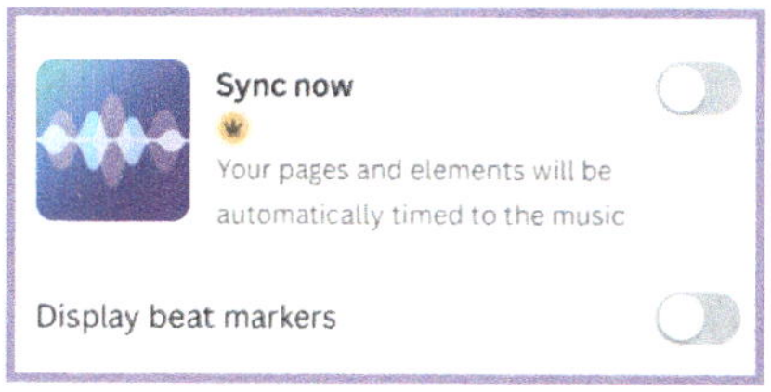

HOW TO MAKE YOUR DESIGNS LOOK REAL WITH MOCKUPS

Mockups are a great way to demonstrate how a finished product you're making or selling will look with your image or logo on it.

Step 1: Click on the **Elements** tab, then click **Mockups**.

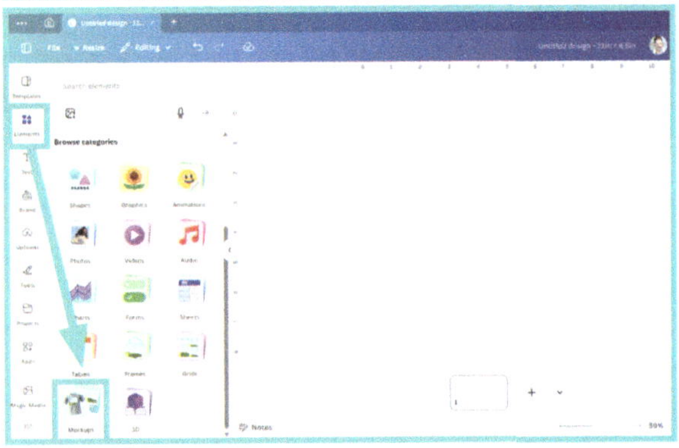

Step 2: Click **See all** on a Mockup category to see all available Mockups.

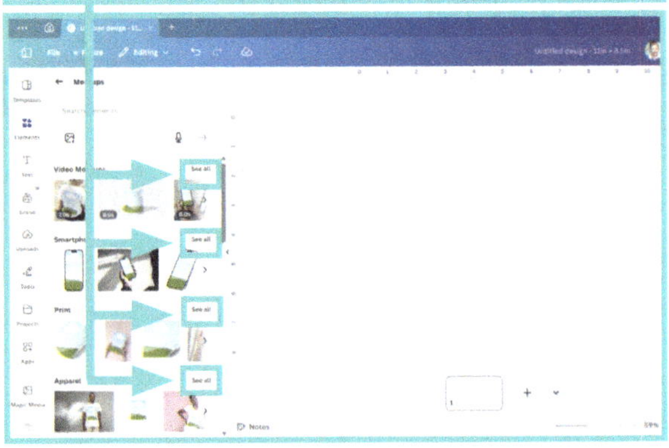

Step 3: Look through the Mockups to find the one you want to use.

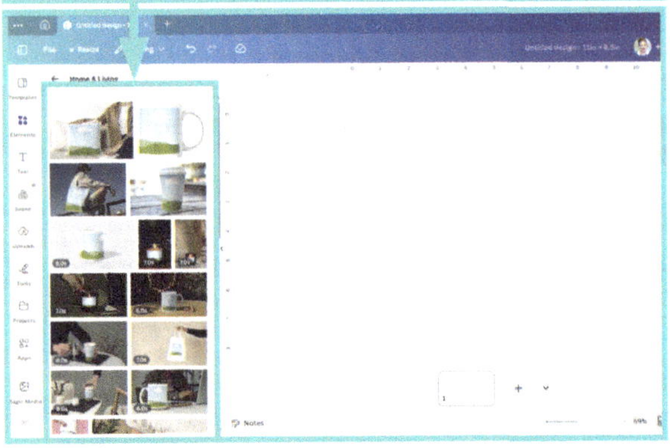

Step 4: Click to add the **Mockup** to the canvas, then click on the mockup to select it.

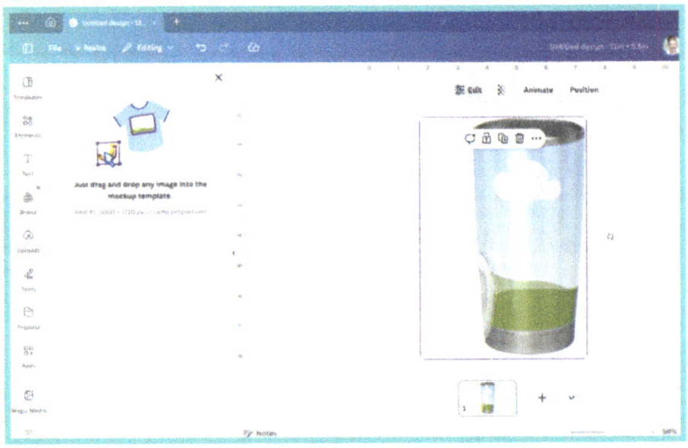

Step 5: Click the **Uploads** tab. Upload your image. Click, hold and drag the image to add it to the canvas.

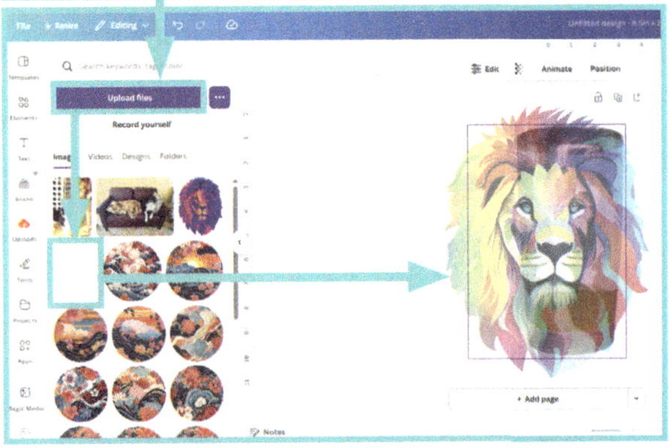

Step 6: Click and hold the image over the Mockup to combine them.

HOW TO CREATE CHARTS TO VISUALIZE DATA

Charts are a great way to display data in a presentation. Canva includes a variety of charts to help you visualize your data clearly.

Step 1: Click the **Elements** tab, then click **Charts**.

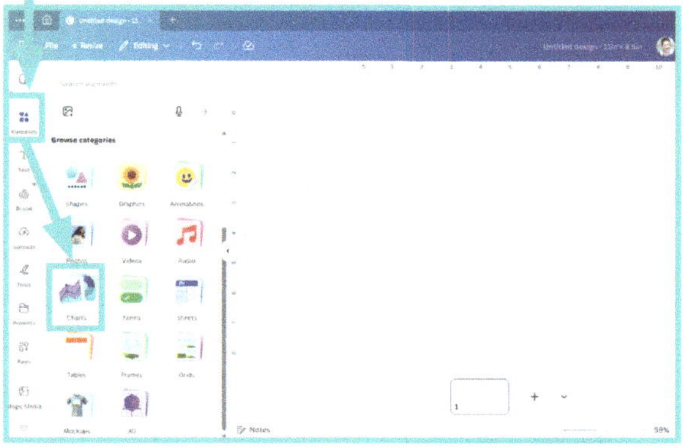

Step 2: Look for the chart you want to use, then click to add it to the canvas.

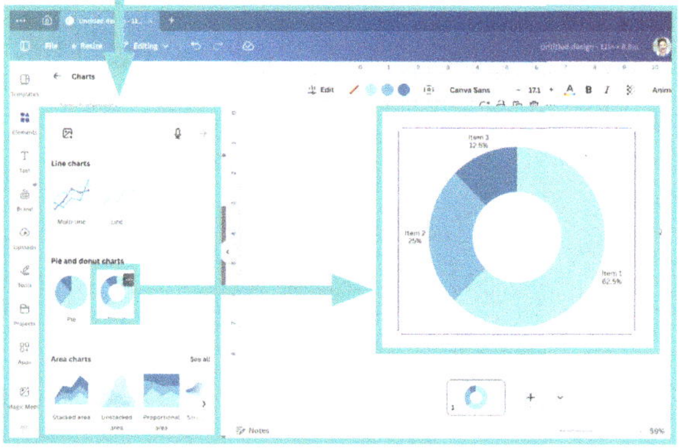

Step 3: Enter your data labels into the chart.

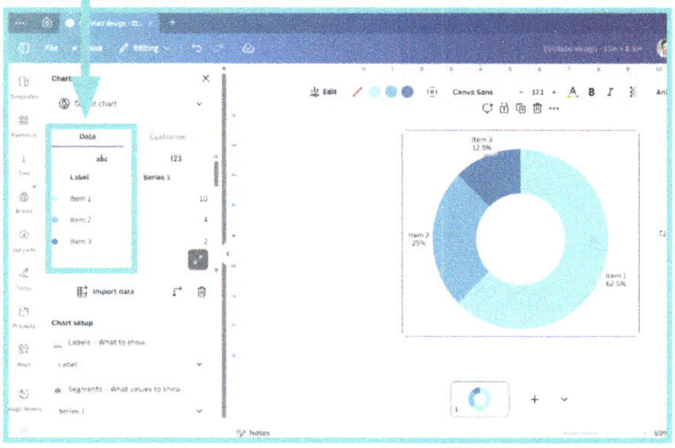

Step 4: Input your numerical data into the chart.

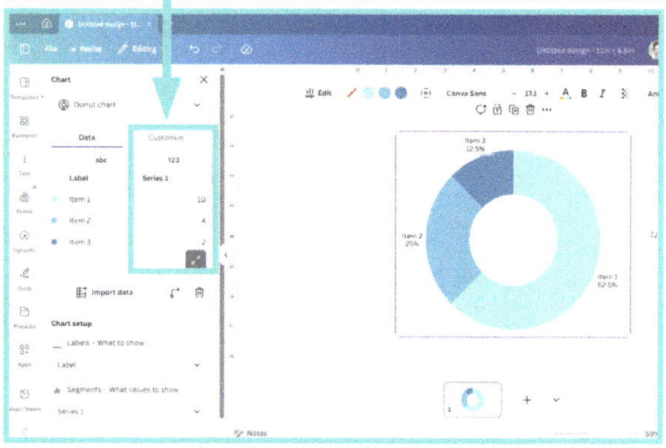

Step 5: Click **Customize** and choose the settings you want to use.

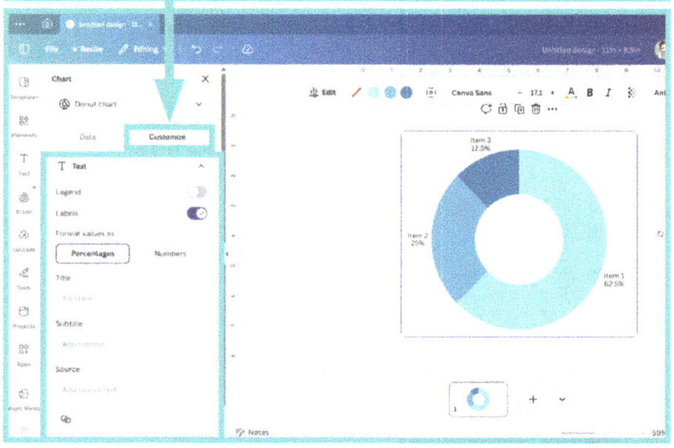

Step 6: Click on a chart segment and use the menu bar to change colors and fonts.

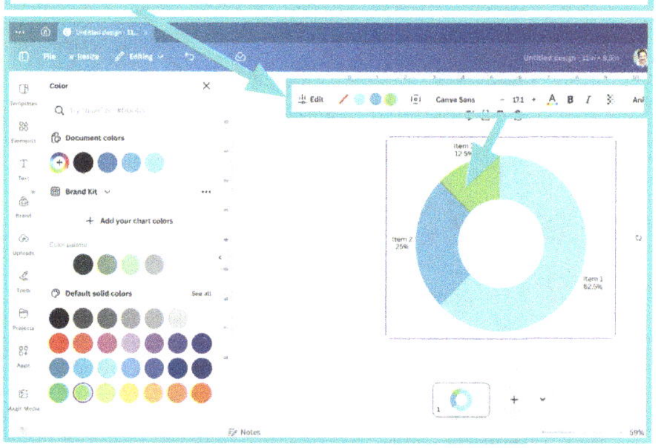

HOW TO ARRANGE PHOTOS AND ELEMENTS WITH GRIDS

Grids are organized collages for elements such as graphics, photos, stickers, and more. Canva has a library of grids available for you to use.

Step 1: Click on **Elements**, then find **Grids** and click to open.

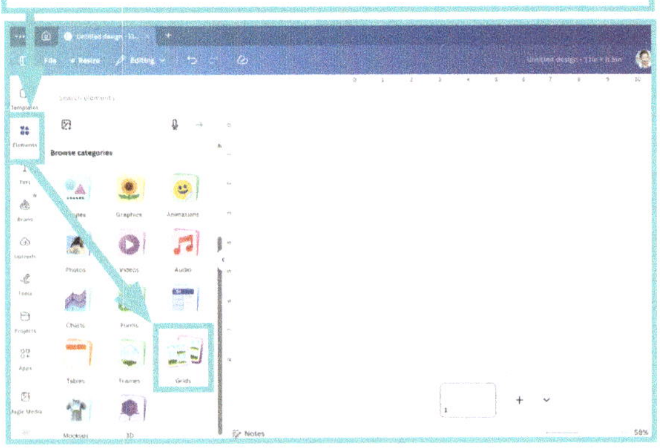

Step 2: Look through the library of Grids to find the one you want to use.

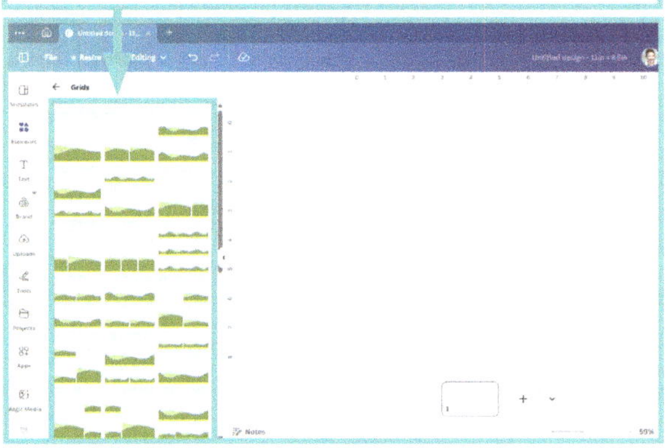

Step 3: Click on the Grid to add it to your canvas.

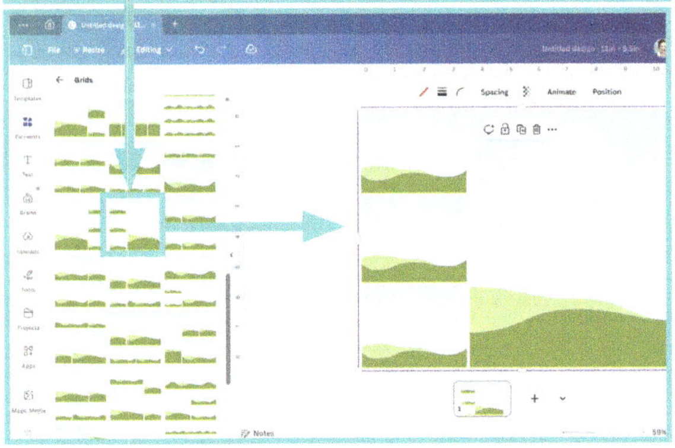

Step 4: Click on **Elements** again to find elements to add to your grid.

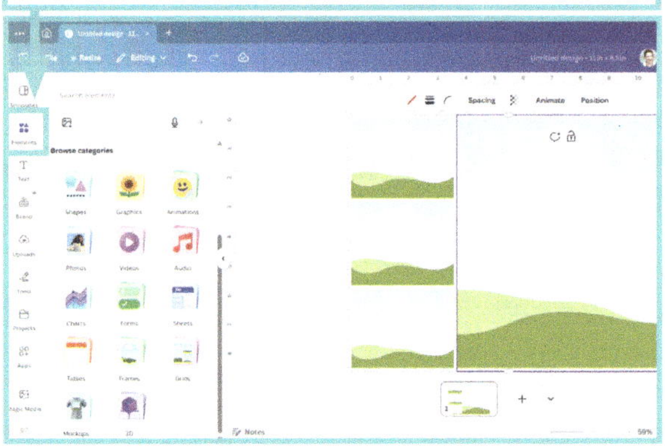

Step 5: Search for elements to add, then click and drag to each Grid space.

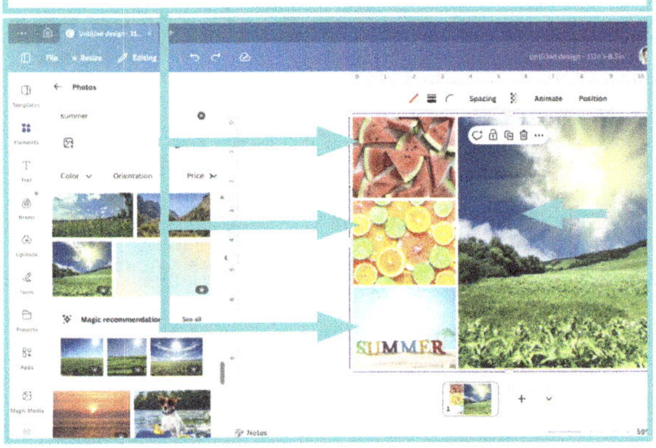

Step 6: Adjust Grid spacing – Click on the **Grid**, click **Spacing**, then use the **sliding bar**.

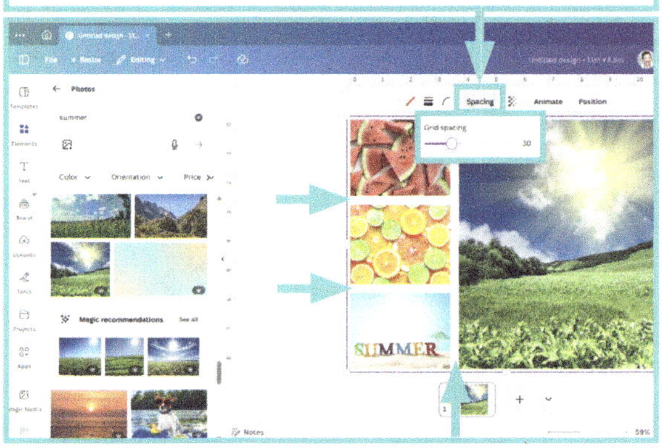

HOW TO FIND CURATED ELEMENT COLLECTIONS

Collections are curated groups of design elements organized around a specific topic or theme. They help you quickly find related graphics, photos, and other assets.

Step 1: Click on the **Elements** tab, click on **Graphics**, and then scroll down to **Collections**.

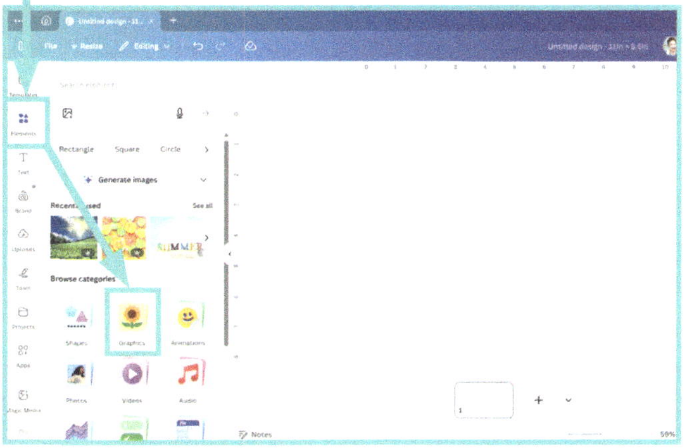

Step 2: Scroll through the **Collections** to find one that you want to look at.

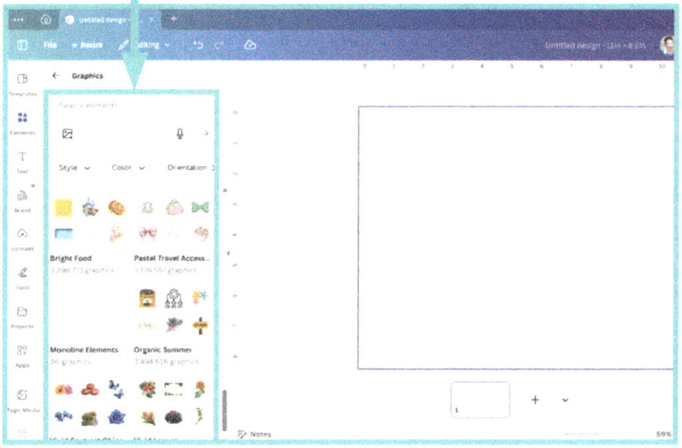

Step 3: Click on the Collection to look through the images within the Collection.

Step 4: Click on images to add them to the canvas.

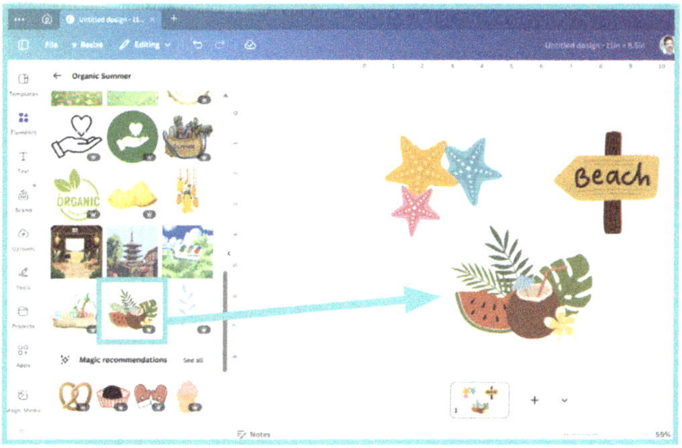

DESKTOP

HOW TO ADD STICKERS FOR FUN DESIGNS

Stickers are cute animated graphics that can be used to catch your eye on digital finished projects.

Step 1: Click on the Elements tab and click Animations.

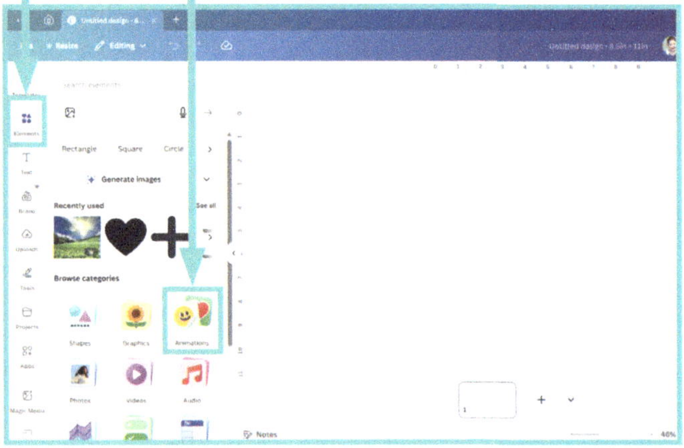

Step 2: Click See all next to a category or refine your search in the search box.

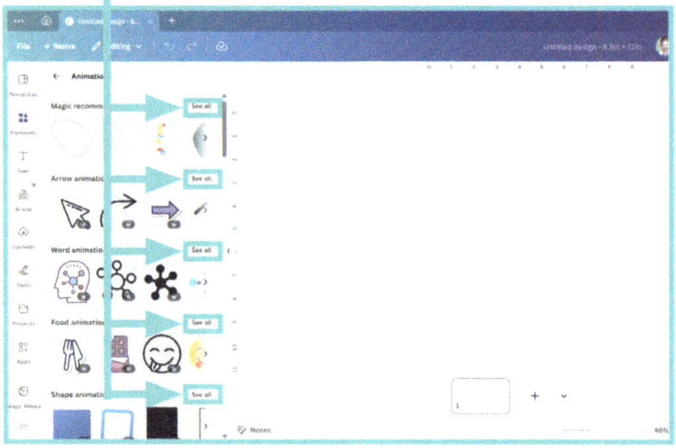

Step 3: Look through the stickers within the category.

Step 4: Click on stickers to add them to the canvas. The animation will start.

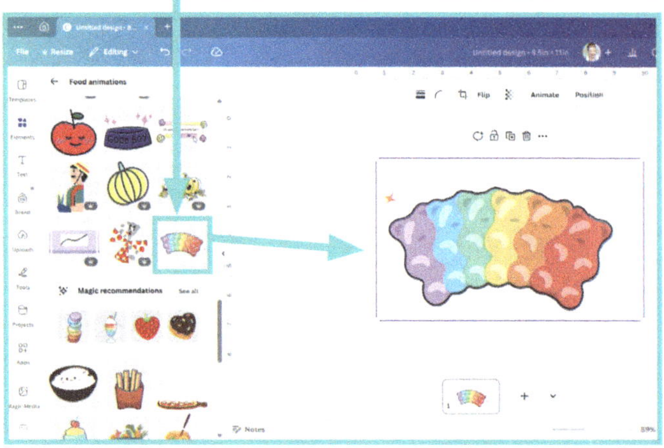

NOTE: Most stickers are only for digital finished projects since they are animated.

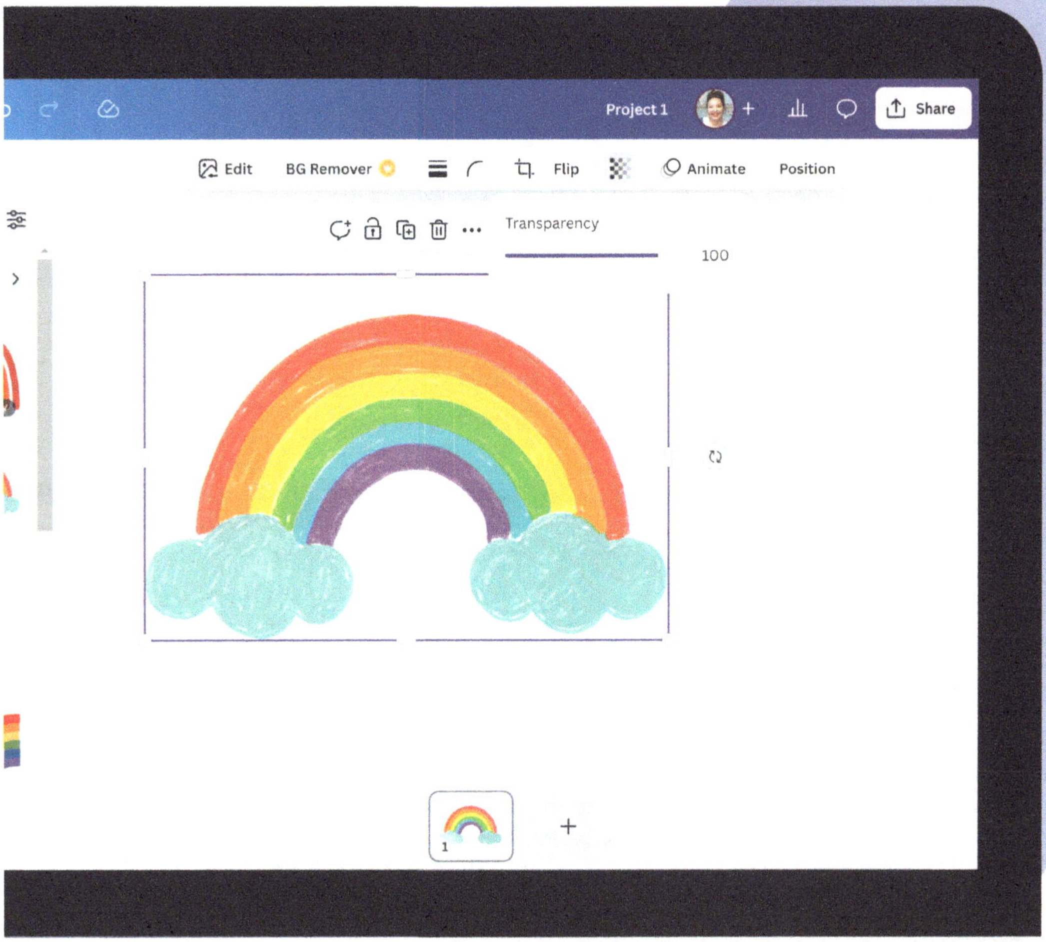

DESKTOP: PRECISION EDITING AND ENHANCEMENTS

HOW TO:

- ✔ GROUP MULTIPLE ELEMENTS TOGETHER
- ✔ RESIZE ELEMENTS TO THE SIZE YOU NEED
- ✔ ROTATE ELEMENTS FOR THE PERFECT LOOK
- ✔ CROP ELEMENTS AND IMAGES TO FIT YOUR DESIGN
- ✔ ADJUST ELEMENT TRANSPARENCY FOR A COOL LOOK
- ✔ MAKE YOUR DESIGN STAND OUT WITH ANIMATION

HOW TO GROUP MULTIPLE ELEMENTS TOGETHER

You can group elements together so that they move as one if you want to move them all to a certain area on your canvas while still keeping their spacing relative to one another.

Step 1: Click and drag your mouse over all of the elements that you want to group together.

Step 2: Each element you want to group should have a purple box around it.

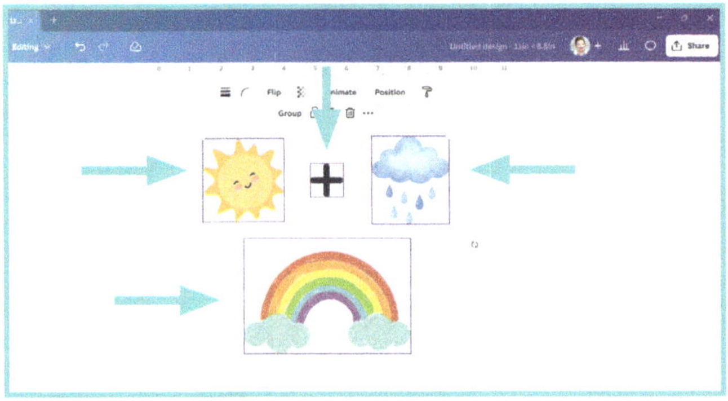

Step 3: Click on the word "Group" that appears in the small menu toolbar on the canvas.

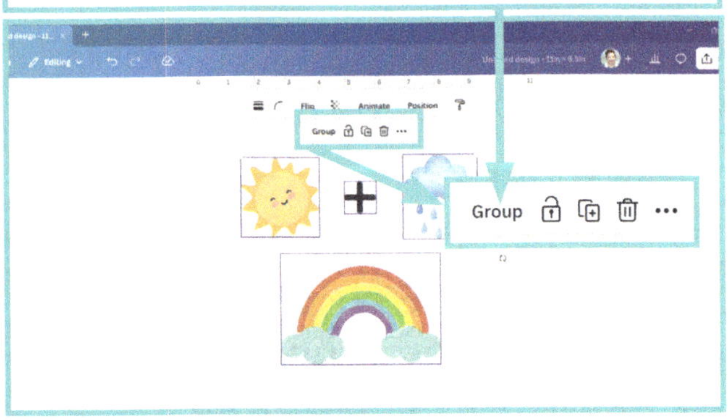

To Ungroup elements, click on the group, then click the word "Ungroup" in the toolbar.

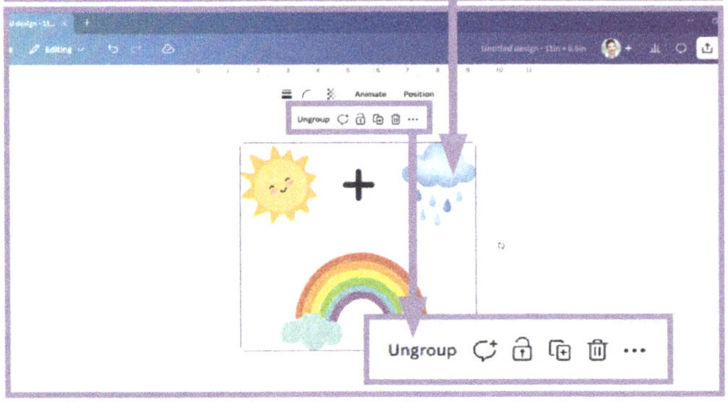

To edit an element inside a group, click the group, then click the specific element you want to adjust.

NOTE: Grouping is not permanent and can always be undone.

TIP: To group only specific elements that may be spread out across your canvas, hold down the Shift key on your keyboard and click on each element you want to group.

TIP: To ungroup only one element, click on the group and the element you want to ungroup, then click ungroup in the toolbar above the element.

HOW TO RESIZE ELEMENTS TO THE SIZE YOU NEED

You will need to resize and reposition almost every element that you add to your canvas in order to create the projects you envision.

Step 1: Add an element to your canvas.

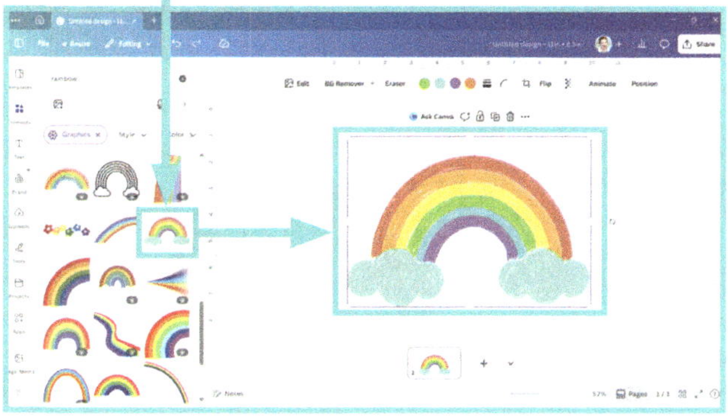

Step 2: Click on the element on your canvas.

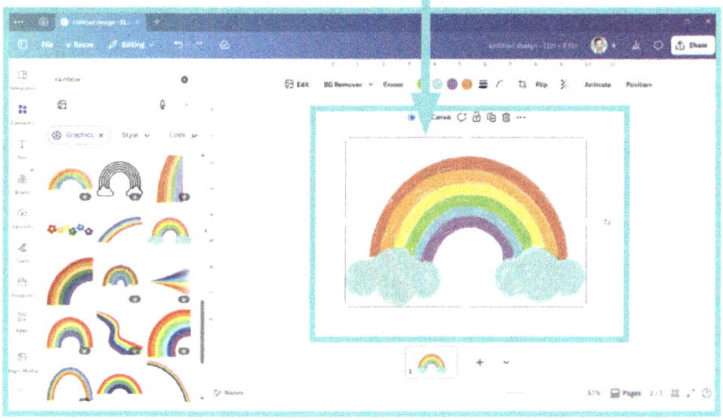

Step 3: Click and hold one of the circles at each corner of the element.

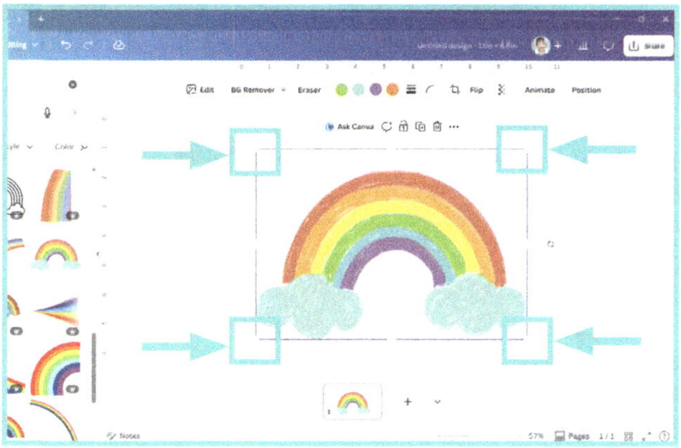

Step 4: Drag your mouse inward to shrink the element and outward to enlarge the element.

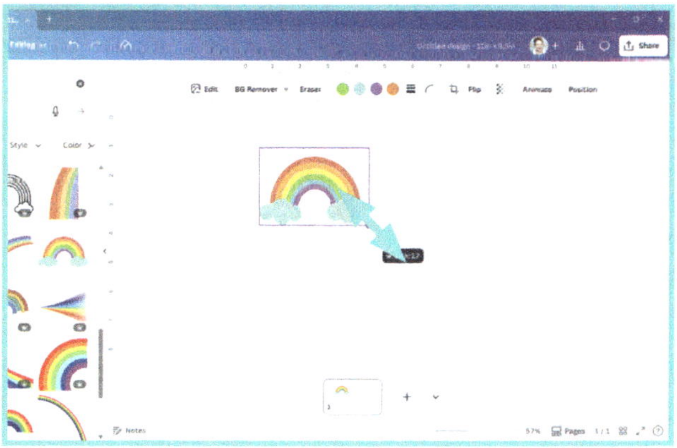

NOTE: You can resize an element as many times as needed.

NOTE: The dimensions of the element will appear as you are resizing the element. w: 4 h: 2.7

HOW TO ROTATE ELEMENTS FOR THE PERFECT LOOK

You can rotate elements and text to any angle on your canvas.

Step 1: Add an element to your canvas.

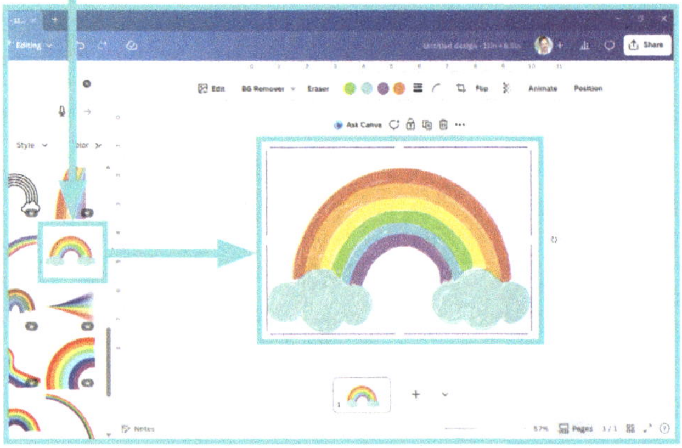

Step 2: Click on the element on your canvas. The Rotate icon will appear next to or below the element.

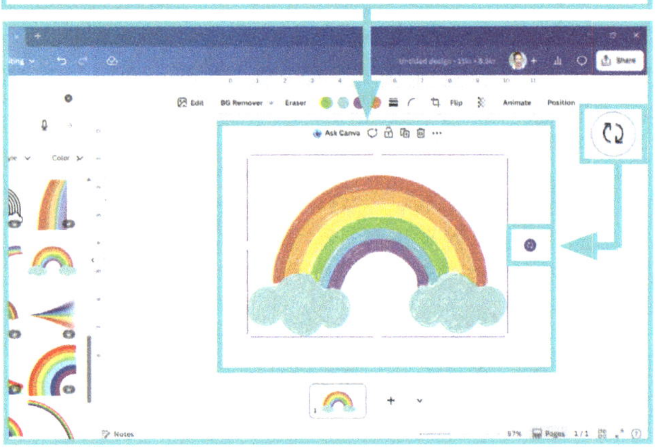

Step 3: Click and hold on the Rotate icon. Drag your mouse right or left to rotate the element.

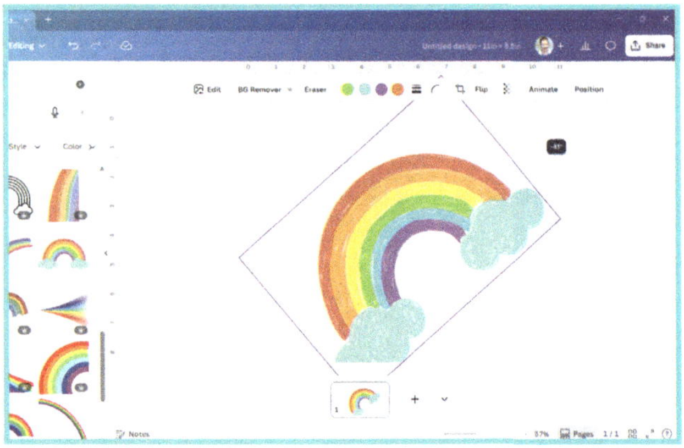

Step 4: If you want to lock the element in a specific place and at that angle, click the Lock.

NOTE: The degree of the angle will appear as you rotate an element.

-62°

DESKTOP

HOW TO CROP ELEMENTS AND IMAGES TO FIT YOUR DESIGN

You may need to crop an element if you only want a part of it. You can uncrop an element you have cropped if you decide you want the whole image.

Step 1: Add an **element** to your canvas.

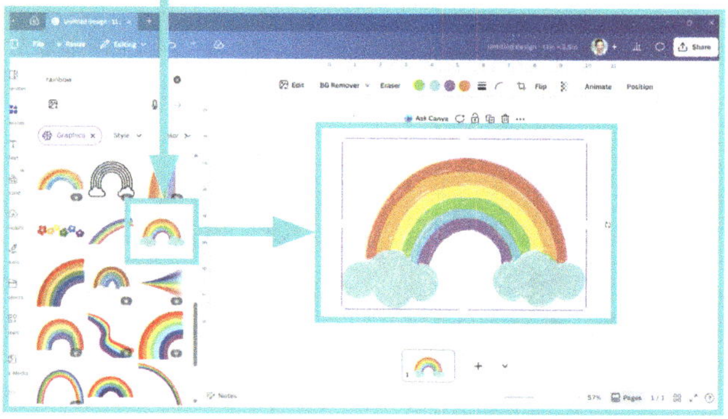

Step 2: Click on the **element** on your canvas.

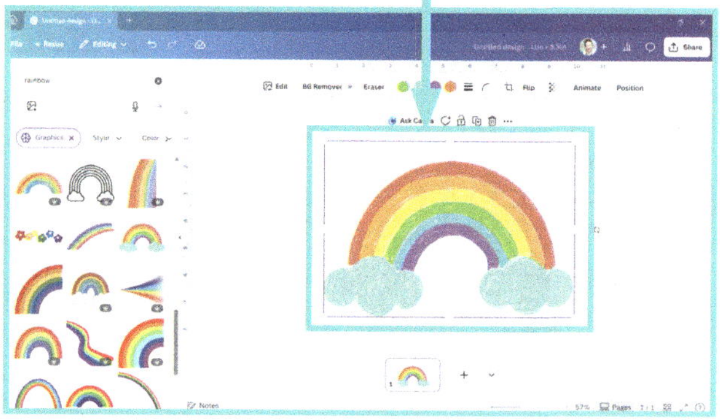

Step 3: Click and drag one of the four **bars** in the center of each side of the element to crop.

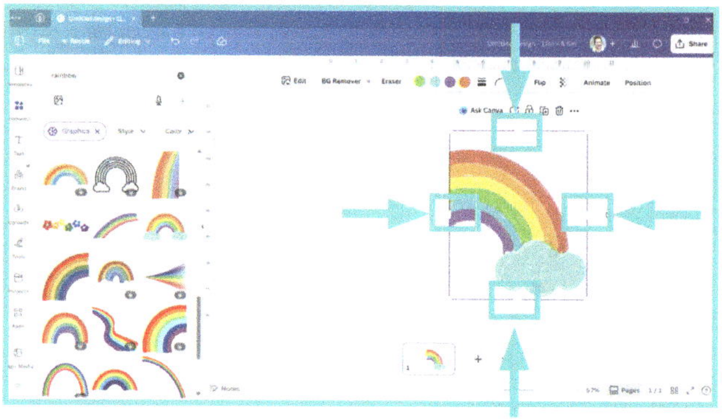

To **uncrop** an element, click on the same **bar** you used to crop it, then drag outward.

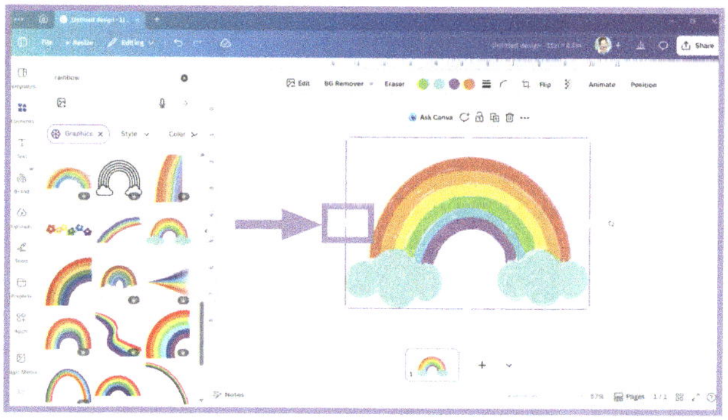

DESKTOP

HOW TO ADJUST ELEMENT TRANSPARENCY FOR A COOL LOOK

You can adjust the transparency of any element or text. This is useful when you need a particular image to stand out or look faded.

Step 1: Add an **element** to your canvas.

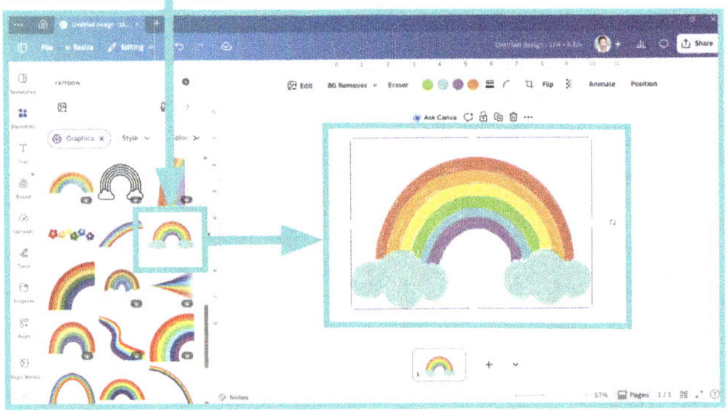

Step 2: Click on the **element** on your canvas.

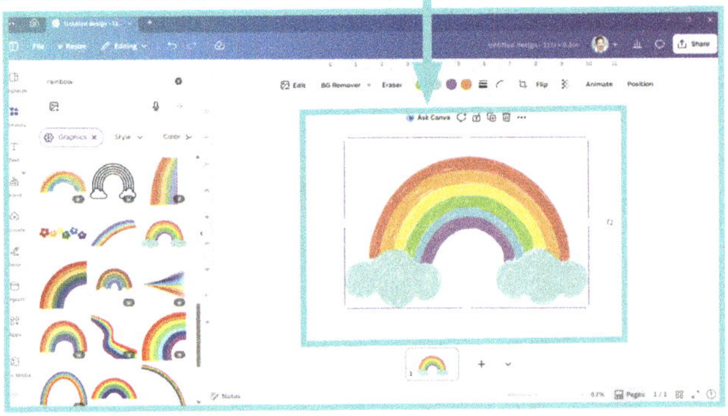

Step 3: Click on the **Transparency icon**, which looks like a fading checkered square.

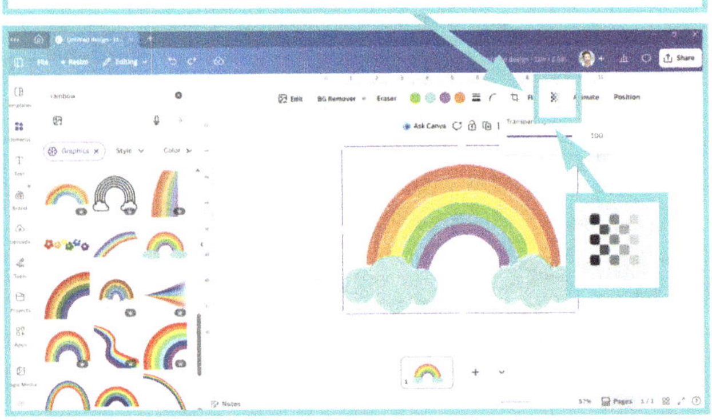

Step 4: Move the **sliding bar** or type a number from 0-100 in the box to adjust transparency.

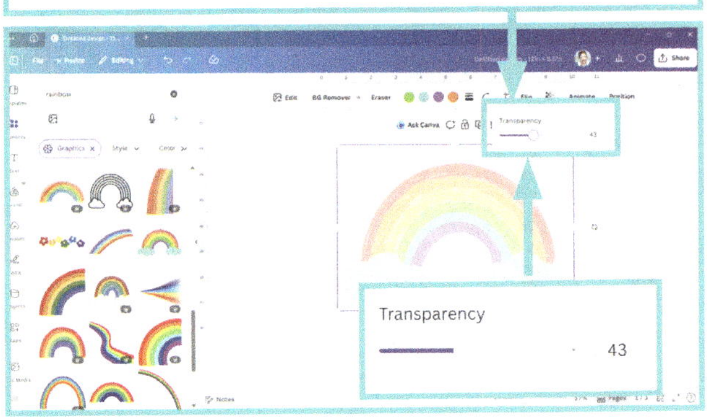

DESKTOP

HOW TO MAKE YOUR DESIGN STAND OUT WITH ANIMATION

Bring your designs to life by animating elements in Canva! Follow these simple steps:

Step 1: Click on the element you want to animate.

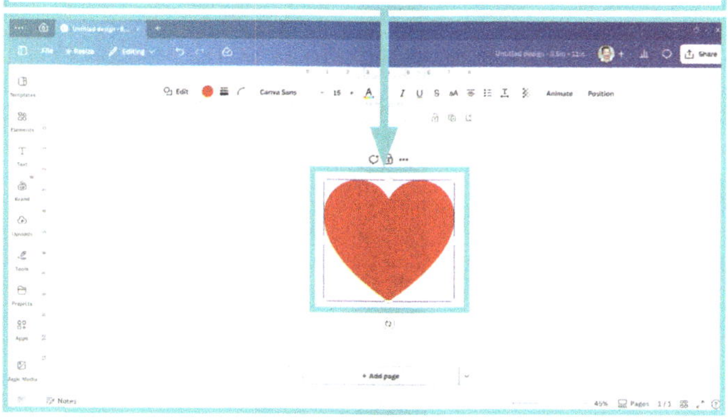

Step 2: In the toolbar at the top, click Animate. A side panel with animation options will appear.

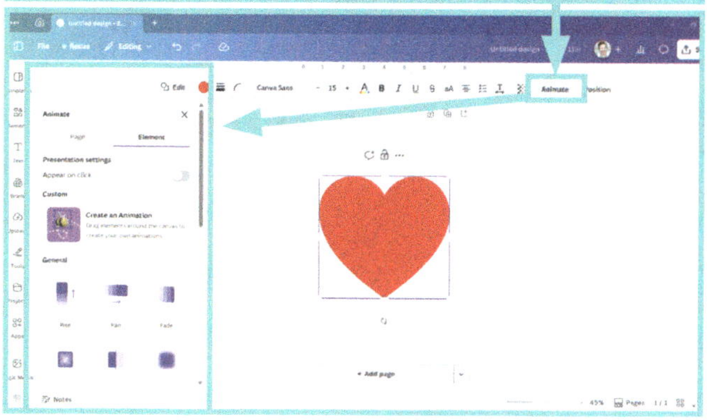

Step 3: Browse the animation effects in the General and Add-on effects categories.

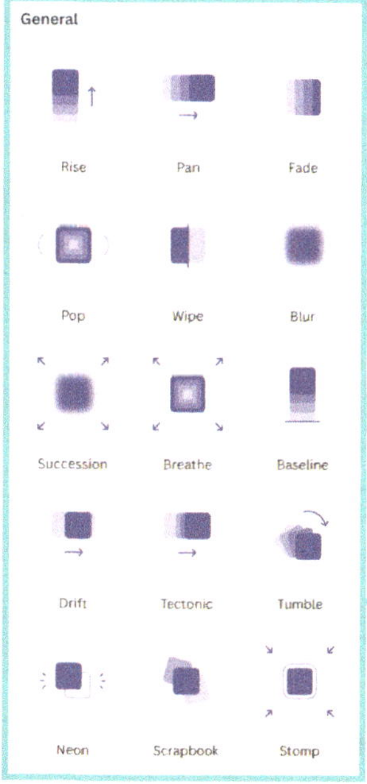

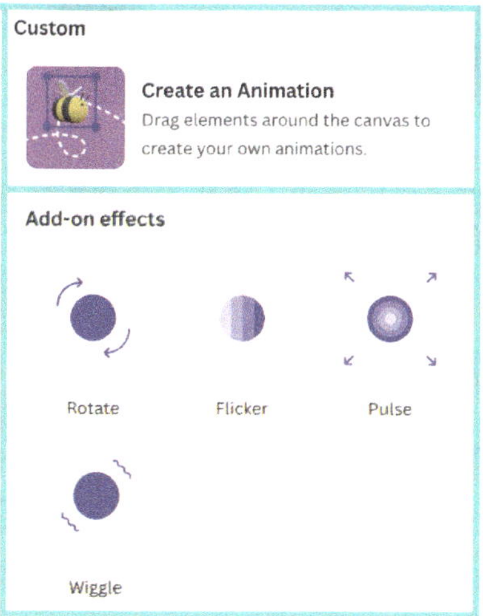

TIP: Hover over each style to see a preview.

Step 4: Click on the desired animation to apply it to your element.

Step 5: Use the settings below the animation preview to tweak the effect's duration, direction, or intensity, if available.

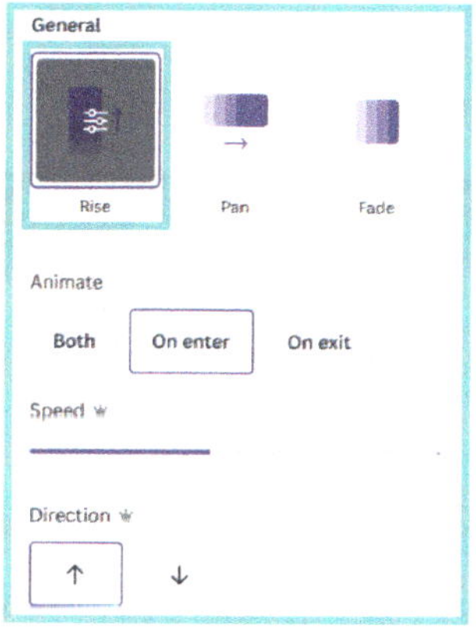

Step 6: Click the Preview button in the top-right corner to preview your animated design.

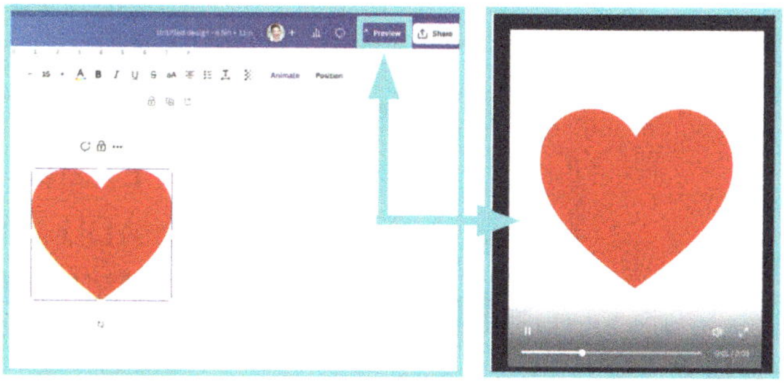

NOTE: To create your own animation, select your element, click Create an Animation in the Animate menu. Then drag the element around the canvas. To create straight lines, hold Shift whilst dragging your element. You can also control the speed of your animation with how fast or slow you move the element. Once finished, simply stop dragging the element.

WARNING: Some animations are marked with a crown icon and require a Canva Pro subscription.

Direction ♛ ← Speed ♛ ←

DESKTOP: MASTERING TEXT IN CANVA

HOW TO:

- ✔ FIND AND USE TEXT TOOLS
- ✔ ADD AND RESIZE TEXT BOXES TO FIT YOUR TEXT
- ✔ PICK AND CHANGE FONTS FOR THE RIGHT LOOK
- ✔ ADJUST TEXT ALIGNMENT AND SPACING
- ✔ EASILY STYLE YOUR TEXT
- ✔ ADD PAGE NUMBERS THAT UPDATE FOR YOU
- ✔ PAIR FONTS LIKE A PRO
- ✔ FADE TEXT FOR A SUBTLE EFFECT
- ✔ MAKE YOUR TEXT POP WITH SPECIAL EFFECTS
- ✔ ADD MOVING TEXT TO CREATE ENGAGING DESIGNS

DESKTOP

HOW TO
FIND AND USE TEXT TOOLS

The Text tab lets you add, format, and style text in your Canva designs. It provides pre-designed text templates to save time and inspire creativity.

Step 1: Open Canva and navigate to your design.

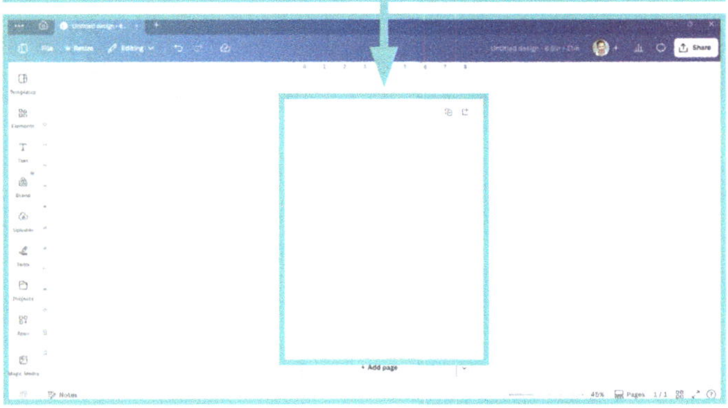

Step 2: Click the Text tab in the left-hand toolbar.

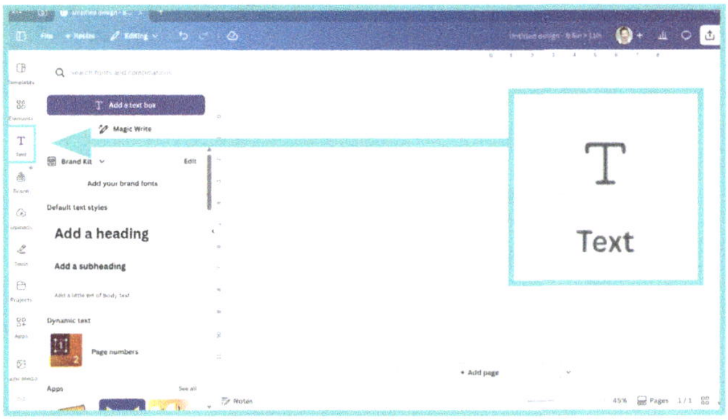

Step 3: Choose an option:
Add a Heading: For titles or large text.
Add a Subheading: Medium-sized text for subtitles.
Add Body Text: Smaller text for paragraphs.

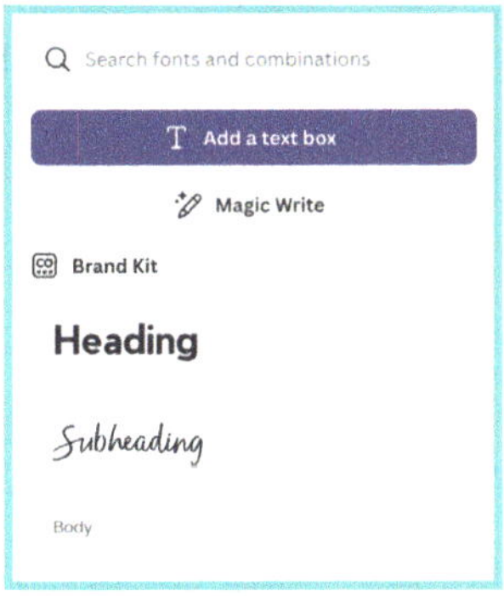

TIP: Click on pre-designed Font combinations to try creative layouts.

Step 4: Type in your desired text!

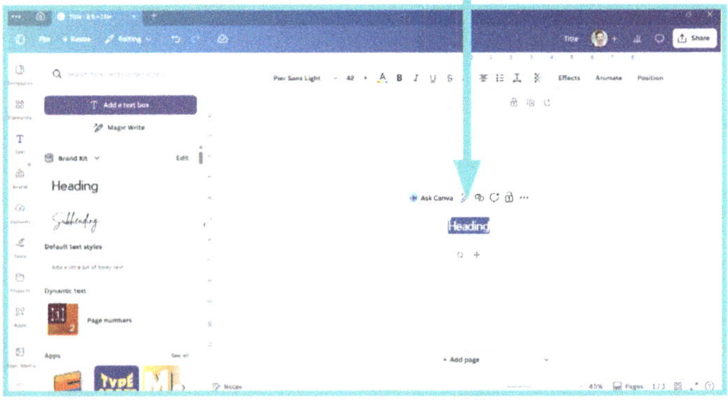

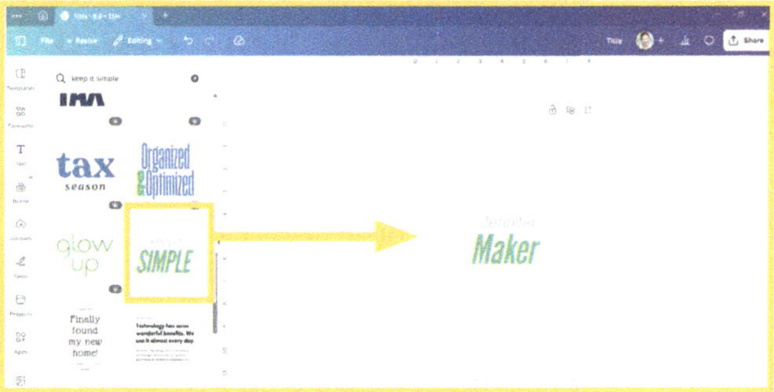

WARNING: Some font combinations are marked with a crown icon and require a Canva Pro subscription.

HOW TO ADD AND RESIZE TEXT BOXES TO FIT YOUR TEXT

Adding and resizing text boxes is essential for organizing text in your design.

Step 1: Click the Text tab and start typing your desired text onto the canvas.

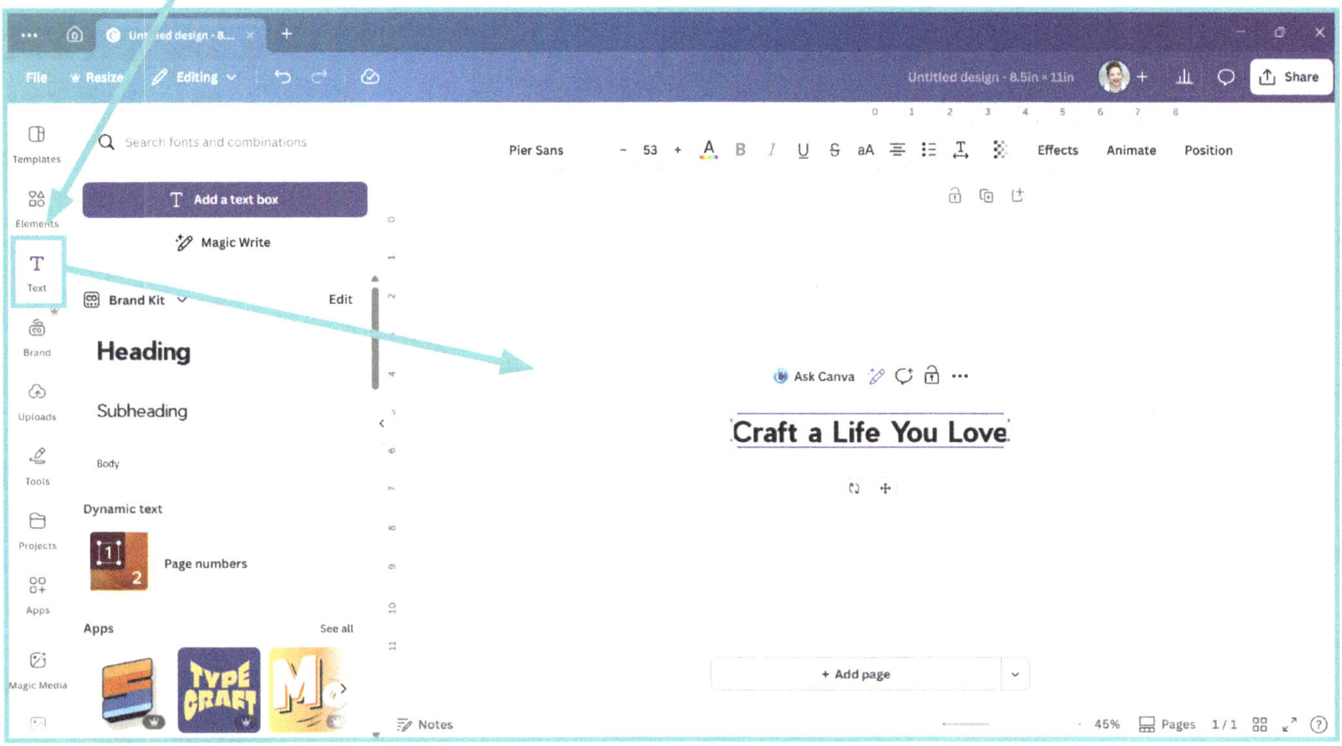

Step 2: Resize your text by clicking the text and either dragging the corner handles or adjusting the Font Size in the toolbar.

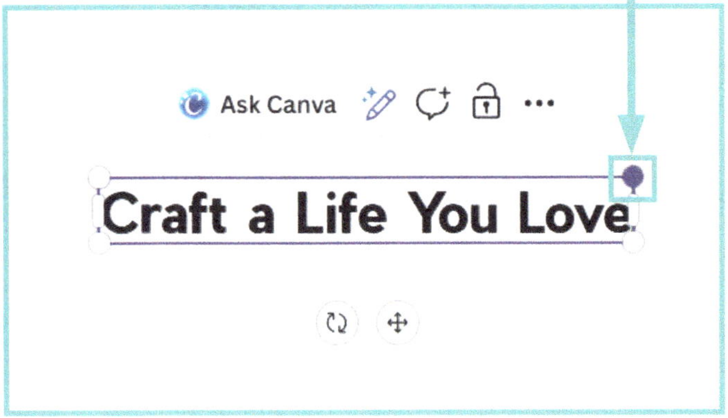

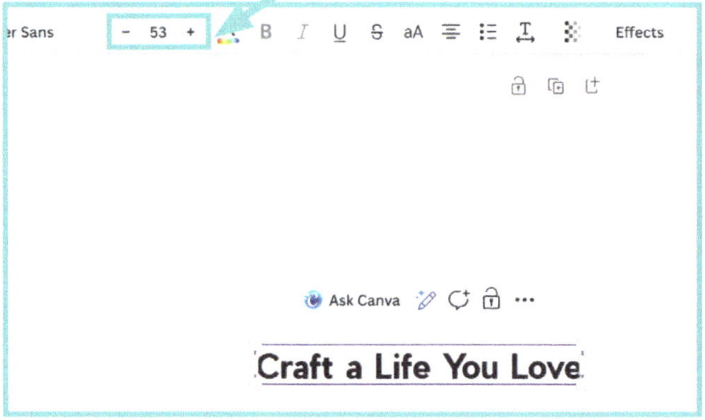

HOW TO PICK AND CHANGE FONTS FOR THE RIGHT LOOK

Customizing fonts and styles enhances the readability and aesthetic of your text.

Step 1: Click the Text tab and start typing your desired text onto the canvas.

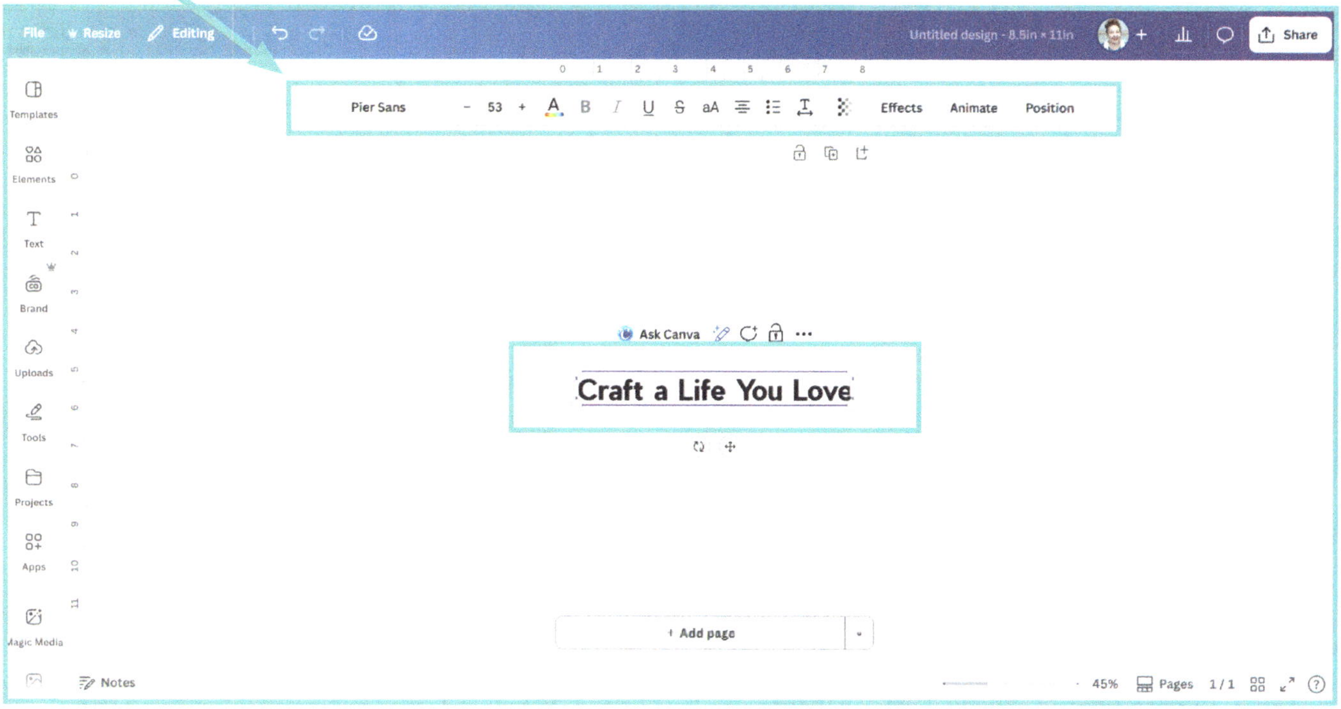

Step 2: To change text font: Access the Font drop-down menu from the top text toolbar.

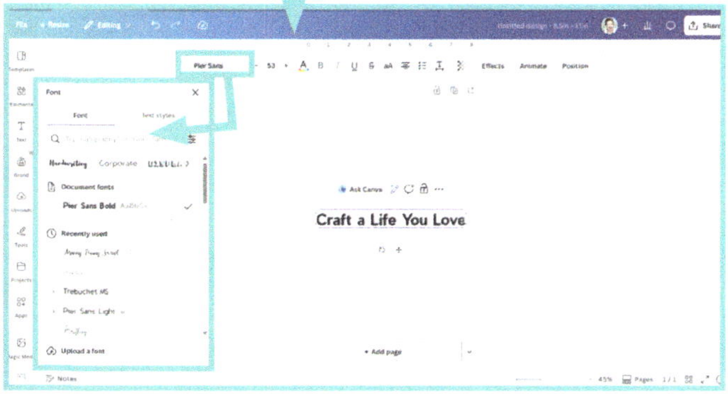

Step 3: To change text style: Use the top text toolbar to apply styles (**Bold**, *Italic*, Underline)

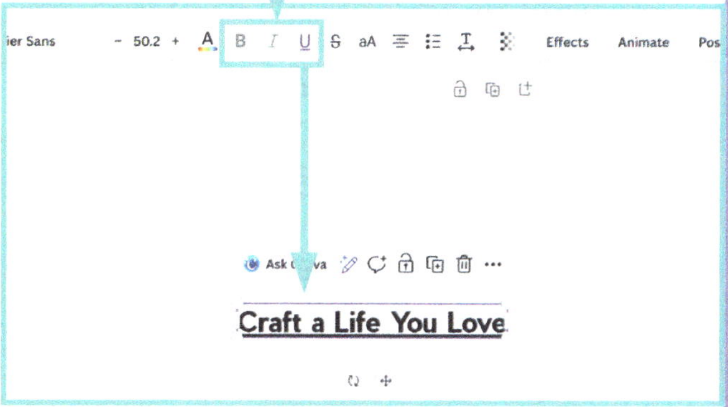

TIP: Play around with different font styles so you can see which you prefer. If you want to go back to a previous font but don't remember which one you chose, simply click the back button at the top.

DESKTOP

HOW TO ADJUST TEXT ALIGNMENT AND SPACING

Text alignment and spacing help structure your text for better readability.

Step 1: Select the text box and click **Alignment** in the text toolbar.

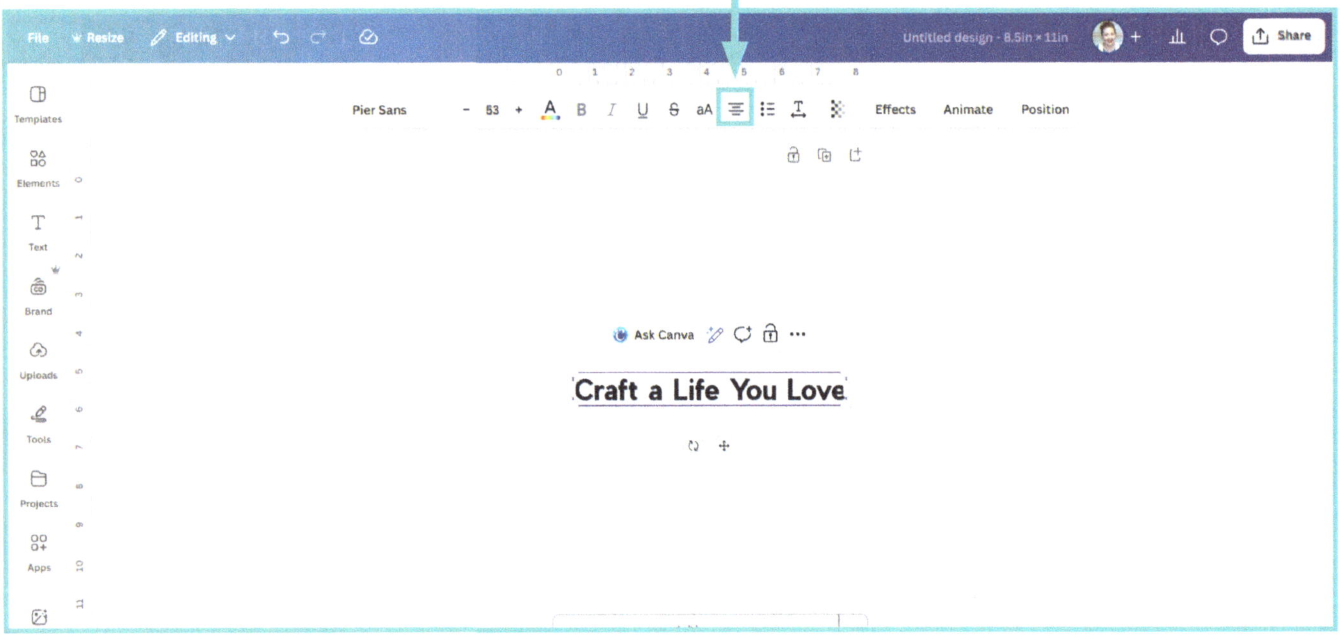

Step 2: Choose **Center**, **Justify**, **Left**, or **Right**.

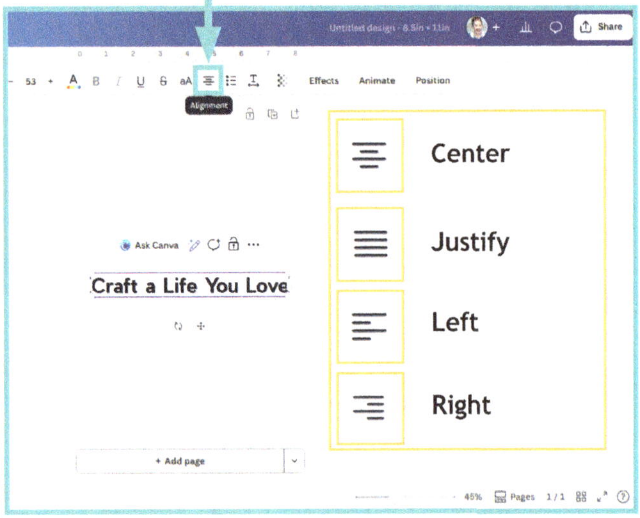

Step 3: Adjust letter or line spacing using the **Spacing tool**.

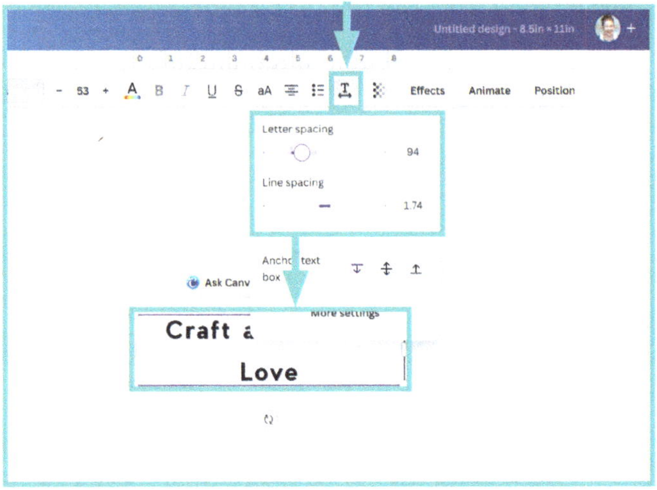

DESKTOP

HOW TO
EASILY STYLE YOUR TEXT

Text styles in Canva allow you to quickly apply pre-designed font combinations, color palettes, and font sets to maintain consistency and save time in your designs. Perfect for creating cohesive visuals with minimal effort.

Step 1: On your design canvas, click the **Template** tab in the left toolbar and click **Styles**.

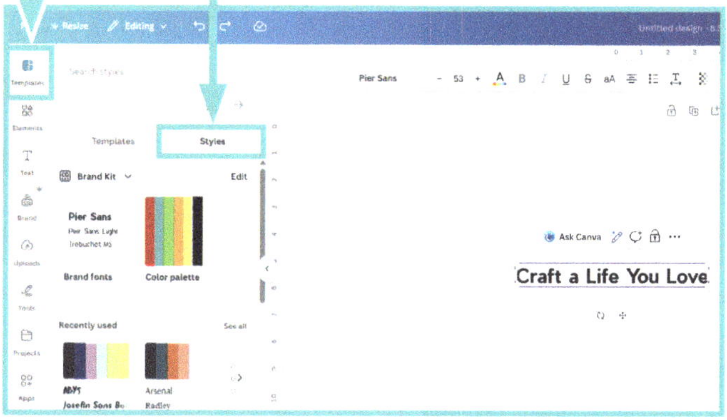

Step 2: Click on a style to apply it to your selected text box.

TIP: Click **See All** to see all the examples in the category.

Step 3: Apply a style by clicking on a style to apply it to your selected text box.

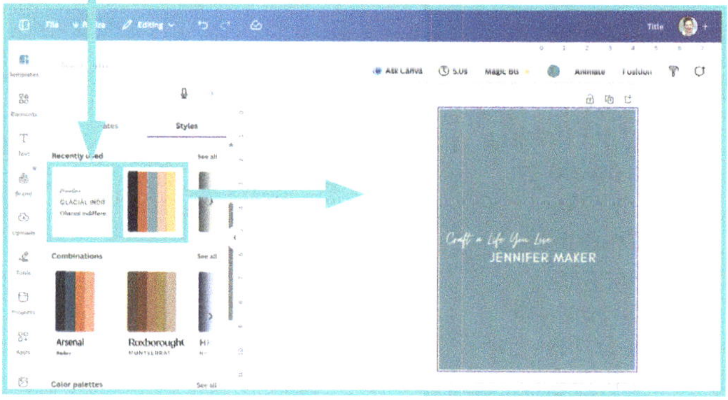

Step 4 (Optional): Click the **Shuffle** button under the **Styles** tab to cycle through different text and color combinations within the selected style.

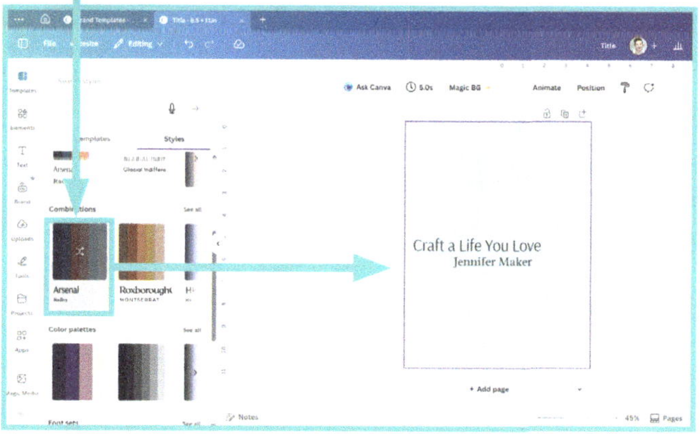

Step 5 (optional): Modify the font, size, or color after applying the style for a personalized touch.

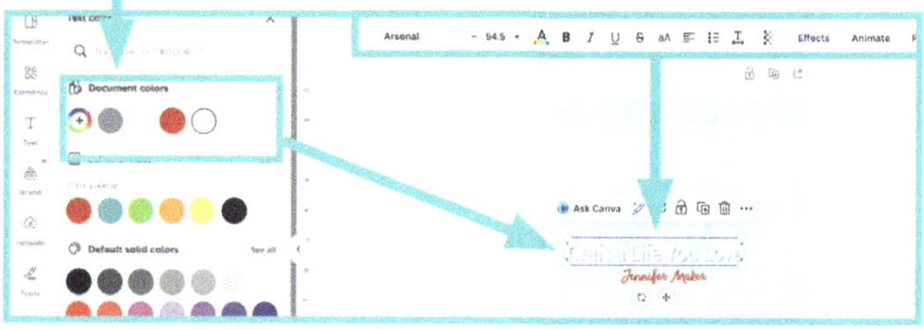

TIP: Use **Text Styles** to align with the aesthetic you're going for by customizing colors to match your color palette.

NOTE: Text Styles save time and ensure consistency, especially in multi-page designs.

DESKTOP

HOW TO ADD PAGE NUMBERS THAT UPDATE FOR YOU

Dynamic text in Canva lets you automatically add page numbers and other document elements that update as your design changes. This is helpful for multi page documents, reports, and eBooks.

Step 1: Create or open a design with multiple pages, such as an eBook, presentation, or catalog. Easily add pages by clicking the **+ sign** on the top right corner.

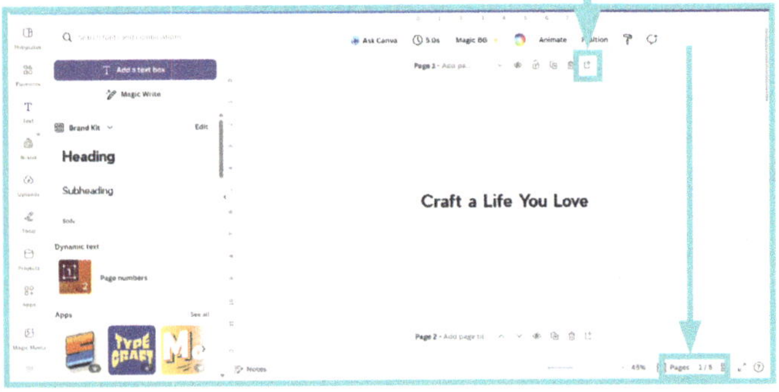

Step 2: Click **Page numbers** under Dynamic Text.

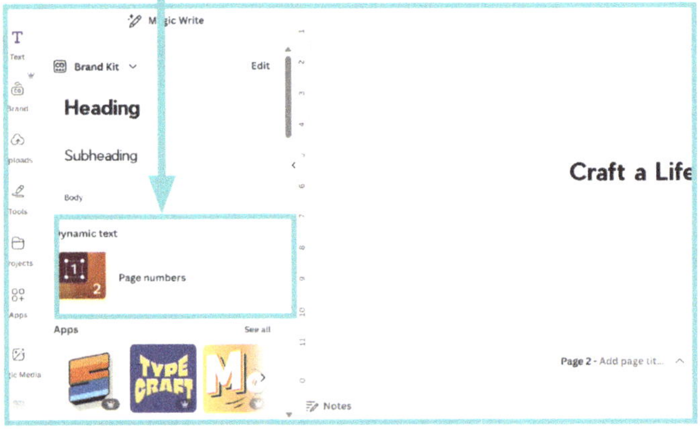

Step 3: Change the settings of your Page numbers by using the drop-down menu under Format, **Show numbers only**, and **Appearance and position**.

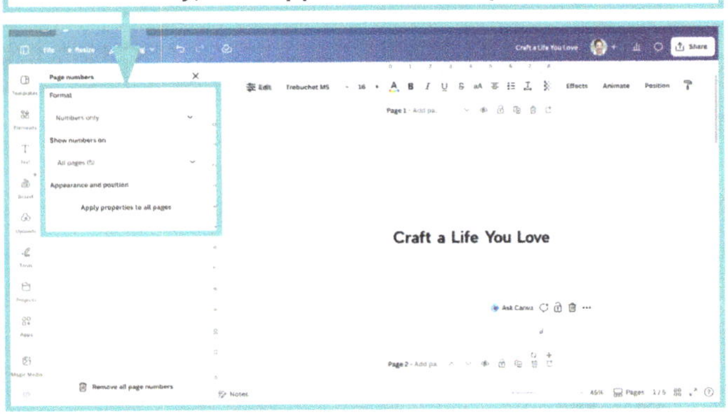

NOTE: If you would only like to add page numbers to certain pages, you can choose them by clicking the drop-down menu under **Show numbers on**. You can also choose **All pages** or just the **Current Page**.

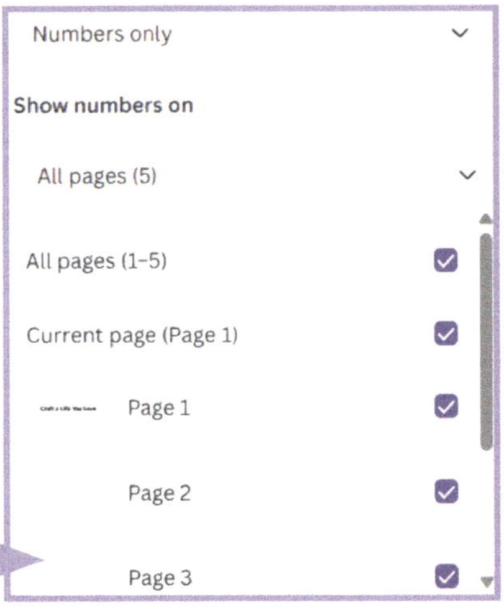

NOTE: You can change the format of your page numbers to **Numbers only**, **Page + number**, or **Page X of Y** depending on what aesthetic you're going for.

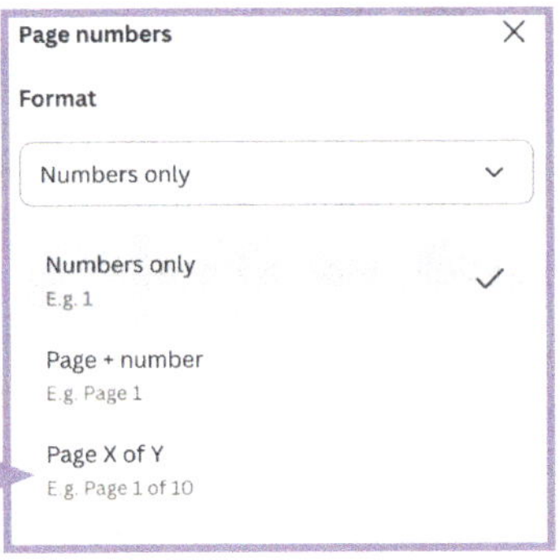

NOTE: Click **Apply properties to all pages** to apply the changes to every page in your document.

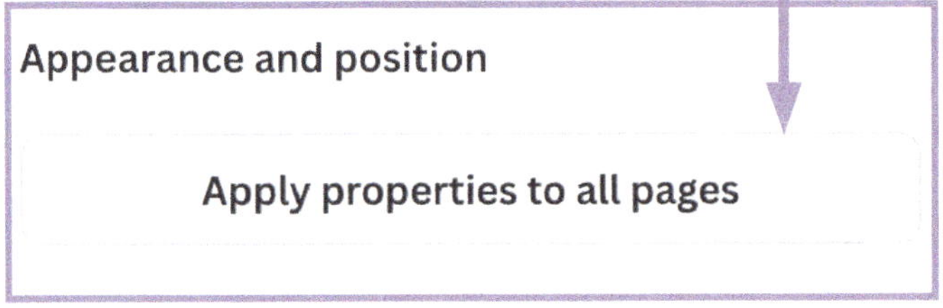

DESKTOP

HOW TO
PAIR FONTS LIKE A PRO

Font combinations in Canva provide pre-paired fonts that work harmoniously together, saving you time and ensuring a visually appealing design. These are great for projects like posters, social media posts, and presentations.

Step 1: On your design canvas, click the **Text** tab in the left toolbar, then the "**Add a text box**" button.

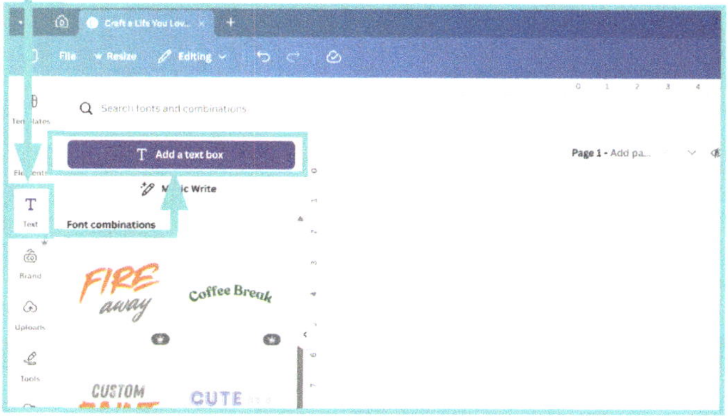

Step 2: Scroll through the pre-designed font pairings under the Font Combinations section.

Step 3: Click on a **Font combination** to add it to your canvas. The fonts will appear as text boxes, grouped for easy positioning.

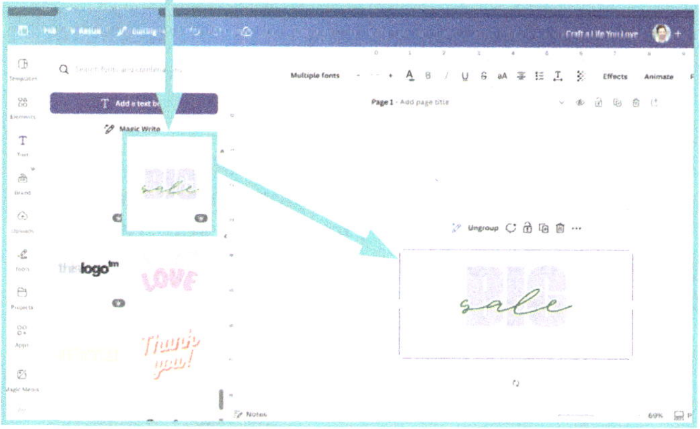

Step 4: Double-click a text box to edit the content. Adjust the **font size**, **color**, or **spacing** if needed.

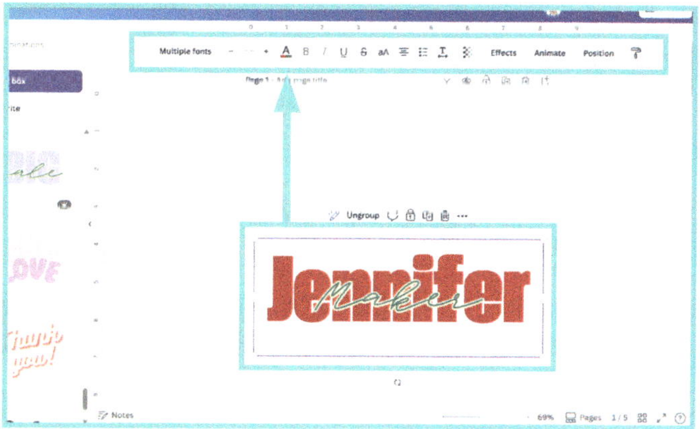

TIP: Swap the colors in the font combination to match your project's aesthetic or palette.

WARNING: Some font combinations are marked with a crown icon and require a Canva Pro subscription.

NOTE: If you like the style of a certain font combination, click the **3 dots** that appear when hovering and you'll get a list of keywords you can click on to view keyword-related font combinations.

HOW TO FADE TEXT FOR A SUBTLE EFFECT

Transparency allows you to tone down text for watermarks, overlays, or subtle effects.

Step 1: Select the text box and click Transparency (checkerboard icon) in the top-right toolbar.

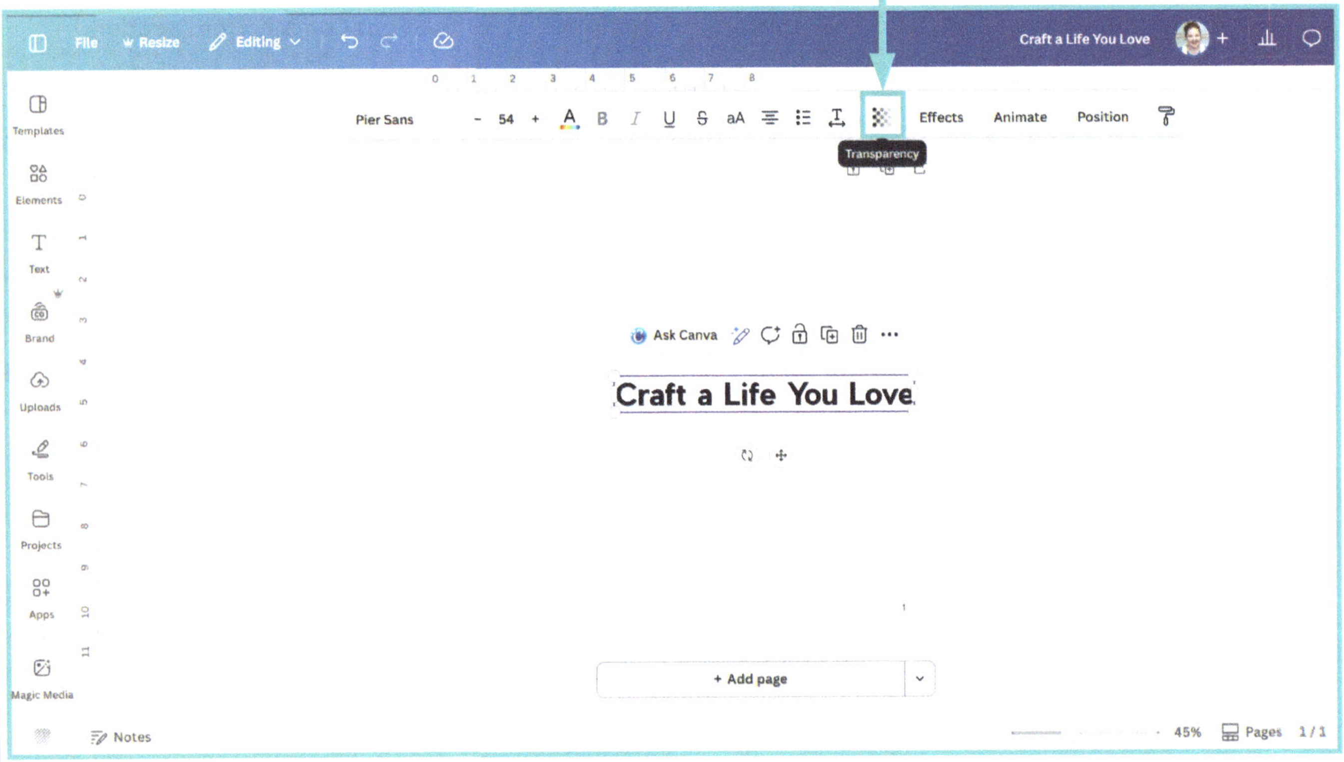

Step 2: Adjust the slider to set opacity.

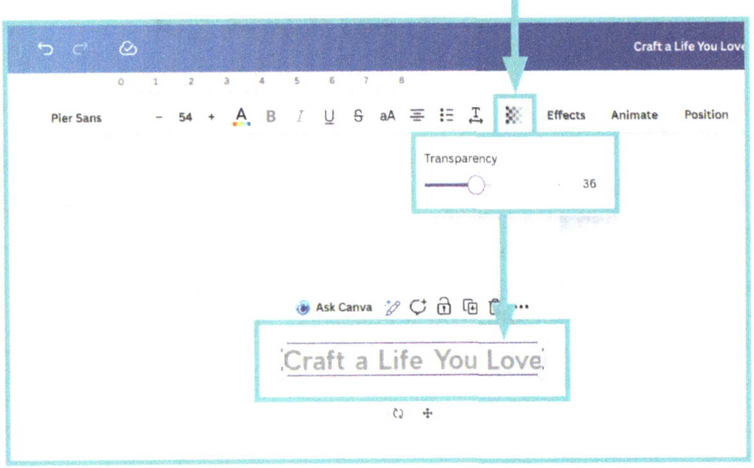

Warning: Too much transparency can make text unreadable; make sure your text is visible before finalizing.

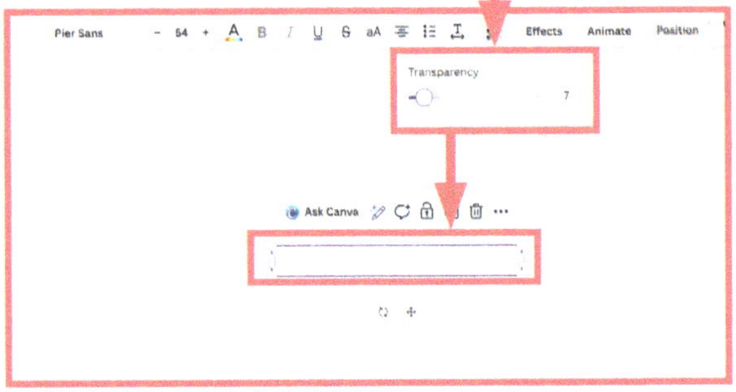

HOW TO MAKE YOUR TEXT POP WITH SPECIAL EFFECTS

Text effects in Canva allow you to add depth and creativity to your designs with features like shadows, glows, and outlines. These effects can make your text stand out and enhance the overall aesthetic of your design.

Step 1: Click on the text box you want to enhance.

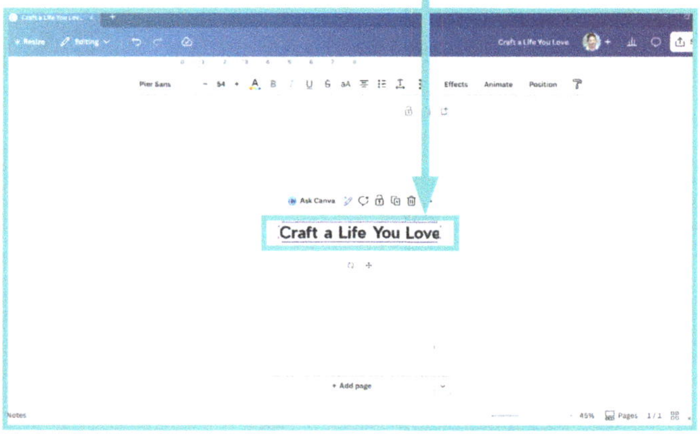

Step 2: Click **Effects** in the top toolbar.

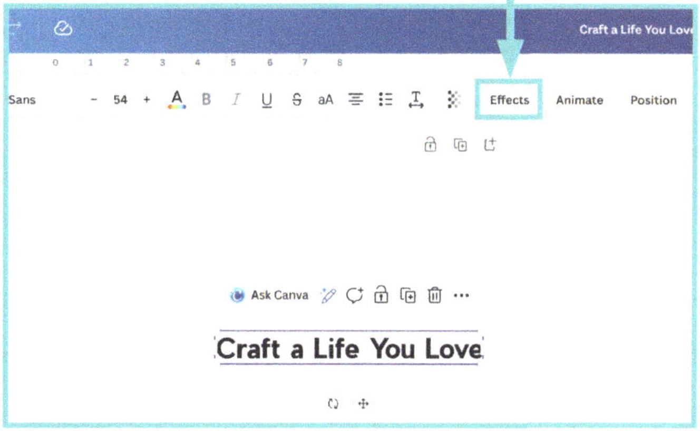

Step 3: Choose an Effect by browsing through the Style and Shapes options such as:
Shadow: Adds a soft or sharp shadow behind the text.
Lift: Creates a subtle 3D effect.
Outline: Frames the text with a border.
Hollow, **Splice**, **Neon**, **Glitch**, **Echo**, or **Background** for more dramatic styles.
Curve: Use if you want to add curvature to text.

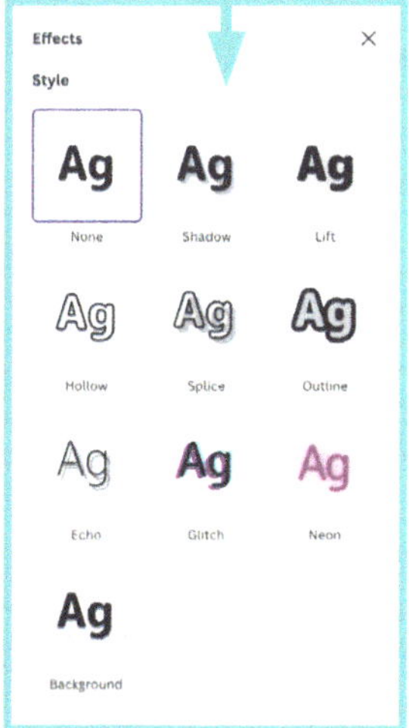

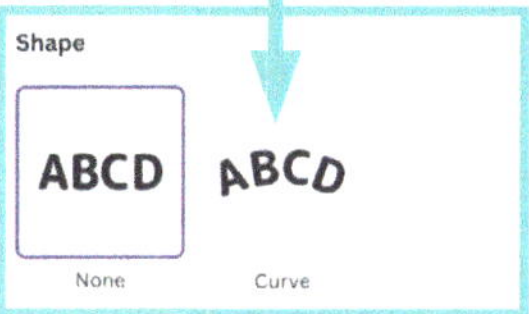

Step 4 (Optional): Customize the effect by using the sliders to adjust properties like **Offset**, **Transparency**, **Blur**, **Thickness**, or **Color**, depending on the selected effect.

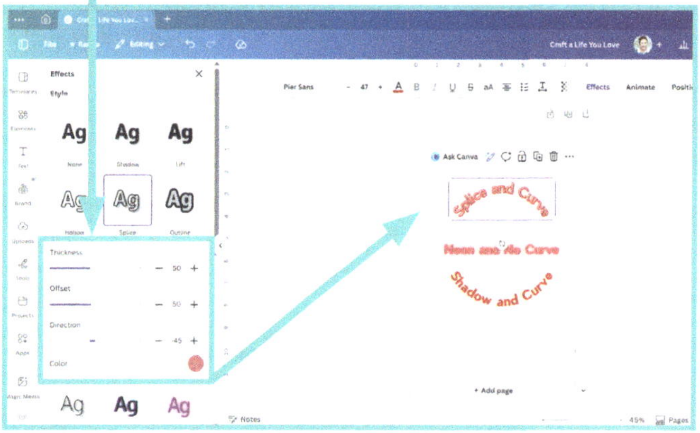

WARNING: Avoid overusing effects as they can make your design look cluttered or unprofessional. Stick to 1-2 effects per project for balance.

NOTE: Effects like **Glitch** and **Neon** work well for digital designs but might not translate well to printed materials.

HOW TO ADD MOVING TEXT TO CREATE ENGAGING DESIGNS

Animating text in Canva adds motion and energy to your designs, making them more engaging and dynamic. This feature is perfect for presentations, social media posts, and video content.

Step 1: Click on the text box you want to animate.

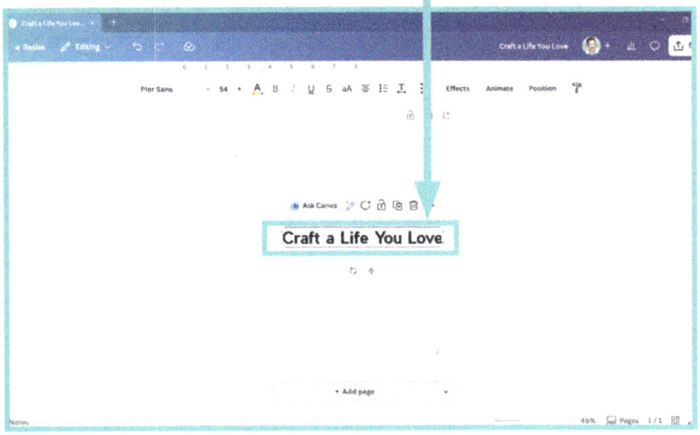

Step 2: Click **Animate** in the top toolbar.

Step 3: Choose an Animation style by browsing through the categories like:

Suggested: Effects suggested to you based on the text on your canvas.

General: General effects you can choose from.

Add-on effects: Styles like Rotate or Wiggle, Flicker, or Pulse that you can add on to an animation.

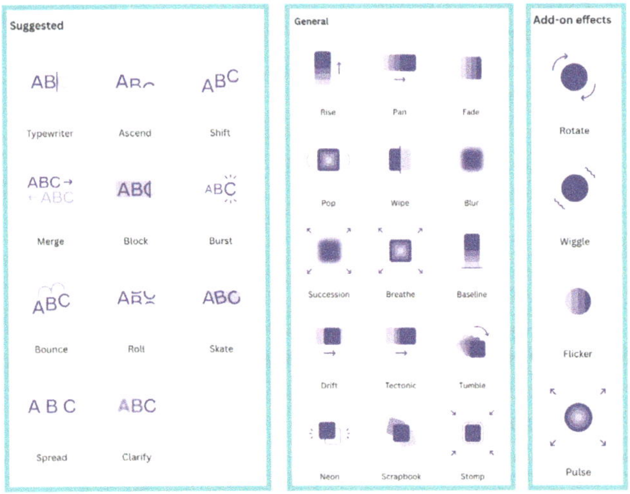

TIP: Hover over an effect to preview it.

Step 4 (Optional): Customize Animation Settings by adjusting the settings such as **Speed** or **Direction** (e.g., left-to-right).

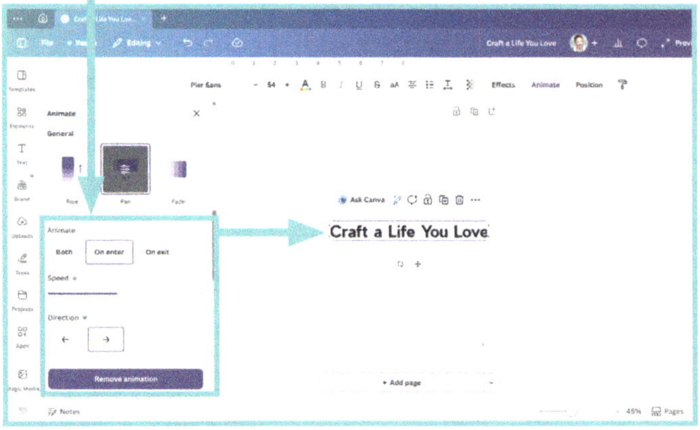

WARNING: Some animation settings are marked with a crown icon and require a Canva Pro subscription.

NOTE: Animations won't appear in static file formats like PNG or PDF; choose MP4 or GIF when exporting.

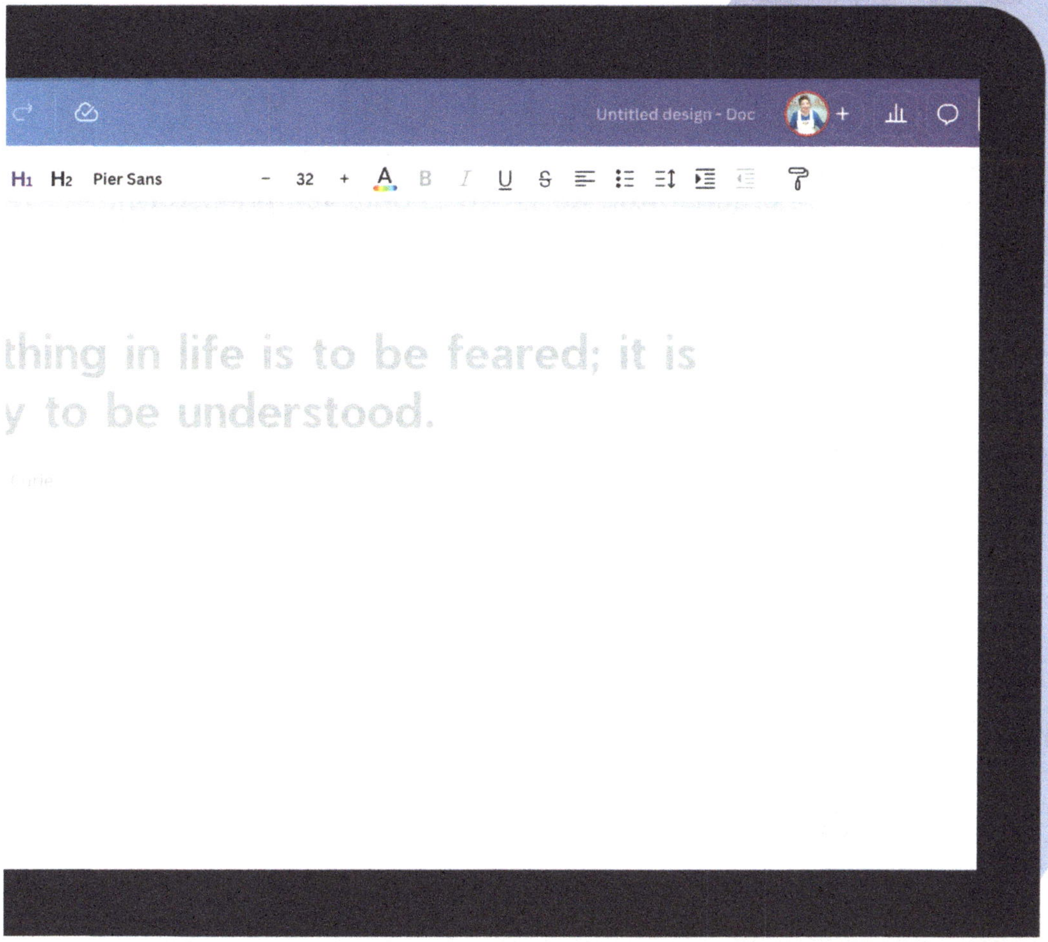

HOW TO:

DESKTOP: ADVANCED CANVA FEATURES

- ✔ USE MAGIC WRITE™ TO GENERATE TEXT FOR YOU
- ✔ UPLOAD AND ORGANIZE YOUR FILES
- ✔ UPLOAD AND USE YOUR OWN IMAGES
- ✔ PLACE AND EDIT YOUR UPLOADED IMAGES
- ✔ SKETCH AND DRAW DIRECTLY IN CANVA
- ✔ FIND YOUR SAVED PROJECTS
- ✔ UNLOCK MORE FEATURES WITH APPS
- ✔ CREATE USING CANVA MAGIC MEDIA™
- ✔ CREATE AI-GENERATED IMAGES WITH MAGIC MEDIA™

DESKTOP

HOW TO USE MAGIC WRITE™ TO GENERATE TEXT FOR YOU

Magic Write™ is Canva's AI-powered text generator, designed to help you brainstorm, create, and polish written content with ease. Whether you need captions or outlines, Magic Write™ saves time and boosts creativity.

Step 1: From the Canva homepage, click on **Docs**.

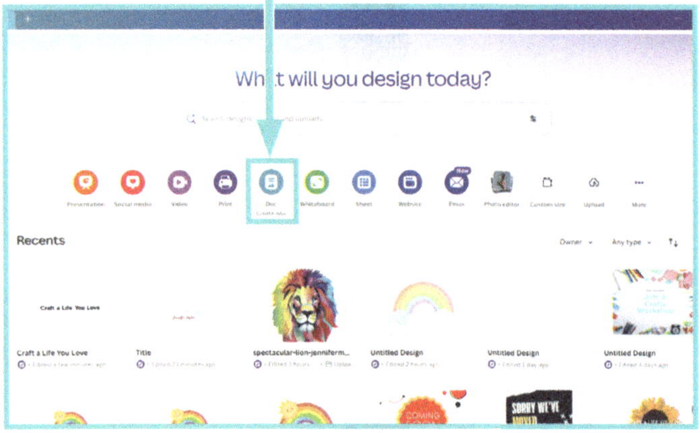

Step 2: In the document editor, click **Magic Write™**.

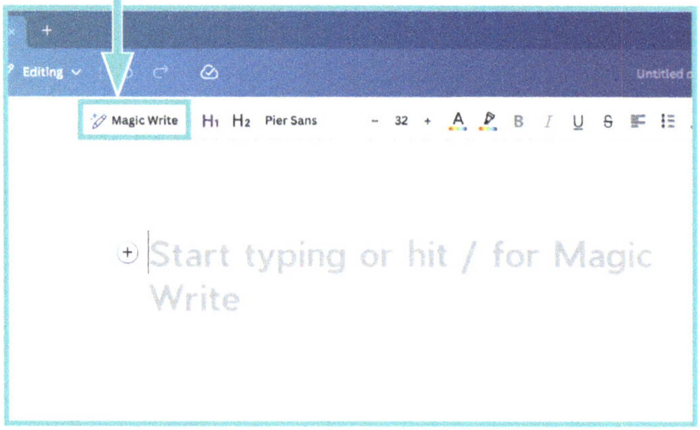

Step 3: Enter a clear and specific prompt, such as

"Create a 3-step guide to better time management while crafting."

You can also use the suggestions that appear to spark new ideas. Press the **Generate** button when finished.

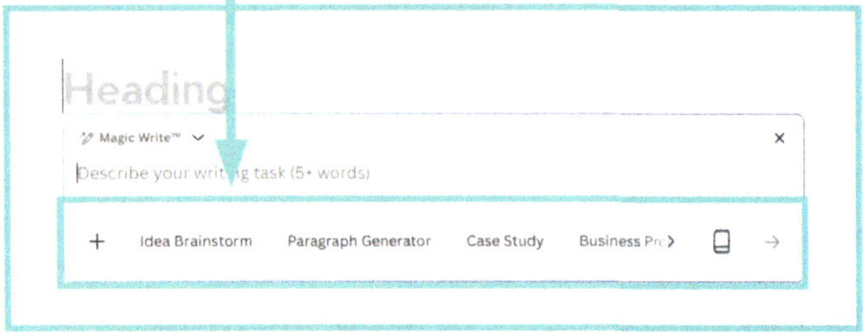

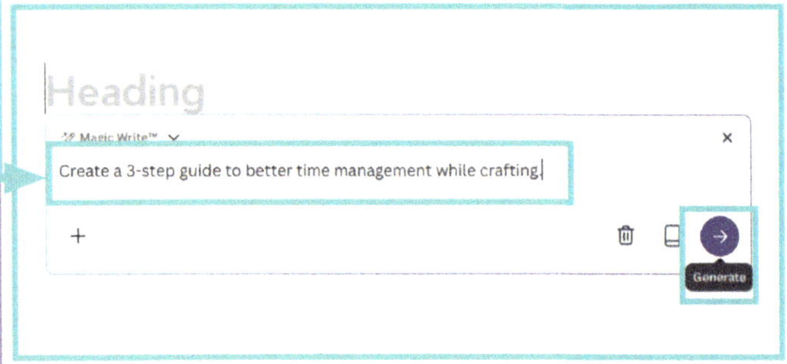

Step 4: Review and Edit - Magic Write™ will create content based on your prompt. Edit the results to align them with your voice or objectives. If you approve, click **Insert** to add it to your doc.

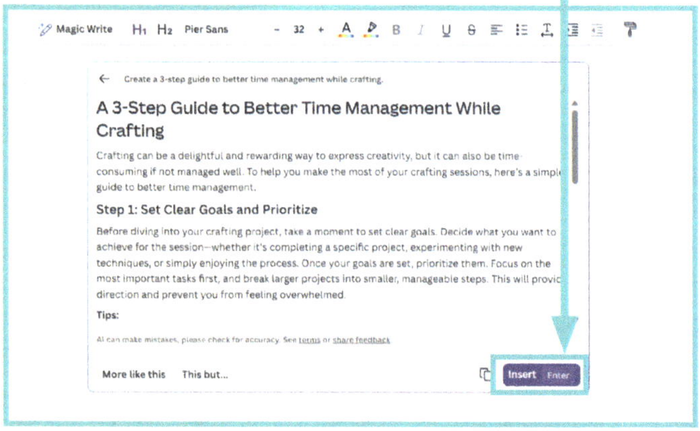

WARNING: Double-check **generated text** for accuracy and relevance, especially for sensitive or industry-specific content.

NOTE: Magic Write™ works best with concise and clear prompts. It may require refinement for complex topics or technical content.

DESKTOP

HOW TO UPLOAD AND ORGANIZE YOUR FILES

The Uploads tab in Canva allows you to add custom images, videos, audio, or other media to your designs, helping you personalize projects or incorporate external assets seamlessly.

Step 1: On your design canvas, click the **Uploads** tab in the left toolbar.

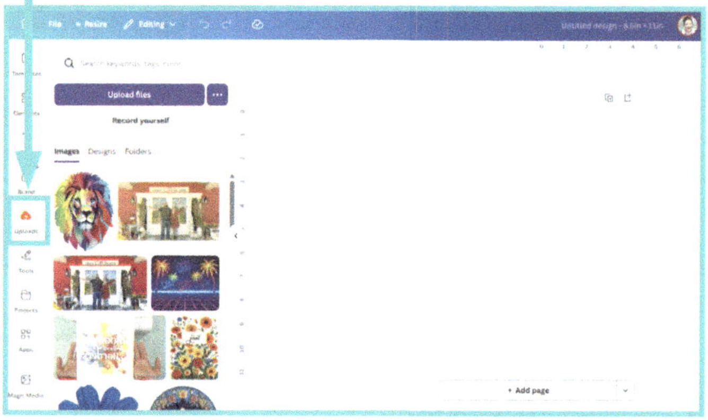

Step 2: Click **Upload files** and select the file(s) you want to upload from your computer. Supported file types include:

- Images: PNG, JPG, SVG, HEIC
- Videos: MP4, MOV
- Audio: MP3, WAV

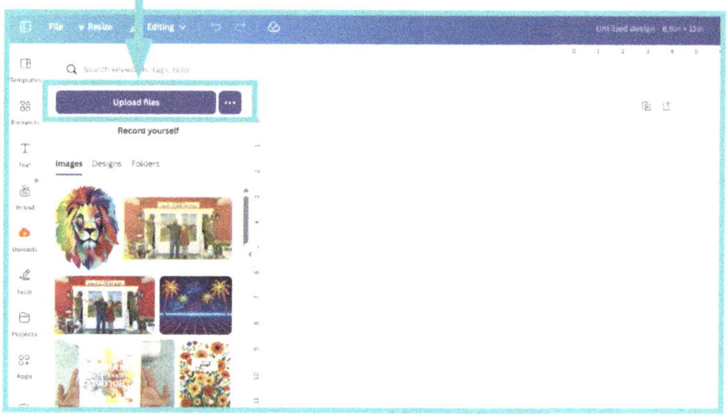

Step 3: Once uploaded, your files will appear in the Uploads library. Click or drag a file to place it on your canvas.

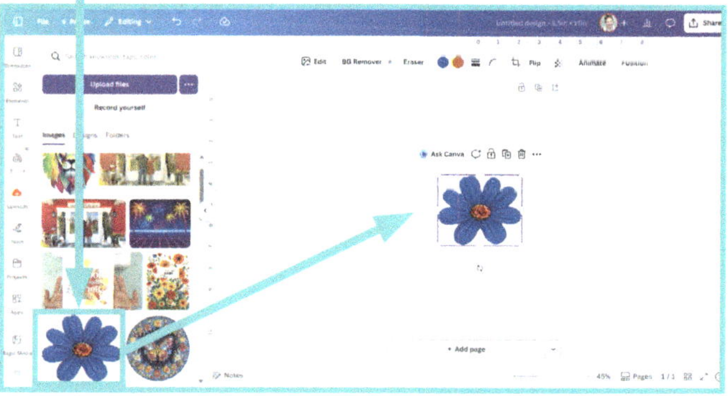

Step 4 (Optional): Use folders to organize frequently used assets. Hover over your image, click the **3 dots**, and click **Move**. Select the folder you want to move the image to can click **Move**.

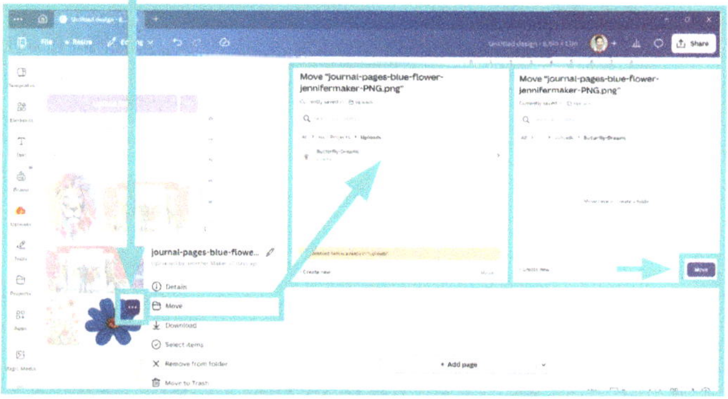

NOTE: Uploaded files remain accessible in your Canva library, so you can reuse them in future projects.

WARNING: Ensure you have the legal rights to use uploaded content, particularly for commercial projects.

TIP: Add relevant image file names and tags to your images so you can easily find them when searching for them in the future.

DESKTOP

HOW TO UPLOAD AND USE YOUR OWN IMAGES

Uploading an image to Canva allows you to add your personal photos, graphics, or other visual elements to your designs, making them more unique and tailored to your needs.

Step 1: On your design canvas, click the **Uploads** tab in the left-hand toolbar.

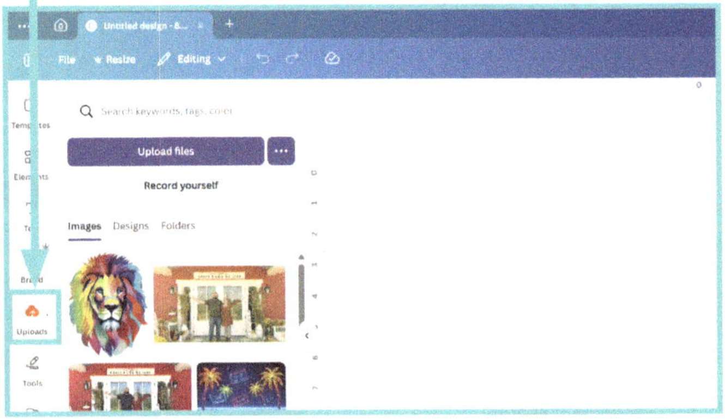

Step 2: Click **Upload files**, and select the image you want to upload from your device.

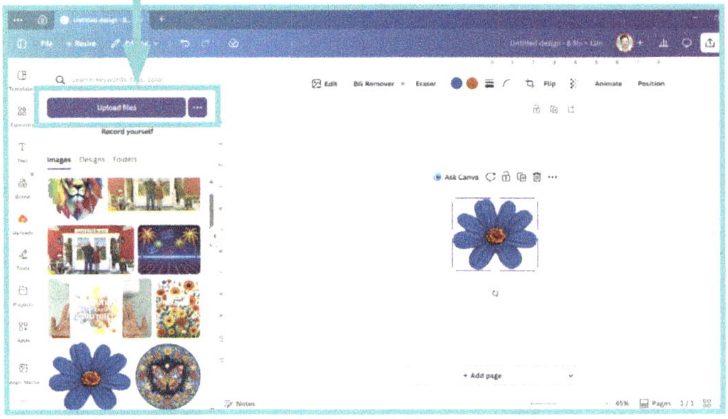

Step 3: As an alternative method, drag and drop the image file directly into the Uploads area. Ensure your image is in one of Canva's supported formats: PNG, JPG, SVG, or HEIC.

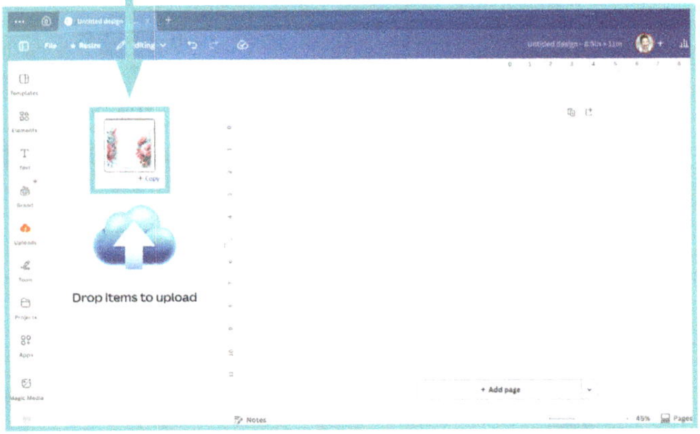

Step 4: After uploading, the image will appear in the Uploads library under the tab.

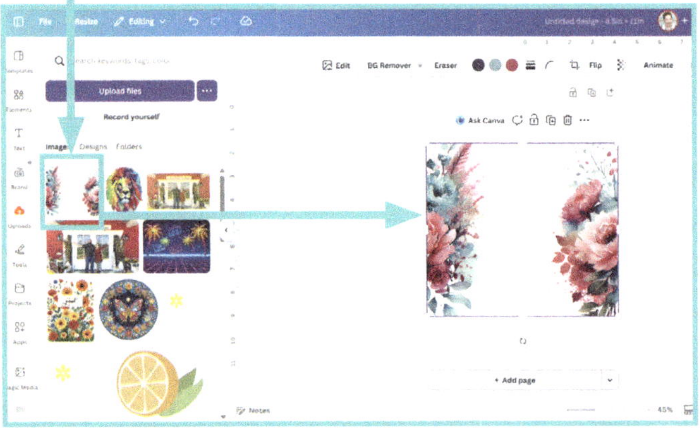

NOTE: Your uploaded image will remain saved in Canva, so you can access and reuse it for future projects without re-uploading.

TIP: Organize your uploads using folders or labels if you plan to use multiple images in your designs.

WARNING: Always verify that you have the legal right to use the uploaded image, particularly for commercial designs.

HOW TO PLACE AND EDIT YOUR UPLOADED IMAGES

Adding an uploaded image to your canvas allows you to incorporate your own visuals into your designs. This step is key to personalizing projects with your unique assets.

Step 1: Click the **Uploads** tab in the left-hand toolbar to access your uploaded files.

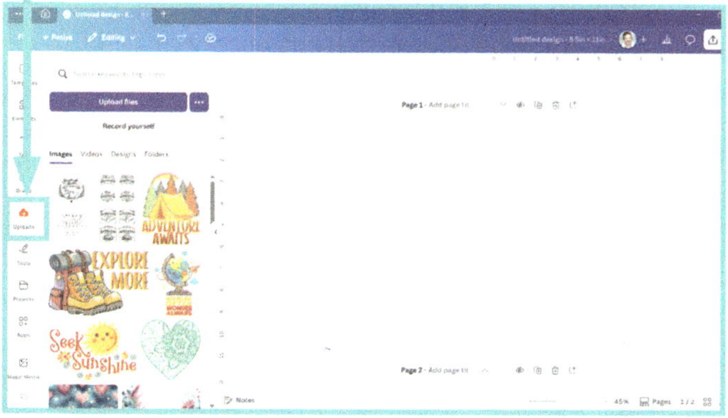

Step 2: Scroll through your uploads or use the search bar to find the image you want to use.

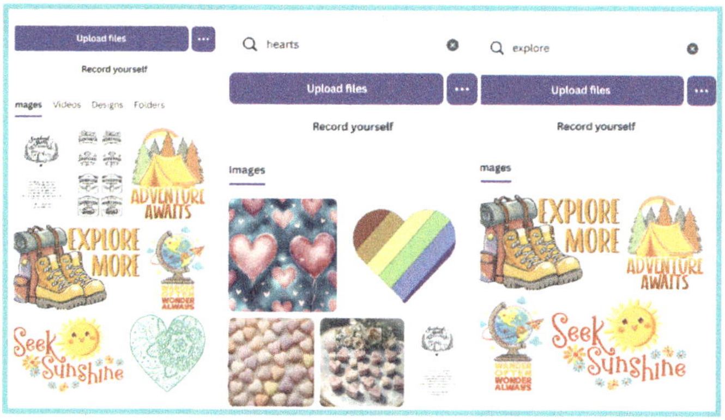

Step 3: Click the image to automatically place it on the canvas, or drag and drop the image onto your desired location.

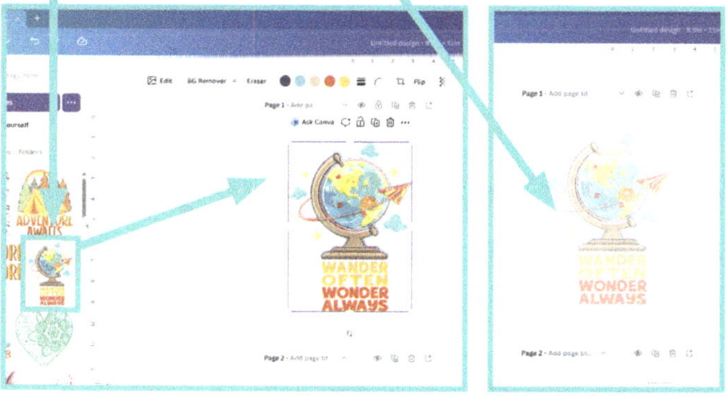

Step 4 (Optional): Use the **corner handles** to resize the image. Click and drag to reposition it anywhere on the canvas.

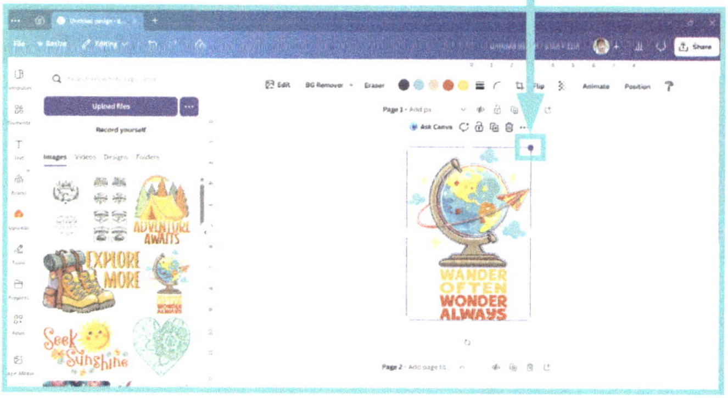

Step 5 (Optional): Customize your image by using tools in the top toolbar to **edit**, **crop**, **flip**, **adjust the transparency**, or **animate** your image.

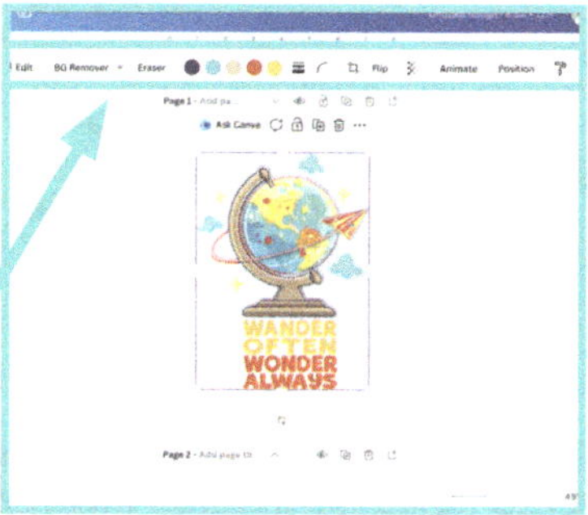

NOTE: Once placed on the canvas, your image becomes part of your design and can be layered, grouped, or edited like any other element.

WARNING: Ensure your uploaded image has a high enough resolution for print projects to avoid pixelation.

DESKTOP

HOW TO SKETCH AND DRAW DIRECTLY IN CANVA

The Tools tab in Canva lets you create freehand drawings directly on your design. It is a helpful tool for adding personal touches, sketches, or creative elements to a project.

Step 1: On your design canvas, click the **Tools** tab in the left toolbar.

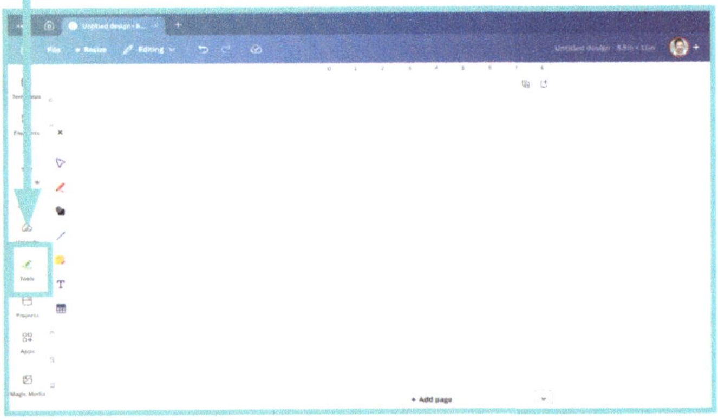

Step 2: Select a brush style from the available options, such as:

- **Pen**: For smooth lines.
- **Marker**: For bold strokes.
- **Highlighter**: For transparent accents.

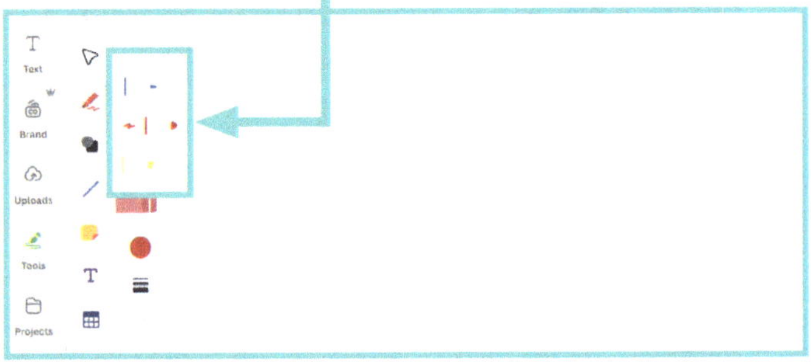

Step 3: Adjust your brush settings by customizing the **size** of the brush for thinner or thicker strokes. Select a **color** from the palette or use a HEX code.

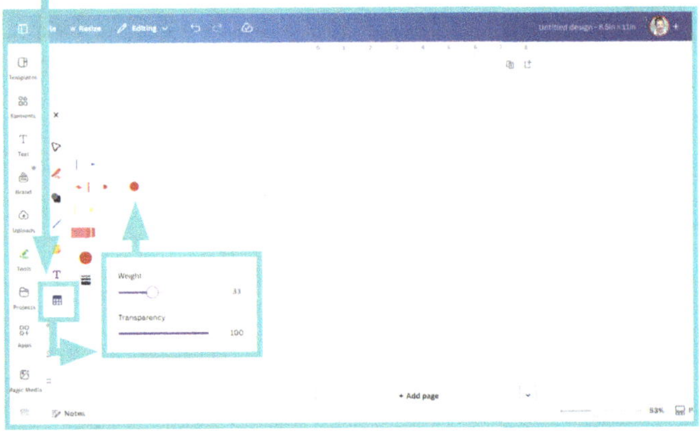

Step 4: Click and drag your mouse to draw directly on your canvas.

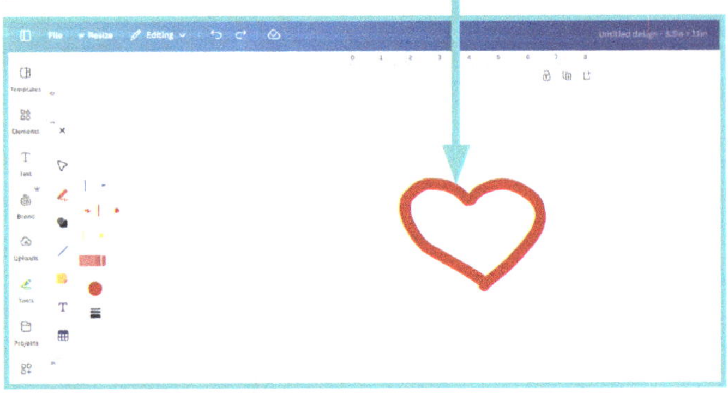

Step 5 (Optional): Edit your drawing by using the **Eraser** tool to remove specific parts of your drawing. Adjust the **position**, **size**, **color**, or **opacity** of your drawing after you finish.

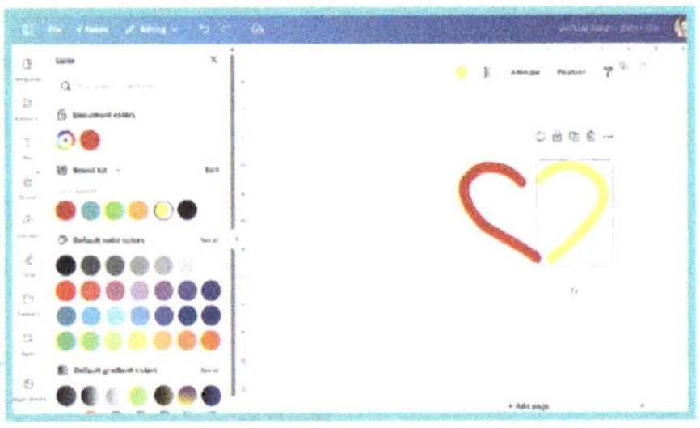

Tip: Move individual strokes around if you need to by clicking on them.

WARNING: Freehand drawings cannot be edited like vector shapes, so undo any mistakes immediately or use the eraser to correct them.

DESKTOP

HOW TO FIND YOUR SAVED PROJECTS

The Projects tab is where all your saved content is stored, including designs, folders, images, and videos. It provides easy access to organize and reuse your work efficiently.

Step 1: From your Canva dashboard or design canvas, click the **Projects** tab in the left-hand toolbar.

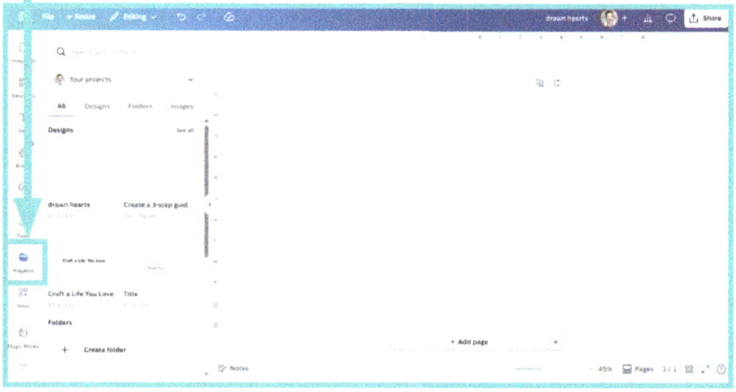

Step 2: The **All** section shows every file stored in your Projects tab, including designs, uploads, and folders, in one centralized view. Use the **Search Bar** to quickly find a specific design by name.

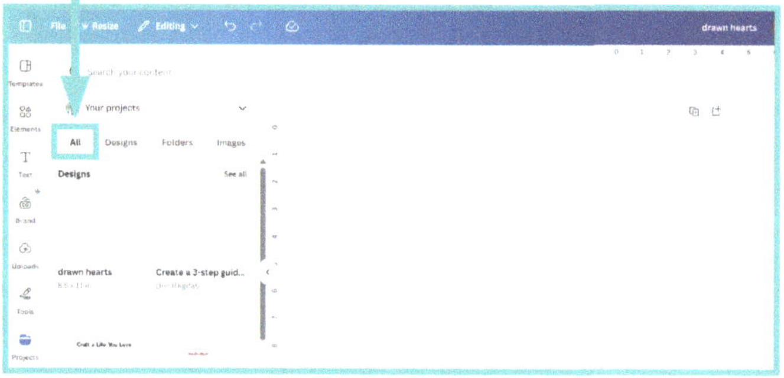

Step 3: The **Designs** section lists all the Canva designs you've created or saved.

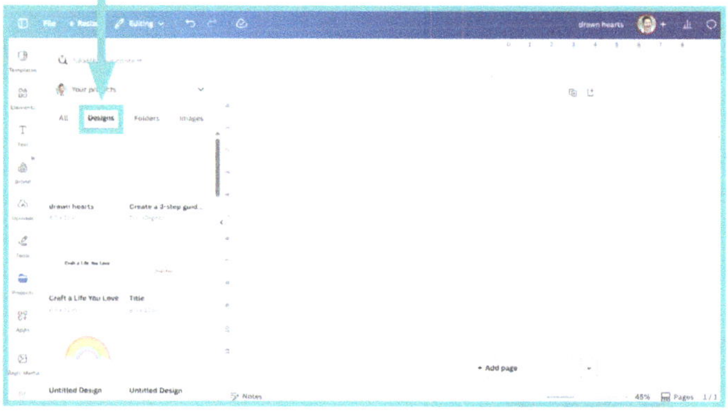

Step 4: The **Folders** section lets you organize your designs and files into labeled groups for better management.
To create a new folder:
Click the **+ Create Folder** button. Enter a folder name and click **Continue**.

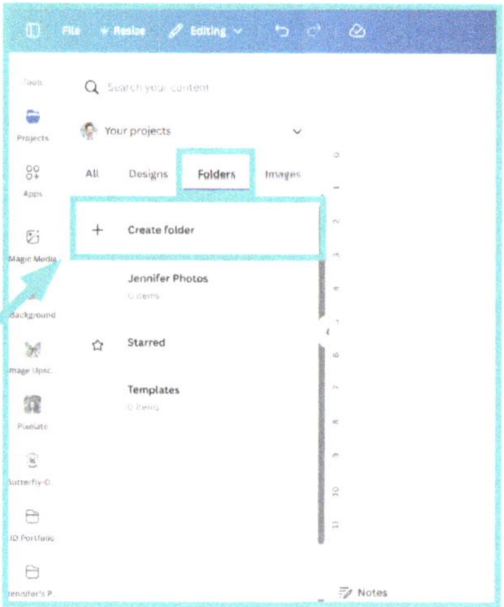

Step 5: The **Images** section displays all the photos or graphics you've uploaded to Canva.

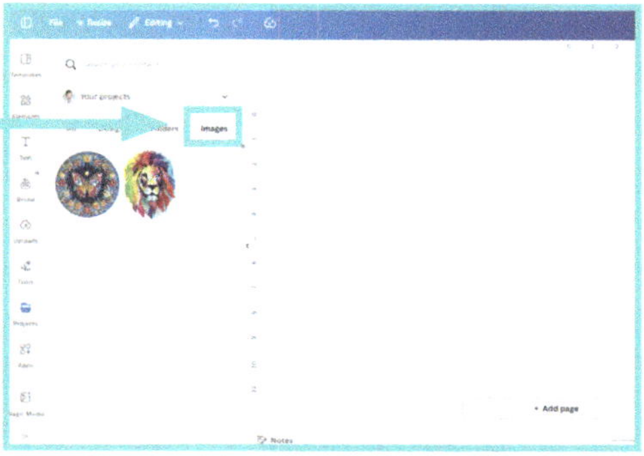

HOW TO UNLOCK MORE FEATURES WITH APPS

The Apps tab in Canva lets you integrate third-party tools, access stock media, and unlock creative features like AI-powered tools or dynamic content. It's a hub for extending Canva's capabilities and streamlining your workflow.

Step 1: From your Canva design canvas, click the Apps tab in the left toolbar.

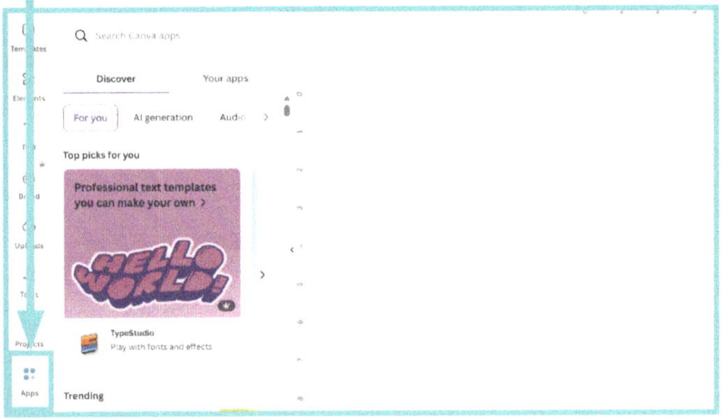

Step 2: Browse popular apps or use the Search Bar to find specific tools.

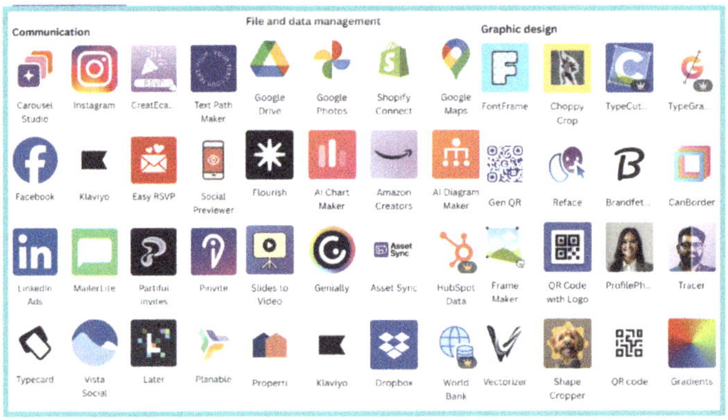

Step 3 (Optional): For apps like Google Drive or Dropbox, follow the prompts to log in and connect your account.

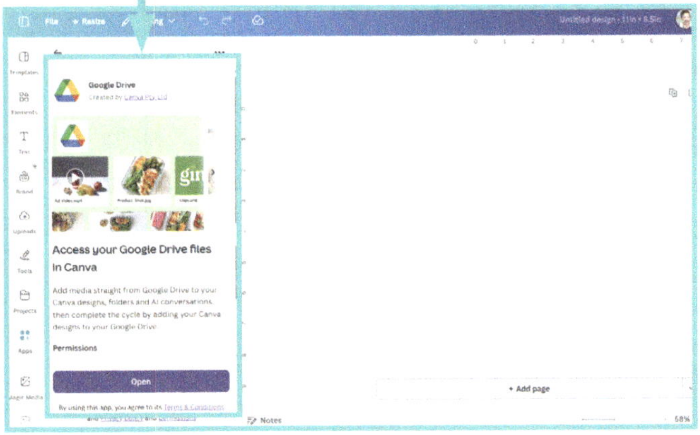

Step 4: Select an app and browse its content (e.g., search for stock images in Pexels).

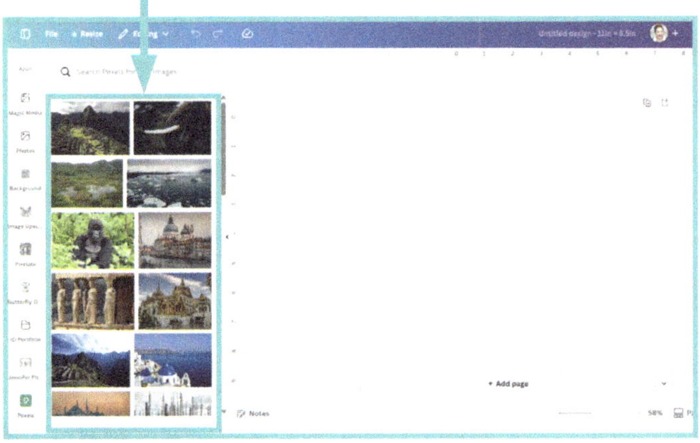

NOTES:

- Some apps may require a Canva Pro account for full functionality.
- All connected accounts (e.g., Google Drive) can be managed under Account Settings in Canva.

TIPS:

- Use Giphy or Stickers to add playful, animated elements to social media designs.
- Integrate Google Drive or Dropbox to pull in assets and save time.
- Use apps like QR Code Generator to enhance marketing materials with scannable links.

DESKTOP

HOW TO CREATE USING CANVA MAGIC MEDIA

Canva AI is a great tool to use when you aren't quite sure what the idea in your head should look like, as well as create multiple options of a design for you to choose from.

Step 1: Click on the **Canva AI** icon in the vertical menu on the left side of the screen.

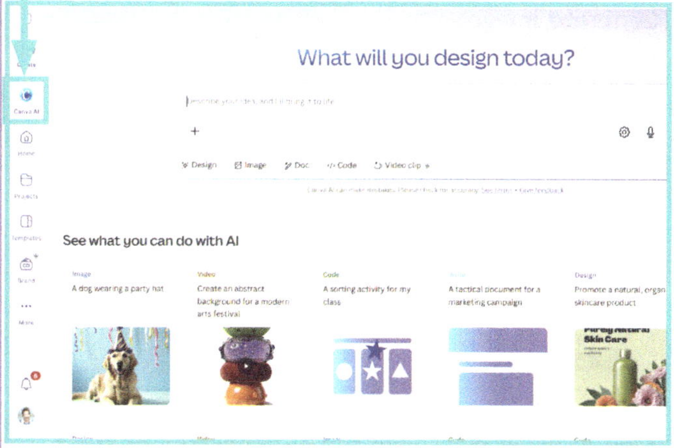

Step 2: Type what you'd like to create into the search bar. Don't press Enter or click the arrow icon yet.

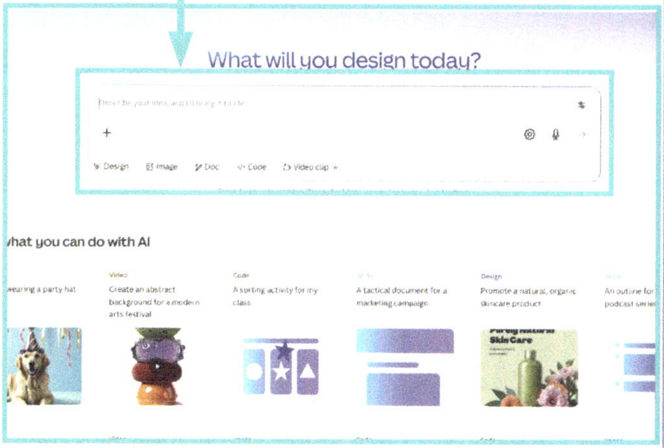

Step 3: Click **Design**, **Image**, **Doc**, **Code**, or **Video Clip**, depending on what you'd like to generate. Choose options in each submenu. Press Enter or the arrow button.

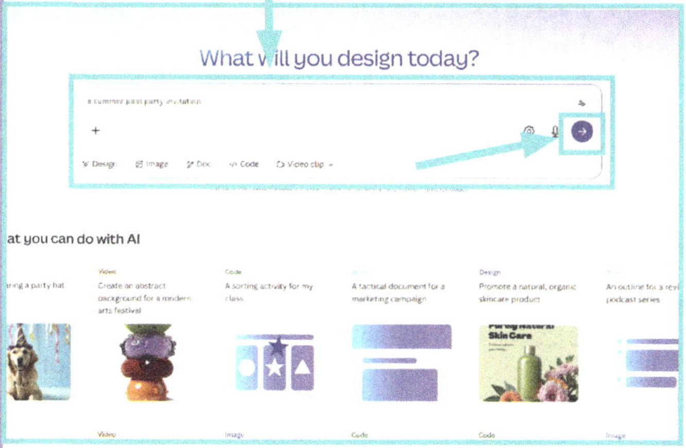

Step 4: Canva AI will generate four options for your design. You can click **More designs** to generate more options, or further refine your design by typing the changes you want into the **search bar**.

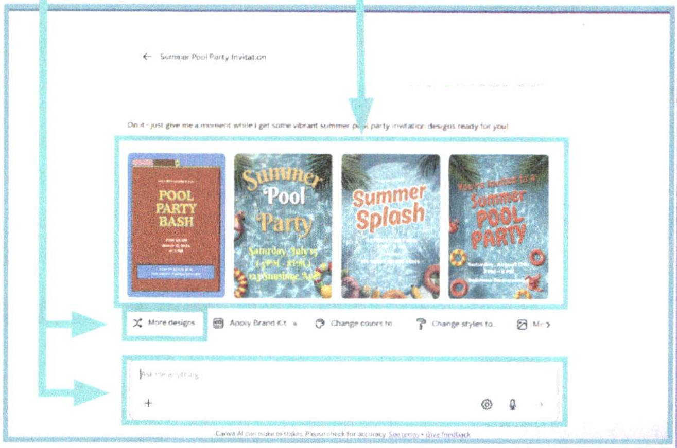

NOTE: These are the submenu options for each of the AI design choices:

- **Design:** Social media, Presentation, Marketing, Cards & Invitations, Logo, Learning Activity
- **Image:** Style, Aspect Ratio
- **Doc:** Type
- **Code:** Grocery list builder, Interactive certificate, Biology quiz
- **Video Clip:** Style, Aspect Ratio, Audio, Framing, Lighting

HOW TO CREATE AI-GENERATED IMAGES WITH MAGIC MEDIA™

The Magic Media™ tab in Canva is an AI-powered tool that helps you discover or generate unique visuals for your designs. It's perfect for finding stock media or creating custom images based on text prompts, saving time and boosting creativity.

Step 1: From your design canvas, click on the **Apps** tab in the left toolbar. Search for and select **Magic Media™** to open the tool.

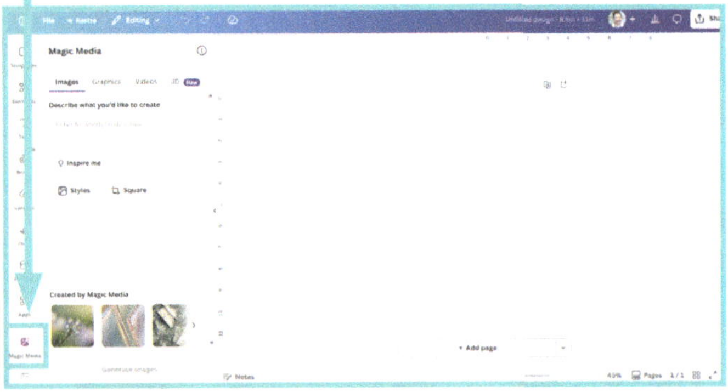

Step 2: **Enter keywords** in the search bar to find stock media like images, videos, or animations. Example: **Type** "seamless heart pattern." Click **Generate image**.

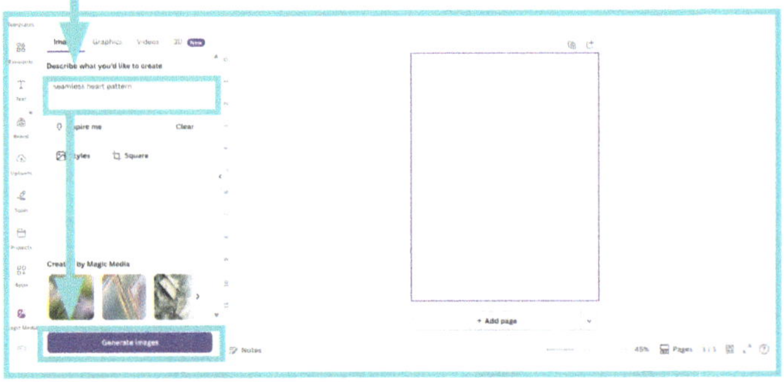

Step 3 (Optional): Click **Styles** and choose one such as **Dreamy** and click **Generate again** to get an array of different options to choose from based on the prompt you chose.

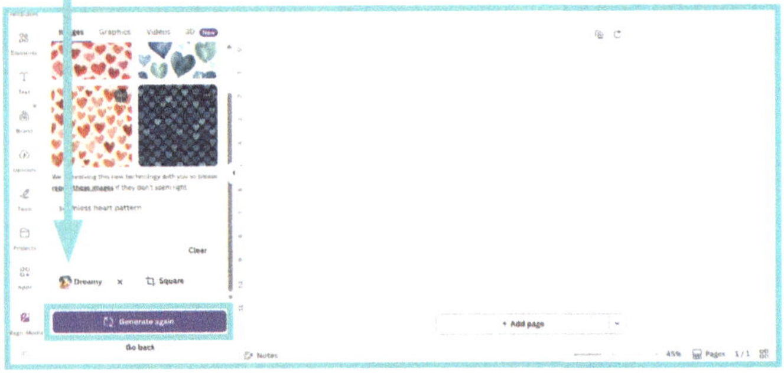

Step 4: Browse through the AI-generated or stock media results. Click on the item you want to use, and it will be added to your canvas.

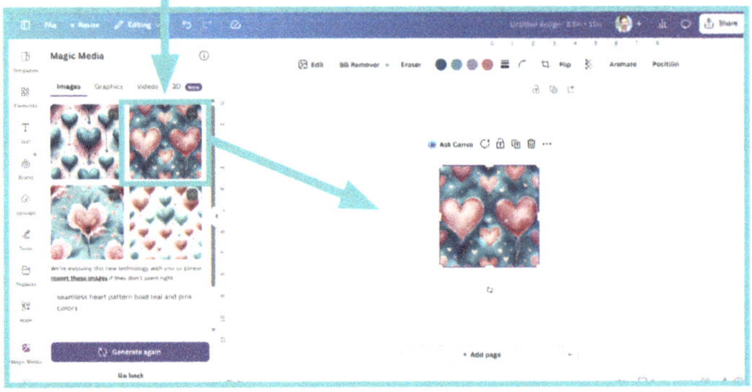

Step 5: Once added, **resize**, **crop**, or **adjust** the media as needed. Use Canva's editing tools to tweak colors, apply filters, or add effects.

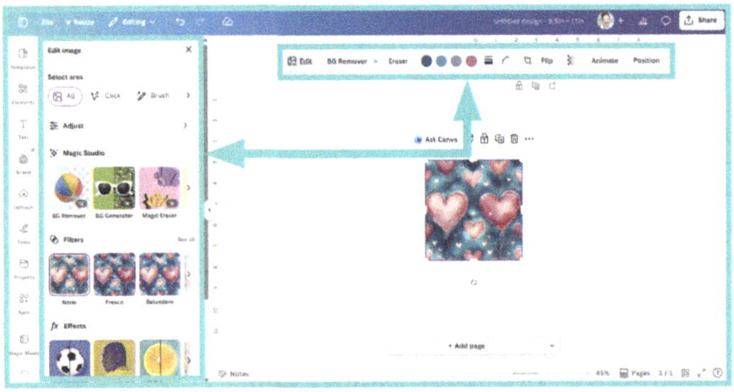

NOTES:

- Play around to get a feel of all the amazing capabilities that Magic Media™ has to offer.
- Some stock content may have usage limitations for commercial projects; review the licensing terms.

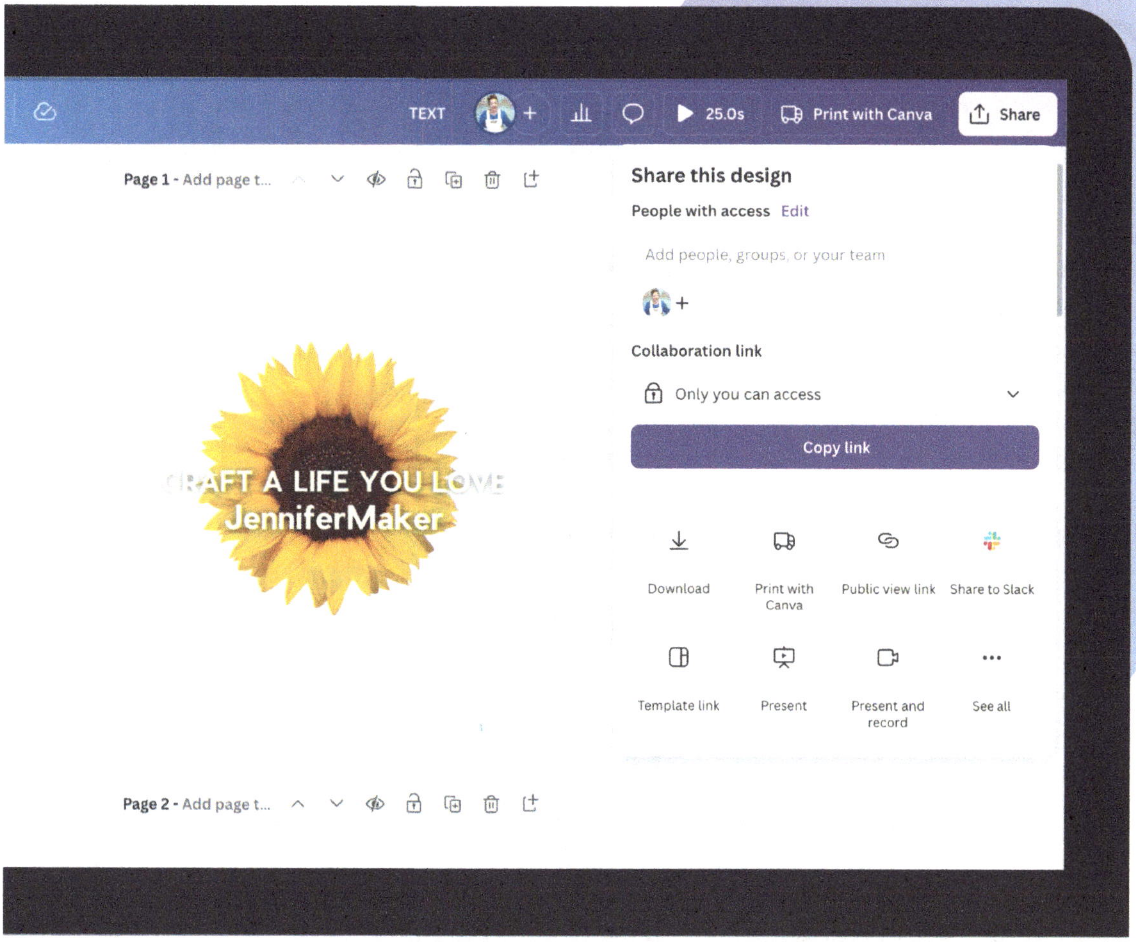

HOW TO:

DESKTOP: EXPORTING, SHARING, AND SAVING TIME

- ✔ CHOOSE THE BEST FILE TYPE FOR YOUR DESIGN
- ✔ SHARE YOUR PROJECT WITH OTHERS
- ✔ DOWNLOAD YOUR PROJECT IN THE BEST FORMAT
- ✔ SPEED UP YOUR WORKFLOW WITH KEYBOARD SHORTCUTS FOR MAC
- ✔ SPEED UP YOUR WORKFLOW WITH KEYBOARD SHORTCUTS FOR WINDOWS

HOW TO CHOOSE THE BEST FILE TYPE FOR YOUR DESIGN

Choosing the right file type in Canva helps ensure your design looks its best for digital use, printing, or sharing. Each file type has features suited to different purposes.

PNG (Portable Network Graphics)
Best For: High-quality images and designs with transparency.
Key Features:

- Retains sharp details.
- Supports transparent backgrounds.

SVG (Scalable Vector Graphics)
Best For: Vector-based designs that need to scale without losing quality.
Key Features:

- Ideal for web and digital applications.
- Fully editable in vector design.

PDF (Portable Document Format)

PDF (Standard):
Best For: Lightweight, shareable documents.
Key Features: Optimized for on-screen viewing.

PDF (Print):
Best For: High-resolution designs for professional printing.
Key Features: Includes crop marks and bleed.

WARNING:

- Certain features like resizing and transparent backgrounds (PNG) are exclusive for Canva Pro users.
- Low-resolution settings can result in pixelation when printed; use PDF (Print) for high-quality results.

JPG (JPEG Image)
Best For: Compressed images with smaller file sizes.
Key Features:

- Quick to load.
- No transparency support.

GIF (Graphics Interchange Format)
Best For: Short, looping animations.
Key Features:

- Limited color palette.
- Small file size.

MP4 (Video Format)
Best For: Animated or video-based designs.
Key Features:

- Supports motion and audio.
- High-quality playback.

PPTX (PowerPoint Presentation)
Best For: Presentations created in Canva that you want to edit or present in PowerPoint.
Key Features:

- Compatible with Microsoft PowerPoint.
- Editable after export.

TIPS: For web use, opt for JPG when file size matters, or PNG for high-quality visuals.

DESKTOP

HOW TO SHARE YOUR PROJECT WITH OTHERS

Sharing projects in Canva allows you to collaborate with others, present your designs, or share them with clients or team members. You can share as a link, email, or directly via presentation mode.

Step 1: Open the design you want to share.

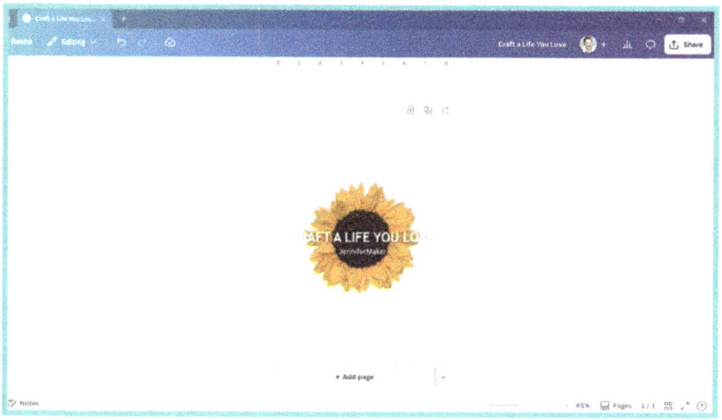

Step 2: In the top-right corner, click the **Share** button.

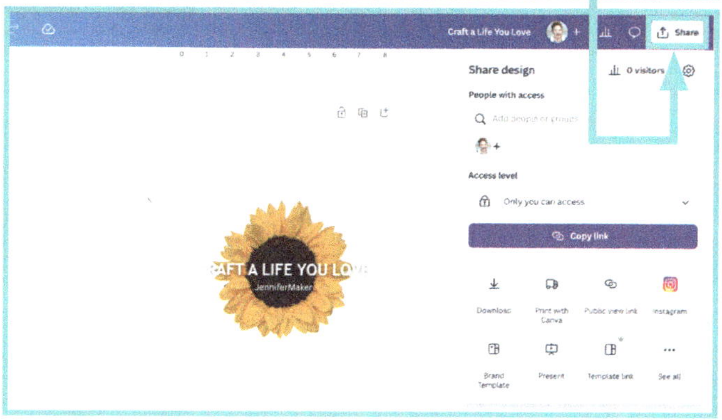

Step 3: Choose a Sharing Option - There are many ways to share a project on Canva. Scroll through and choose the option you prefer. Some of the more popular options include:

- **Public view link**: Share a read-only link for others to see your design without making changes.
- **Template Link**: Create a template link that lets others duplicate your design and edit their own copy.

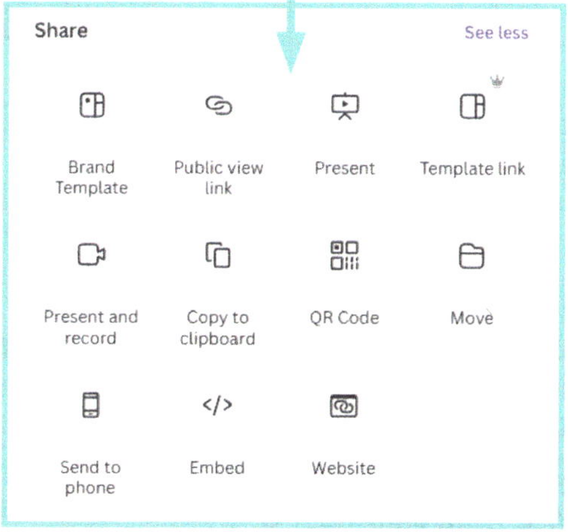

Step 4 (Optional): Enter email addresses to share the project directly with specific people.
Assign permissions:

- **Can Edit**: Grants them full access to modify the design.
- **Can Comment**: Allows them to add comments to the design.
- **Can View**: Allows them to see the design but not edit.

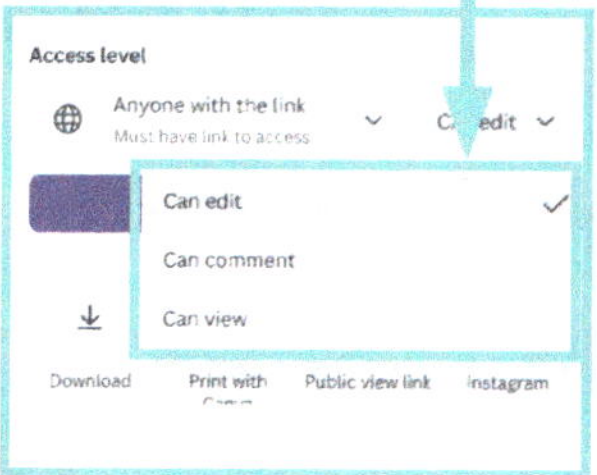

WARNING: Be cautious when granting **Can Edit** access, as collaborators can overwrite or delete content.

DESKTOP

HOW TO DOWNLOAD YOUR PROJECT IN THE BEST FORMAT

Downloading your project in Canva allows you to save it in various formats for digital use, printing, or sharing. Canva offers several file types to match your specific needs, ensuring your design looks professional in any context.

Step 1: From your design canvas, click the **Share** button, then click the **Download** button.

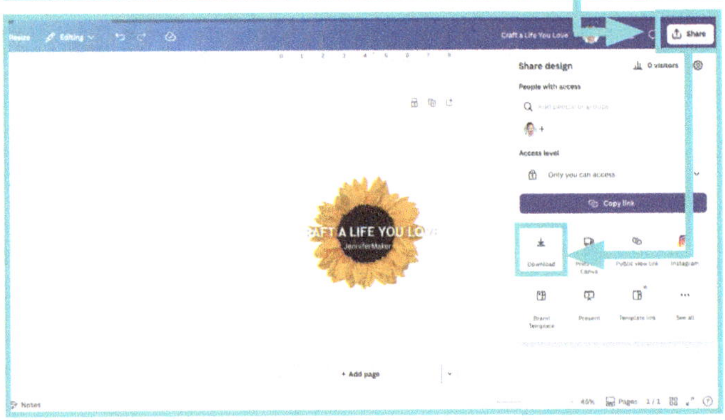

Step 2: Choose a file type. Canva provides multiple file type options such as:

- JPG
- PNG
- PDF Standard
- PDF Print
- SVG
- MP4 Video
- GIF
- PPTX

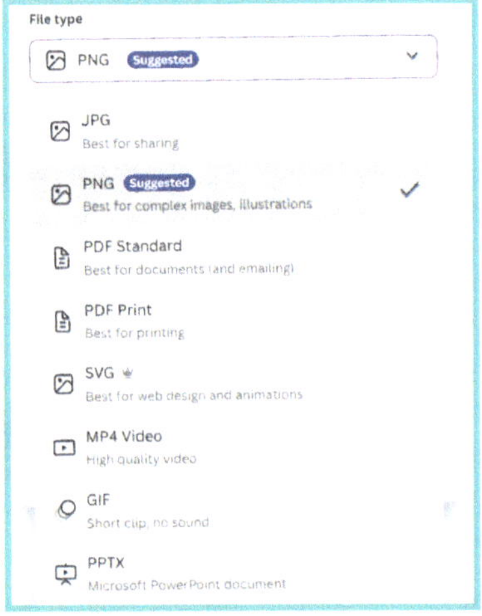

Step 3 (Optional): Depending on the selected file type, you can adjust:

- **Size**: Resize your design dimensions (e.g., for social media or web use).
- **Quality**: Choose higher quality for sharper visuals (especially for PNG and JPG).
- **Transparent Background**: Available for PNG and SVG (Canva Pro required).
- **Crop Marks and Bleed**: Enable for PDF (Print) to prepare designs for professional printing.

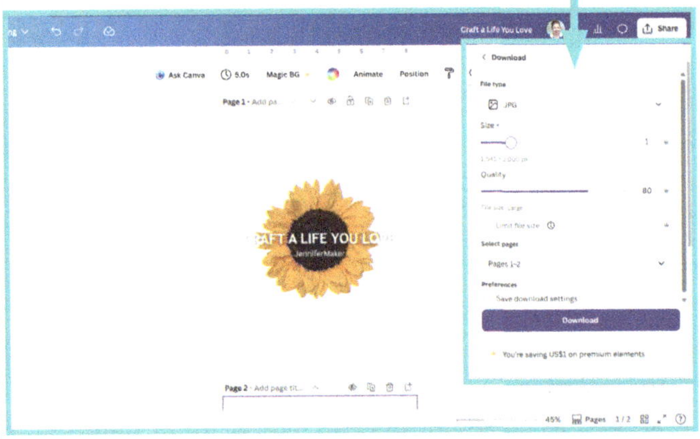

Step 4: Once you've chosen your file type and settings, click **Download** to save the file to your device.

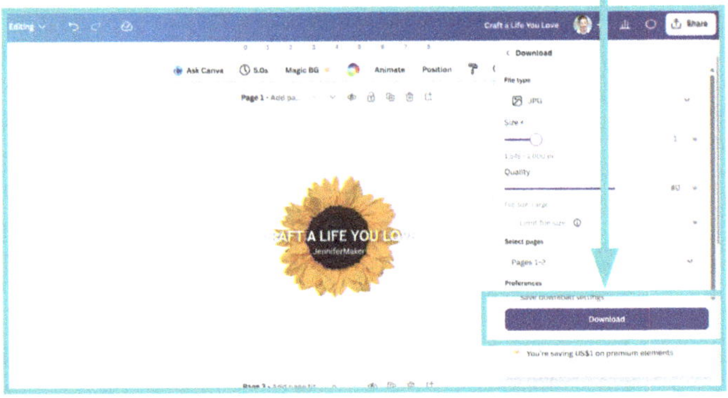

NOTES:

- Canva Pro users can access advanced features like transparent backgrounds and resizing for multiple platforms.
- When exporting animations, MP4 is recommended for video presentations, while GIF works best for short loops.

WARNING: You CANNOT print directly from Canva. You must first download your design, then print it from your device.

HOW TO SPEED UP YOUR WORKFLOW WITH KEYBOARD SHORTCUTS FOR MAC

You can do many tasks in Canva easier and faster using keyboard and mouse shortcuts. Here is a list of the most useful keyboard and mouse shortcuts on Mac:

Function	Mac
Undo	Command + Z
Redo	Command + Y
Save	Command + S
Select All	Command + A
Add Text	T
Add Empty Page	Command + RETURN
Delete Empty Page	Command + Delete
Navigate to Toolbar	Command + F1
Quick Actions	/
Delete Selected Elements	Delete
Group Elements	Command + G
Ungroup Elements	Command + Shift + G
Lock Element	Option + Shift + L
Arrange Element Forward	Command +]
Arrange Element Backward	Command + [
Arrange Element to Front	Option + Command +]
Arrange Element to Back	Option + Command + [
Zoom in	Command + +
Zoom Out	Command + -
Zoom to Actual Size	Command + 0
Zoom to Fit	Option + Command + 0
Zoom to Fill	Shift + Command + 0

Function	Mac
Open Font Menu	Shift + Command + F
Find and Replace	Command + F
Bold Text	Command + B
Italicize Text	Command + I
Underline Text	Command + U
Uppercase	Shift + Command + K
Left Align	Shift + Command + L
Center Align	Shift + Command + C
Right Align	Shift + Command + R
Justify Text	Shift + Command + J
Numbered List	Shift + Command + 7
Bulleted List	Shift + Command + 8
Copy Text Style	Option + Command + C
Paste Text Style	Option + Command + V
Play/Pause Video	Space
Mute/Unmute Video	M
Loop Video	Option + Command + L
Scrolling View	Option + Command + 1
Thumbnail View	Option + Command + 2
Grid View	Option + Command + 3
Presentation Mode	Option + Command + P

HOW TO SPEED UP YOUR WORKFLOW WITH KEYBOARD SHORTCUTS FOR WINDOWS

You can do many tasks in Canva easier and faster using keyboard and mouse shortcuts. Here is a list of the most useful keyboard and mouse shortcuts on Windows:

Function	Windows
Undo	Ctrl + Z
Redo	Ctrl + Y
Save	Ctrl + S
Select All	Ctrl + A
Add Text	T
Add Empty Page	Ctrl + E
Delete Empty Page	Ctrl + Backspace
Navigate to Toolbar	Ctrl + F4
Quick Actions	Ctrl + E
Delete Selected Elements	Backspace OR Delete
Group Elements	Ctrl + G
Ungroup Elements	Ctrl + Shift + G
Lock Element	Alt + Shift + L
Arrange Element Forward	Ctrl +]
Arrange Element Backward	Ctrl + [
Arrange Element to Front	Alt + Ctrl +]
Arrange Element to Back	Alt + Ctrl + [
Zoom in	Ctrl + -
Zoom Out	Alt + Ctrl + 0
Zoom to Actual Size	Ctrl + 0
Zoom to Fit	Alt + Ctrl + 0
Zoom to Fill	Shift + Ctrl + 0

Function	Windows
Open Font Menu	Shift + Ctrl + F
Find and Replace	Ctrl + F
Bold Text	Ctrl + B
Italicize Text	Ctrl + I
Underline Text	Ctrl + U
Uppercase	Shift + Ctrl + K
Left Align	Shift + Ctrl + L
Center Align	Shift + Ctrl + C
Right Align	Shift + Ctrl + R
Justify Text	Shift + Ctrl + J
Numbered List	Shift + Ctrl + 7
Bulleted List	Shift + Ctrl + 8
Copy Text Style	Alt + Ctrl + C
Paste Text Style	Alt + Ctrl + V
Play/Pause Video	Space
Mute/Unmute Video	M
Loop Video	Alt + Ctrl + L
Scrolling View	Alt + Ctrl + 1
Thumbnail View	Alt + Ctrl + 2
Grid View	Alt + Ctrl + 3
Presentation Mode	Alt + Ctrl + P

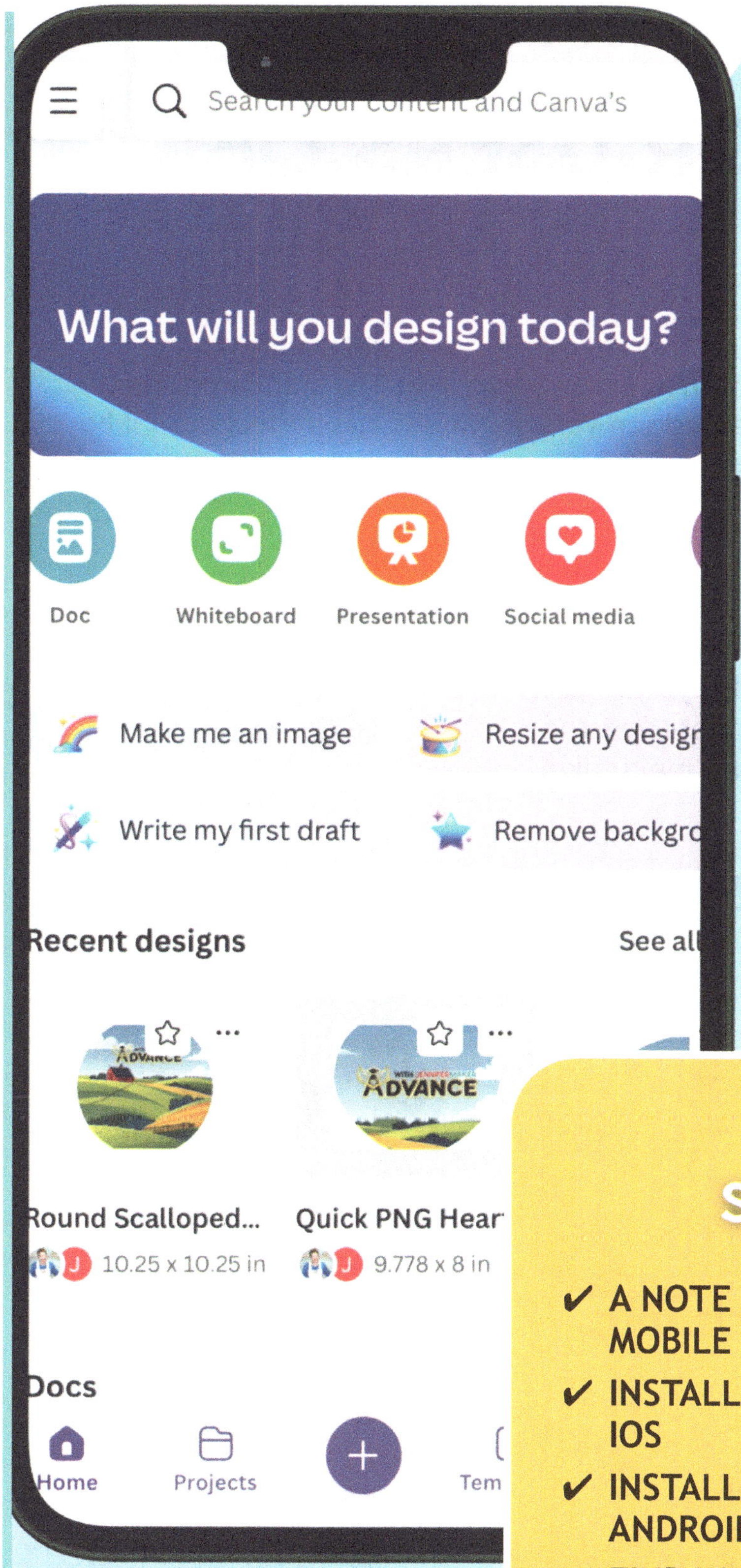

HOW TO:

MOBILE: GETTING STARTED WITH CANVA

- ✔ A NOTE FOR USERS OF CANVA APP ON MOBILE
- ✔ INSTALL AND OPEN THE CANVA APP ON YOUR IOS
- ✔ INSTALL AND OPEN THE CANVA APP ON YOUR ANDROID
- ✔ FIND WHAT YOU NEED ON THE HOME PAGE

A NOTE FOR USERS OF CANVA APP ON MOBILE

The interface for standard-sized iPads and Android tablets looks different than the interface for phones and small tablets (both Apple and Android). The standard-sized tablet interface looks very similar to the Desktop version. In this Mobile section, I'll be showing you the phone/small tablet interface.

Key Difference on the phone app:

Menu Placement: On the phone/small tablet app, the main action buttons, like "Home," "Projects," and "Create a Design (purple '+' sign)", are located at the bottom of the screen, instead of in a side menu like on the tablet.

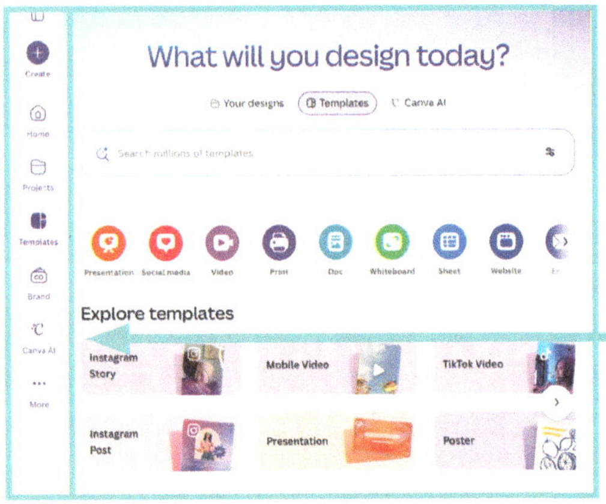

TABLET

PHONE

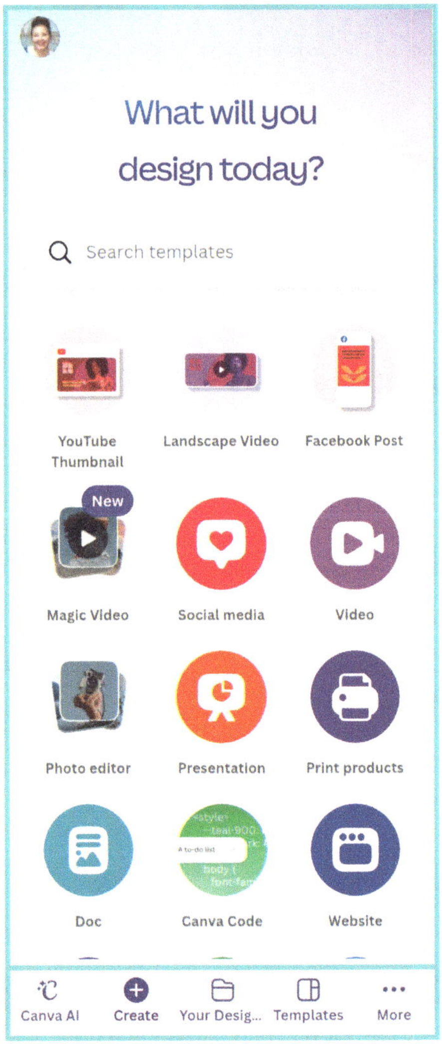

How to Follow This Guide on Standard Tablets

As you work through this playbook, remember that when instructions refer to menus or tools at the "bottom," they are likely located at the side of your tablet screen. Everything else – features, tools, and capabilities – works the same way.

This small adjustment will help you get the most out of Canva on your mobile device. With these differences in mind, **you'll be designing like a pro in no time**, even on a smaller screen!

HOW TO INSTALL AND OPEN THE CANVA APP ON YOUR IOS

It's easy to download, install, and open the Canva app on your iOS device. Follow these steps to learn how.

Step 1: Find the **App Store** on your device and click on it.

Step 2: Click **Search** in the lower menu.

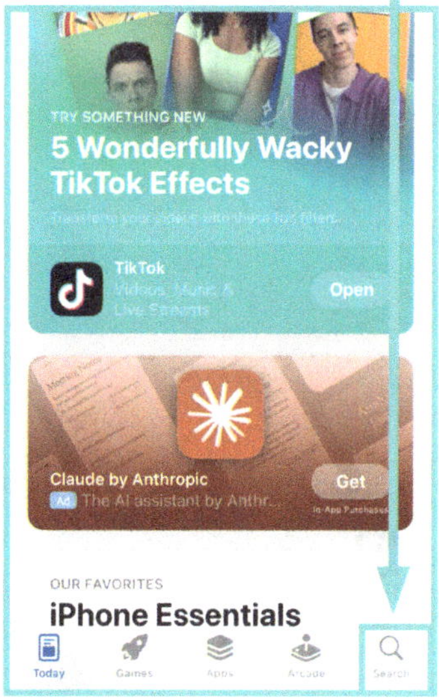

Step 3: Search for **Canva** in the search bar and click **Get**.

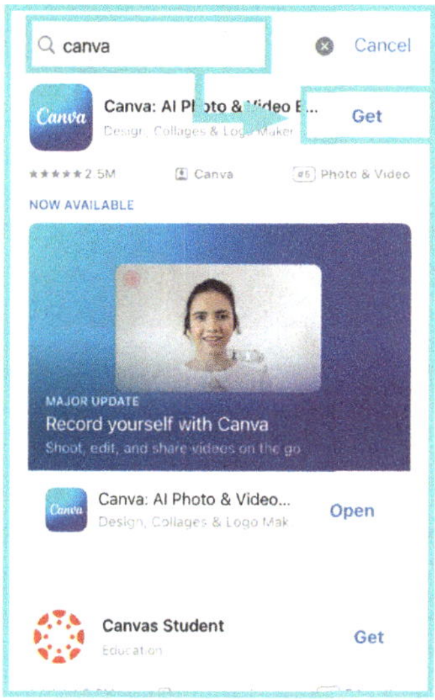

Step 4: The app will start downloading.

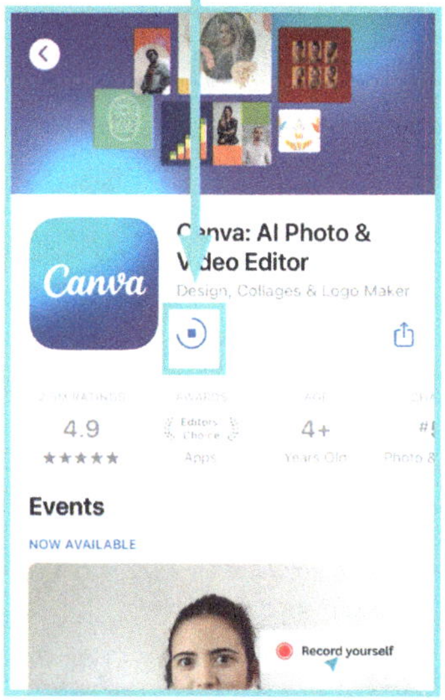

Step 5: Once downloaded, the app will appear in your home screen.

Step 6: Click on the app to open it up.

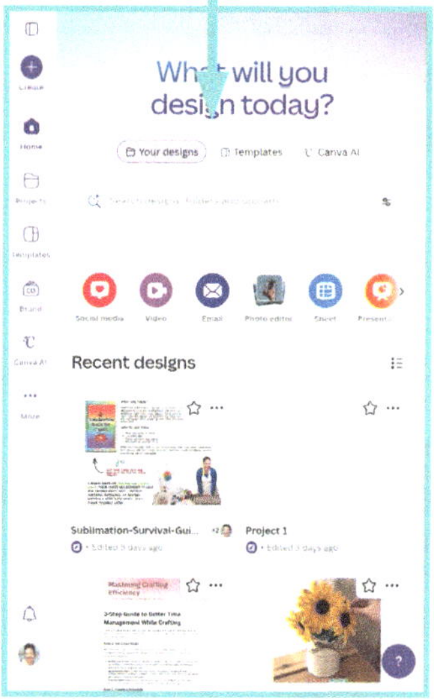

HOW TO INSTALL AND OPEN CANVA APP ON YOUR ANDROID

It's easy to download, install, and open the Canva app on your Android device. Follow these steps to learn how.

Step 1: Tap on the **Play Store** icon on your device.

Step 2: Tap the **Search** icon. Type "Canva" in the search bar. Tap your **Enter/Return** key.

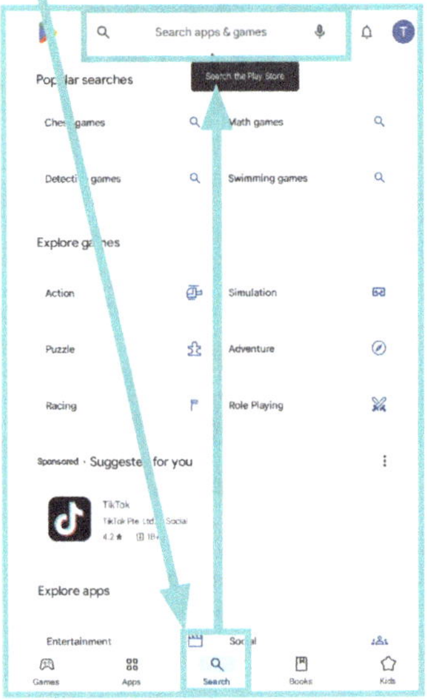

Step 3: Tap the **Install** button next to the Canva search result.

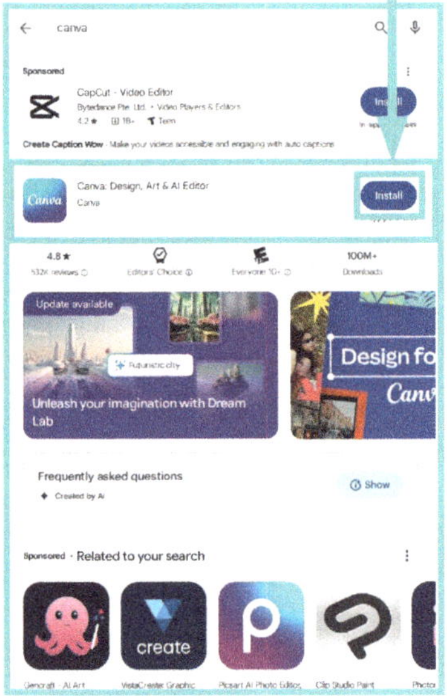

Step 4: The download and installation will start.

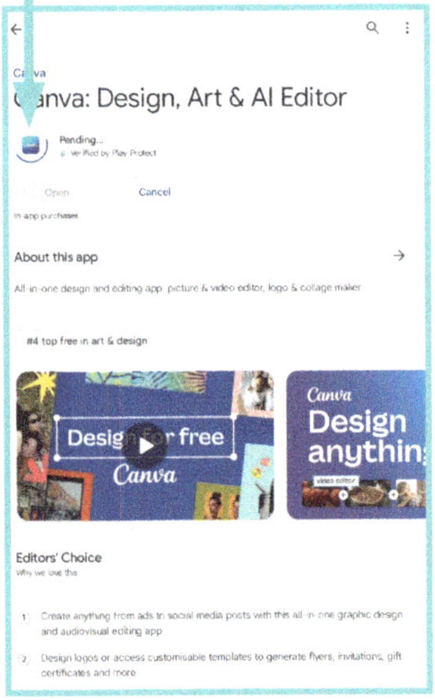

Step 5: Once Canva is installed, look for the Canva icon on your device.

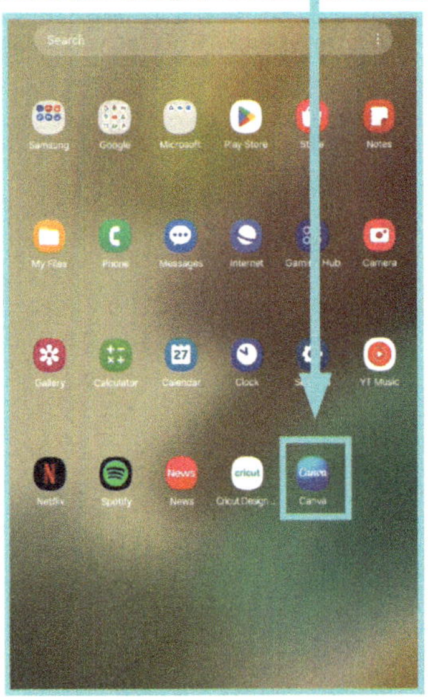

Step 6: Tap the Canva icon. The Canva app will open and the home screen will appear.

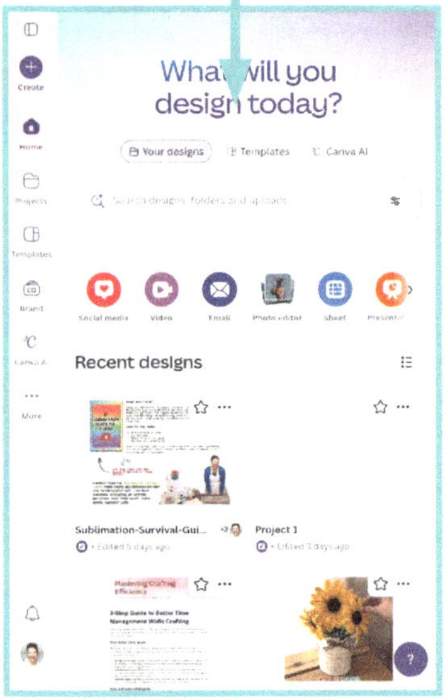

MOBILE

HOW TO FIND WHAT YOU NEED ON THE HOME PAGE

The home page can be overwhelming, so this page will help you find and learn about the basics — everything you need to know to get started.

Search bar

Create a design

Your projects

Find templates

Find apps

Thumbnails of designs you've recently created will appear here.

Your account area — click to find settings and account options.

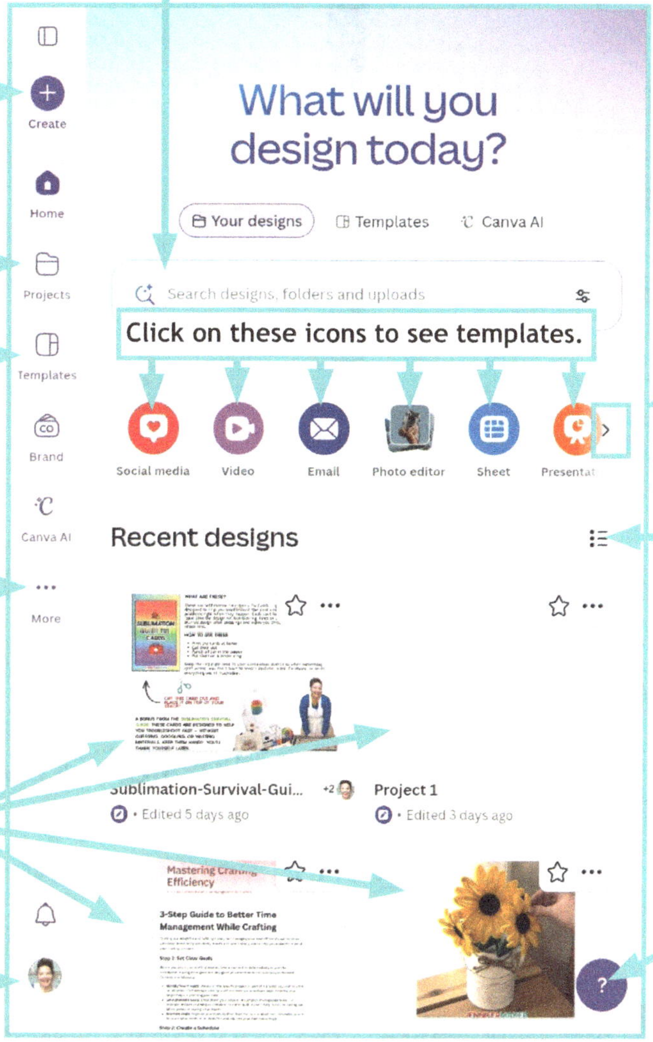

Click on these icons to see templates.

Swipe over to find more template options.

This icon changes the layout of the "Recent designs" area.

Click this icon to get help from the automated Canva assistant.

NOTE: Your dashboard may look slightly different than mine after opening the app.

TIP: Take some time to familiarize yourself with the home page. Explore the other icons after you are familiar with everything pointed out on the map above.

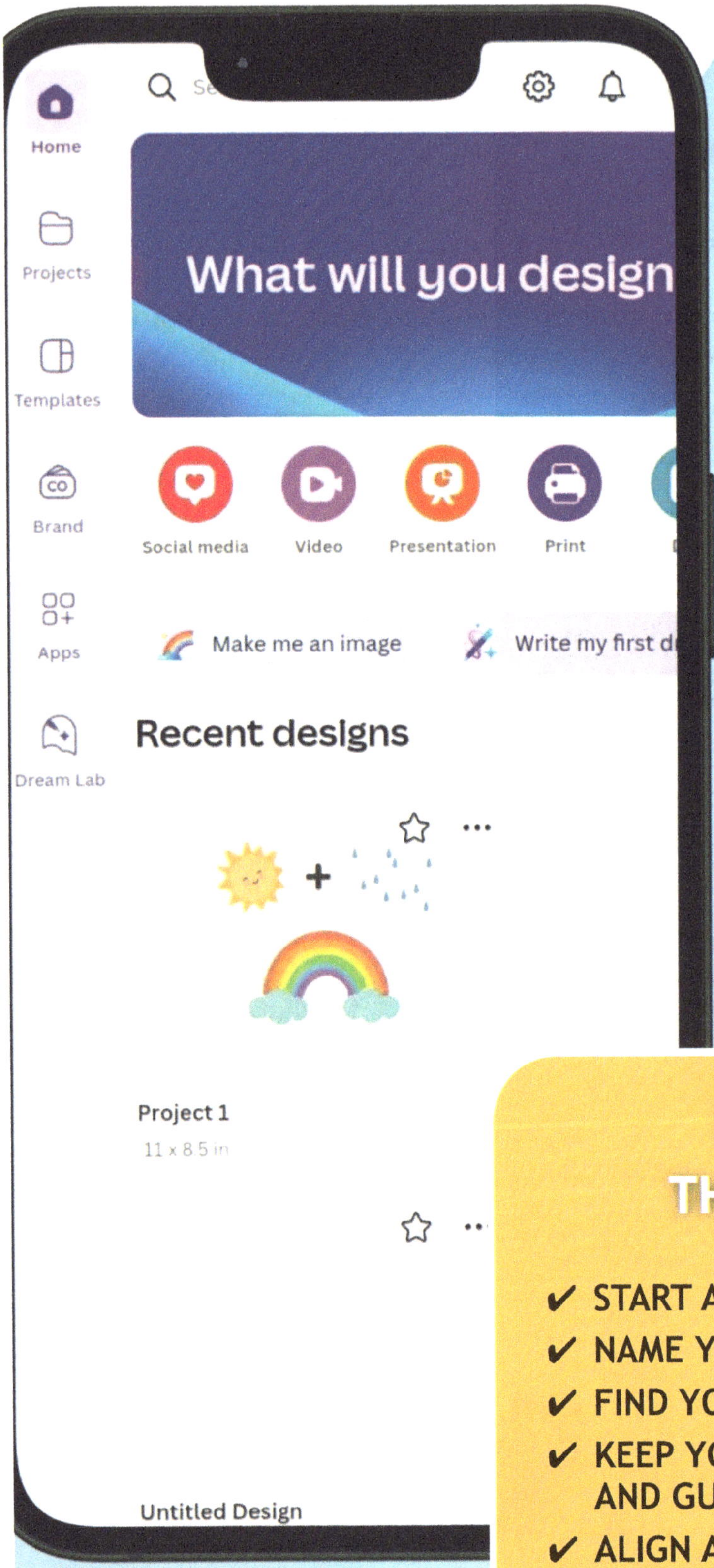

HOW TO:

MOBILE: NAVIGATING THE CANVA WORKSPACE

- ✔ START A NEW DESIGN FROM A TEMPLATE
- ✔ NAME YOUR PROJECTS
- ✔ FIND YOUR TOOLS ON THE DESIGN PAGE
- ✔ KEEP YOUR DESIGN ALIGNED WITH RULERS AND GUIDES
- ✔ ALIGN AND ARRANGE ELEMENTS FOR A CLEAN LAYOUT

MOBILE

HOW TO START A NEW DESIGN FROM A TEMPLATE

You can start a new design using any of the many available pre-made templates on the Canva app.

Step 1: Tap the Create button on the homepage.

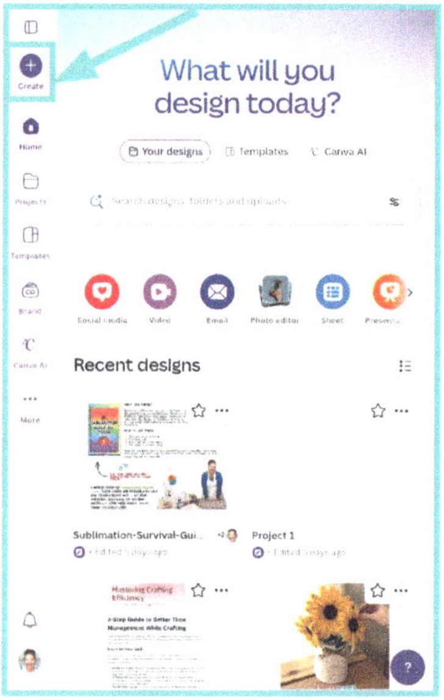

Step 2: Look through the templates in the category to find what you need, then tap it.

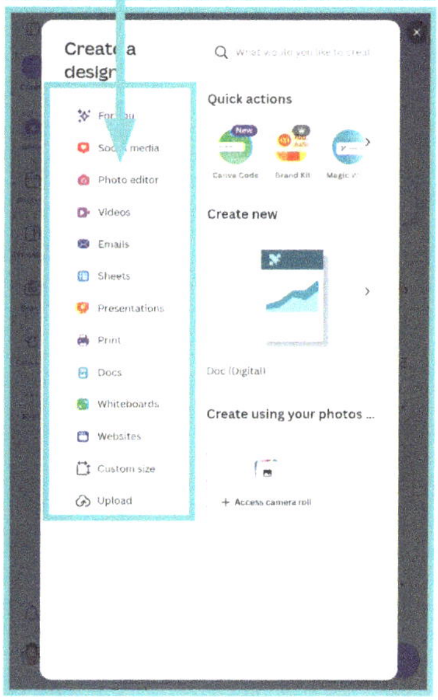

Step 3: The blank template you selected will open on the screen.

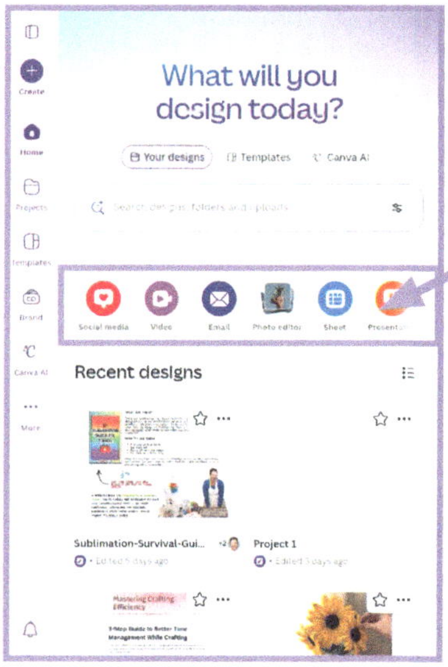

NOTE: You can also tap on any of the template icons below the banner on the home page. Remember to swipe over to see all of the template icons.

WARNING: You MUST create your new design at the size you want if you're using the Free version because you cannot resize it later. You can only resize your designs if you are a Pro member.

TIP: If you can't find a template that works for you, you can create a custom template. Look for "How to Make a Custom Template" on page 93.

HOW TO
NAME YOUR PROJECTS

You should name your projects when you first start them. It's very easy to name a project. Follow the steps below to learn how to do it.

Step 1: Tap the File menu icon in the top left corner of the screen.

Step 2: In the menu that appears, tap the pen icon next to "Untitled design - [your template size]."

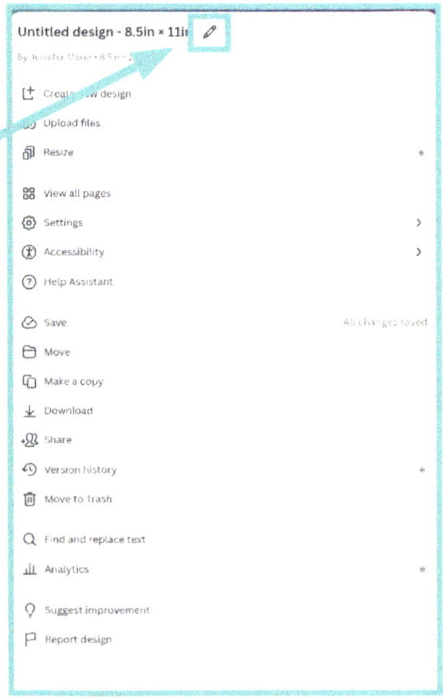

Step 3: Type in whatever you'd like to name your project. I'm going to call mine "Project 1."

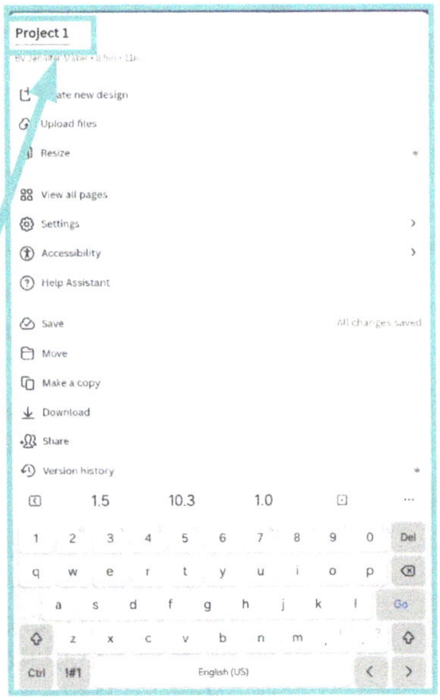

Step 4: Place your finger on the small bar above the menu and swipe down to return to your design page.

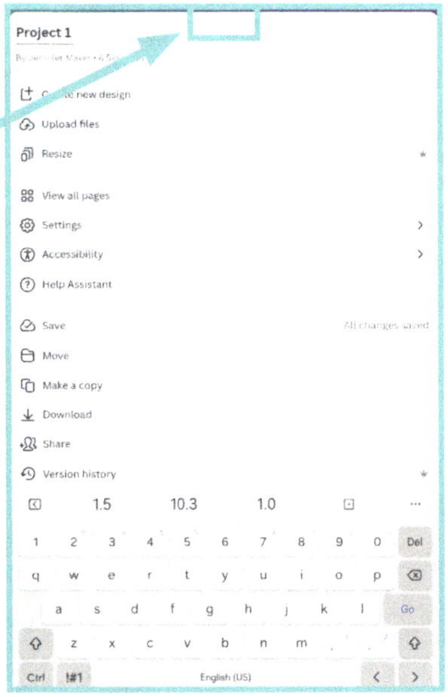

NOTE: You do not have to give your project a name – it will still save automatically and just remain named as the default "Untitled design" followed by the canvas dimensions. But it's a good idea to always give your projects a name so that they are easier to find later.

MOBILE

HOW TO FIND YOUR TOOLS ON THE DESIGN PAGE

The design page looks complicated at first glance, but once you know where all of the tools and functions are, you'll be ready to create!

Home Menu: Create a new design, go to the home page, ask the automated Canva assistant a question, and find recent designs.

Canvas: Where your design will appear

File Menu: Name your project, upload files, access settings, save, share, and more.

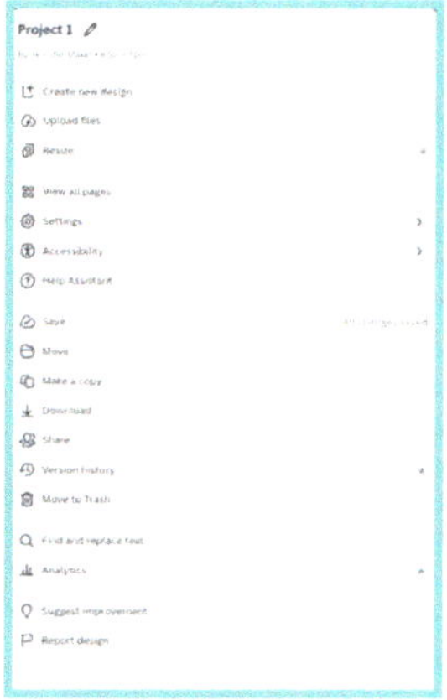

Toolbar: Find all design tools in this area. (see enlarged image below for details)

Elements: Find images, audio and video clips, and more to add to your designs.

Gallery or Camera Roll: Access your mobile device's photo gallery.

Tools: Draw with digital pens, markers, and highlighters.

Apps: Search for and access helpful design apps within Canva's platform.

Templates: Find layout templates, plus curated color palettes, font sets, and recent design styles.

Text: Add text boxes, use an AI text generator, and choose text settings.

Brand: For Canva Pro members only: Set up your brand logo, palette, and images.

Uploads: Upload any image, audio, or video file from your device. You can also record your own audio and video.

Projects: Find your past projects and uploaded elements here.

Magic Media: This feature is Canva's AI art generator.

HOW TO KEEP YOUR DESIGN ALIGNED WITH RULERS & GUIDES

Guides in Canva are visual lines that help you align and position elements precisely on your canvas. They are especially useful for creating professional layouts, balanced designs, and consistent spacing.

Step 1: Tap **File** in the top-left menu. Tap **Settings** in the menu that appears.

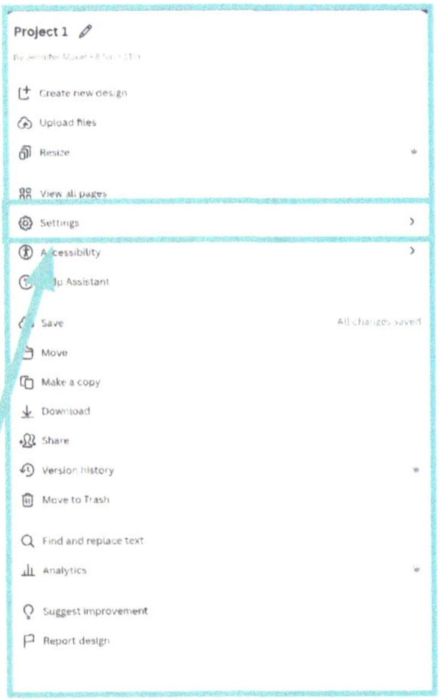

Step 2: In the submenu, tap **Add guides**.

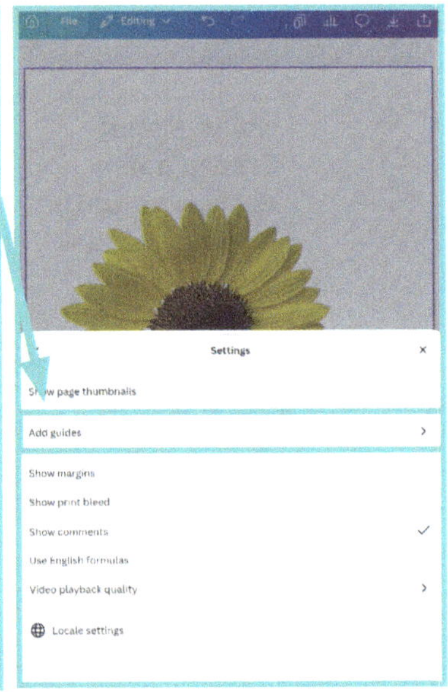

Step 3: Choose which set of guides you would like to use, or tap **Custom** to create your own set of guides.

Step 4: Use the guides to help place your elements as desired. When dragging an element, it will "snap" to the nearest guideline.

NOTES:

- Guides are only visible during editing and will not appear in your exported design.
- To hide guides, go to **File** > **Settings** > **click Show rulers and guides**.

MOBILE

HOW TO ALIGN AND ARRANGE ELEMENTS FOR A CLEAN LAYOUT

Aligning elements to the page in Canva allows you to center, justify, or position elements relative to the entire canvas. Layering helps you organize overlapping design elements.

Align Elements

Step 1: Tap on the element you want to align. Tap **Position** in the bottom toolbar.

Step 2: Tap **Align** at the bottom of the screen. Choose the alignment position you want. I chose **Middle** and **Center** to center the image both vertically and horizontally.

Arrange Elements

Step 1: Tap on the element that you want to change the order of in relation to the other elements on the canvas. Tap **Position** in the bottom toolbar.

Step 2: Tap **Arrange** at the bottom of the screen. Choose the position you want. I chose **To Back** because I wanted the rose to be the very bottom layer.

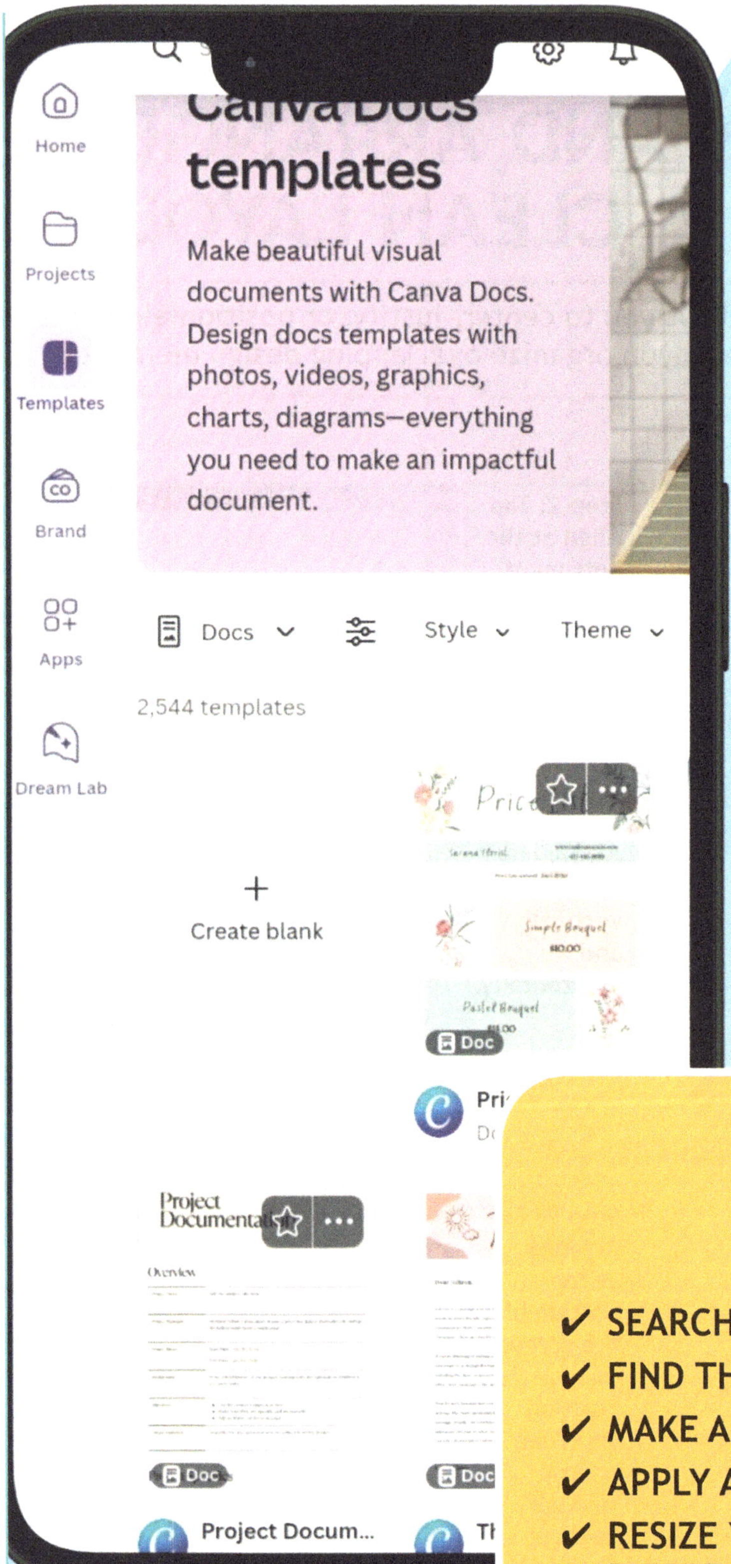

HOW TO:

MOBILE: WORKING WITH TEMPLATES

- ✔ SEARCH FOR ANY TEMPLATE
- ✔ FIND THE MOST POPULAR TEMPLATES
- ✔ MAKE A CUSTOM SIZE TEMPLATE
- ✔ APPLY A PRE-MADE DESIGN TEMPLATE
- ✔ RESIZE YOUR DESIGN IF YOU NEED A DIFFERENT SIZE

CANVA COACH PLAYBOOK

MOBILE

HOW TO SEARCH FOR ANY TEMPLATE

Canva has millions of pre-made templates available for you to customize and make your own. The new Template Search function makes it easy to find what you want!

Step 1: On the homepage, tap on the **Templates** icon above the big search bar.

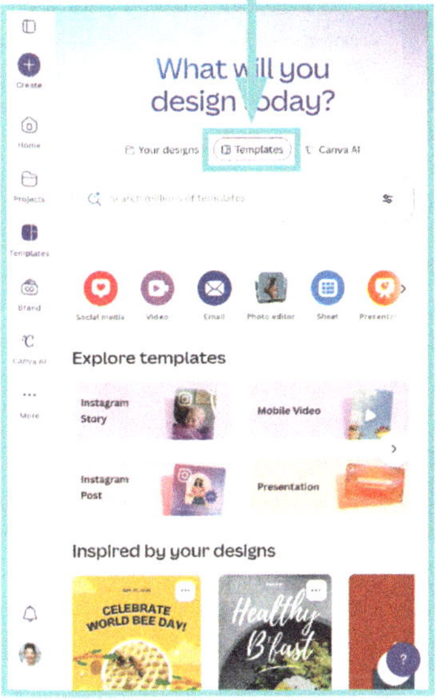

Step 2: On the Templates page, you will see a search bar and some templates to explore.

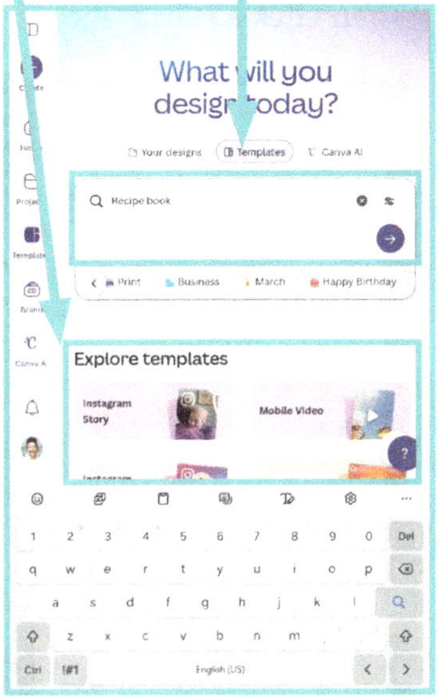

Step 3: Type in a template you want to find, then click **Category** and pick from the dropdown menu.

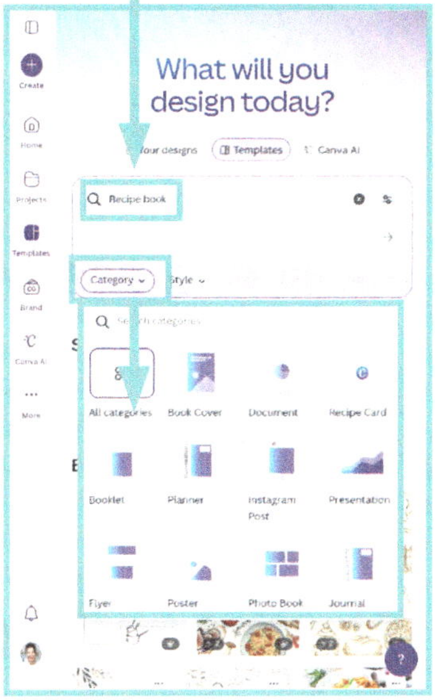

Step 4: Now click **Style** and choose one from the dropdown menu.

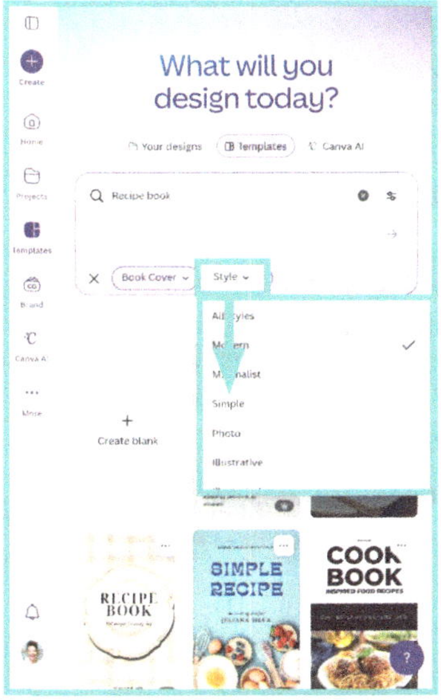

Step 5: Scroll down to look through the all of the templates available.

Step 6: Tap on a template to open it inside the editor.

HOW TO FIND THE MOST POPULAR TEMPLATES

Canva has many pre-made templates for a variety of needs. You can start with any template and then edit it to make it your own.

Step 1: Tap the **Create** button on the homepage.

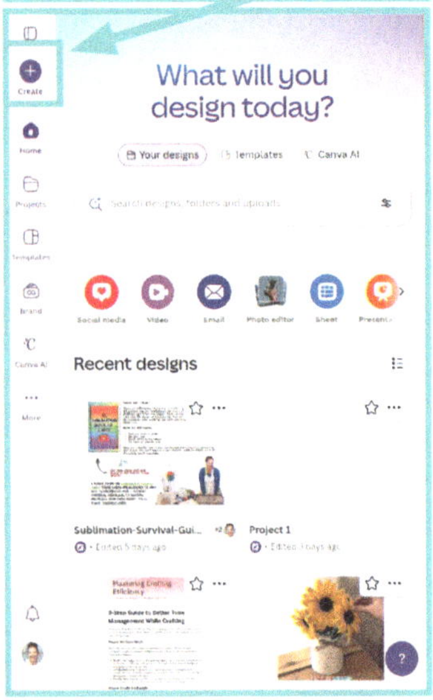

Step 2: Tap one of the template categories: **Docs**, **Whiteboards**, **Sheets**, **Presentations**, **Social Media**, or **Print Products**. Then click a subcategory.

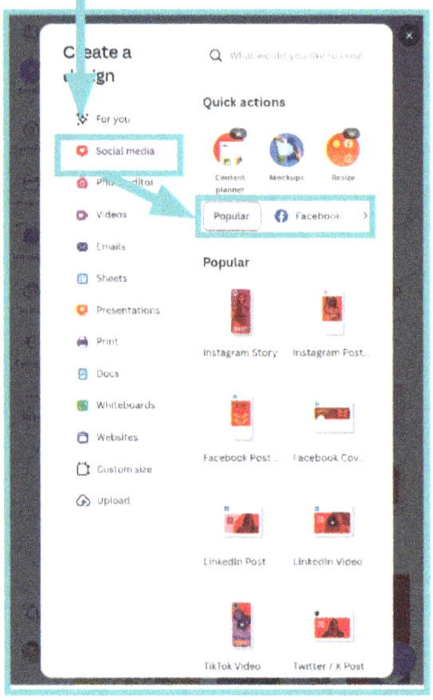

Step 3: Scroll through the available options and tap a template to open it automatically.

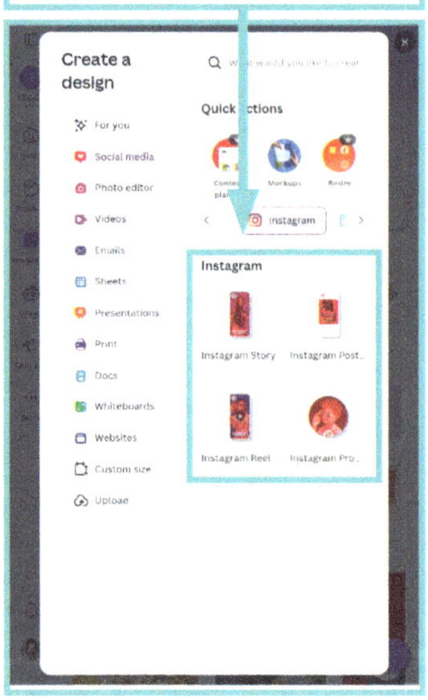

NOTE: Social Media, Video, Print Product templates are divided into categories, so just click on a specific category to see just templates that fit your needs.

TIP: Make sure you choose the category that has templates to fit your purpose:

- **Sheets:** Record data in an organized format.
- **Docs:** Create posters, menus, flyers, and more.
- **Whiteboards:** Map out ideas, plans, and other related works.
- **Presentations:** Create a high-quality multi-slide presentation.
- **Social Media:** Curate styled posts for your social media presence.
- **Videos:** Put together well-design videos.
- **Print Products:** Create and order physical products, such as business cards, invitations, cards, and marketing materials.

NOTE: You can edit everything on the template you choose — colors, fonts, images, and more.

MOBILE

HOW TO MAKE A CUSTOM SIZE TEMPLATE

If there are not any pre-made templates that will work for your design, you can make your own custom template in the exact size you need.

Step 1: On the homepage, tap the **Create** button.

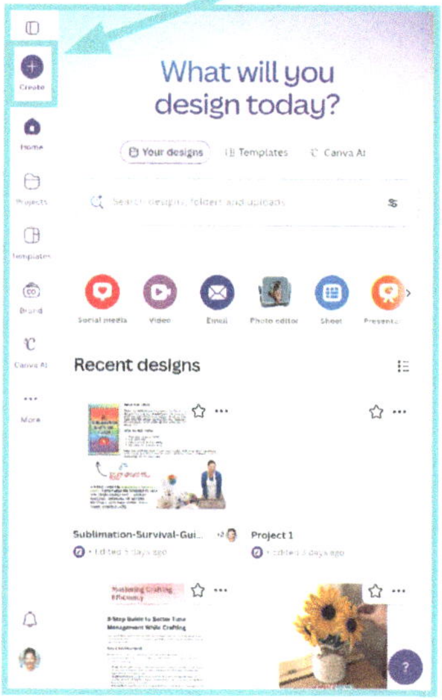

Step 2: Tap **Custom Size**.

Custom size

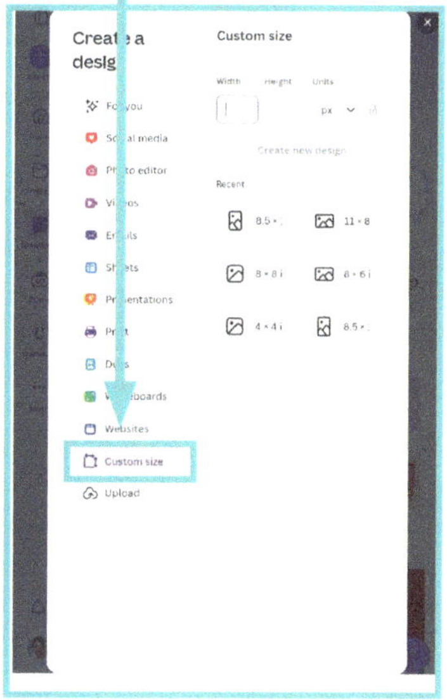

Step 3: Tap the **Units** dropdown box and tap whichever unit you want to use.

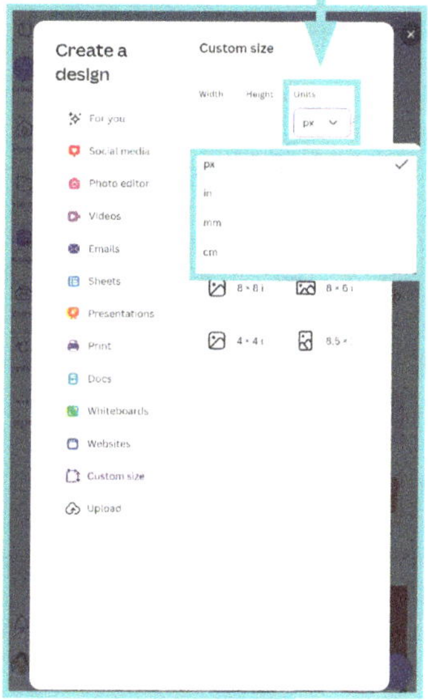

Step 4: Type in your desired **Width** and **Height** dimensions, then tap the **Create new design** button.

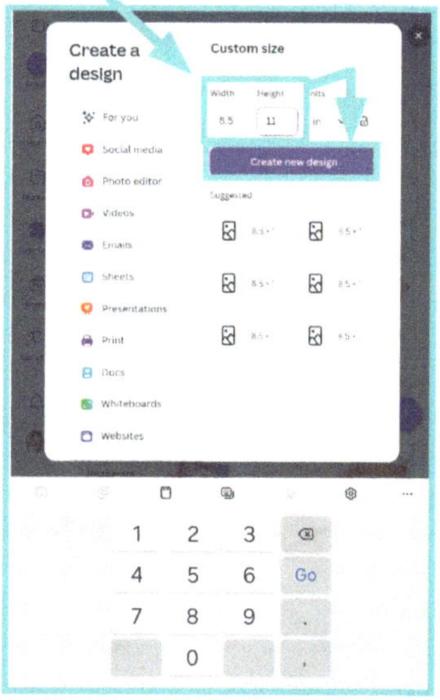

A new project page with your custom template will appear in the window.

WARNING: You MUST create your new design at the size you want if you're using the Free version because you cannot resize it later. You can only resize your designs if you are a Pro member.

HOW TO APPLY A PRE-MADE DESIGN TEMPLATE

Templates are an excellent resource for when you don't want to start a project from scratch. There are a wide variety of templates to suit your needs.

Step 1: Tap on the Design tab, then tap Templates near the top of the screen.

Step 2: Type descriptive words into the search bar to help find your desired templates.

Step 3: Tap the purple arrow button to start the search.

Step 4: Tap on the template you want to use to add it to your canvas.

Step 5: The template will fill up your canvas.

Step 6: To edit the template, tap on an area you want to edit, then change as desired.

HOW TO RESIZE YOUR DESIGN IF YOU NEED A DIFFERENT SIZE

For Pro members only, Canva has a "Resize" feature that allows you to change the size of your canvas after you've already started creating.

Step 1: On the design you want to resize, tap "File" in the top menu bar.

Step 2: When the File menu opens, find and tap "Resize."

NOTE: Only Canva Pro members can use the "Resize" feature.

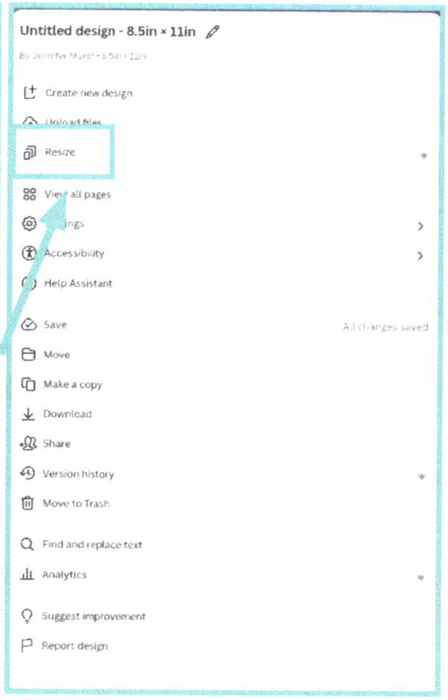

Step 3: If you clicked "Copy & resize," find the resized copy in your Projects. If you clicked "Resize this design," the design you are working on will be resized and the original version will no longer exist.

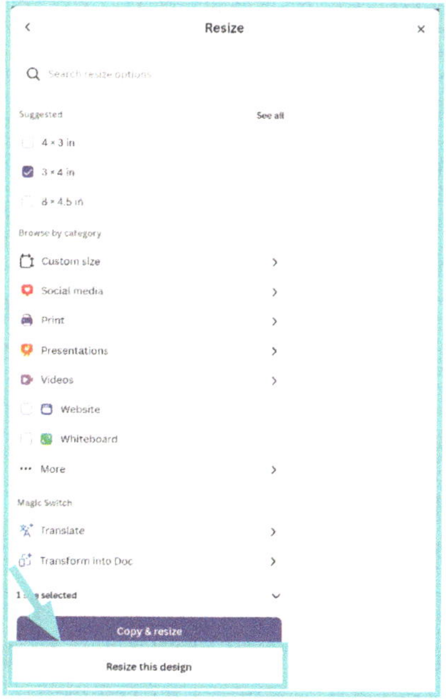

Step 4: Your resized design will appear on the screen. Notice that the size of the elements did not change, but the size of the canvas did.

WARNING: You MUST create your new design at the size you want if you're using the Free version because you cannot resize it later.

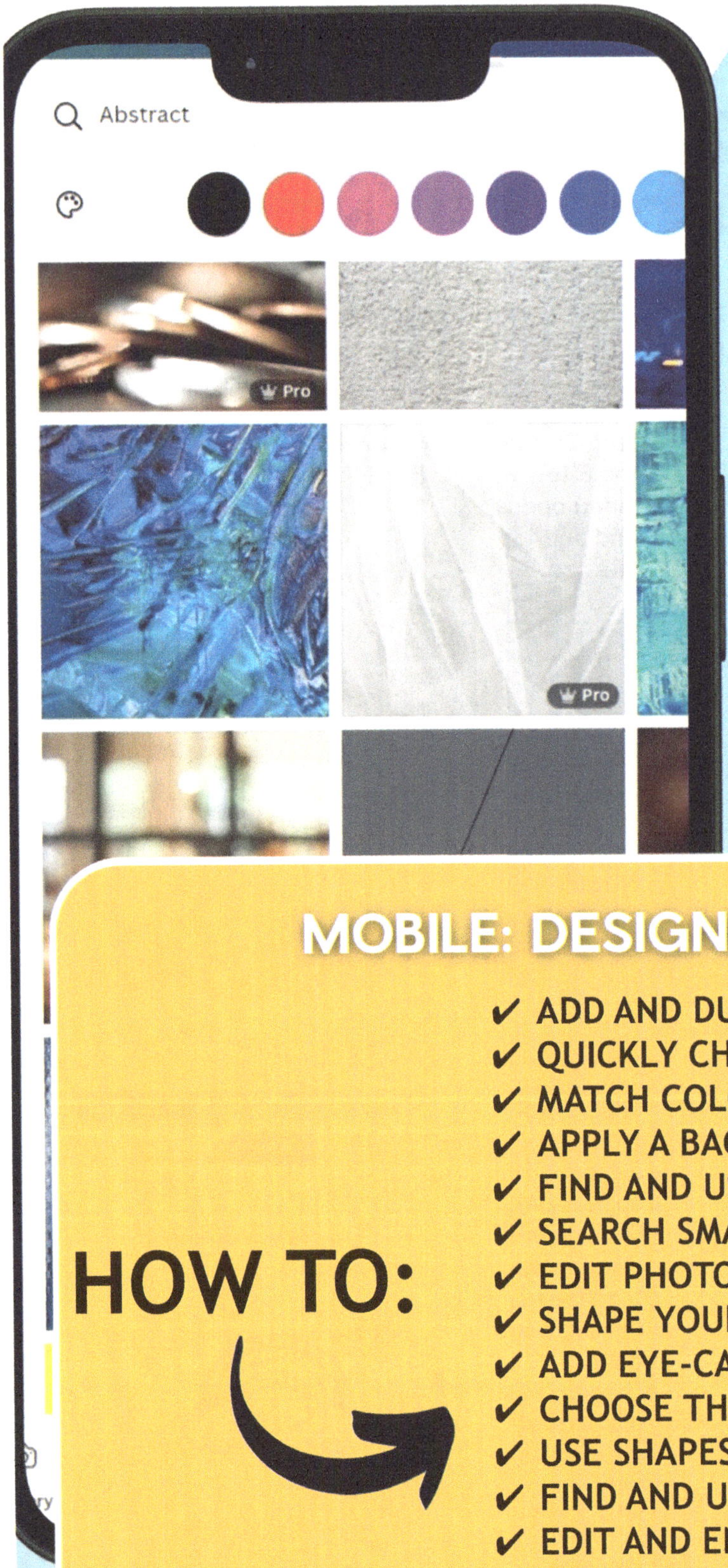

MOBILE: DESIGNING WITH ELEMENTS

HOW TO:

- ✔ ADD AND DUPLICATE PAGES IN YOUR DESIGN
- ✔ QUICKLY CHANGE THE LOOK OF YOUR DESIGN
- ✔ MATCH COLORS AND FONTS WITH CANVA STYLES
- ✔ APPLY A BACKGROUND TO YOUR CANVAS
- ✔ FIND AND USE DESIGN ELEMENTS
- ✔ SEARCH SMARTER FOR GRAPHICS AND IMAGES
- ✔ EDIT PHOTOS
- ✔ SHAPE YOUR IMAGES WITH FRAMES
- ✔ ADD EYE-CATCHING GRAPHICS TO YOUR DESIGN
- ✔ CHOOSE THE RIGHT PHOTOS FOR YOUR DESIGN
- ✔ USE SHAPES TO ENHANCE YOUR LAYOUTS
- ✔ FIND AND USE VIDEOS
- ✔ EDIT AND ENHANCE VIDEOS
- ✔ ADD AUDIO TO YOUR PROJECTS
- ✔ MAKE YOUR DESIGNS LOOK REAL WITH MOCKUPS
- ✔ CREATE CHARTS TO VIZUALIZE DATA
- ✔ ARRANGE PHOTOS AND ELEMENTS WITH GRIDS
- ✔ FIND CURATED ELEMENT COLLECTIONS
- ✔ ADD STICKERS FOR FUN DESIGNS

HOW TO ADD AND DUPLICATE PAGES IN YOUR DESIGN

You can add multiple pages of the same size to your existing project, as well as duplicate a page to create a second identical page. The pages you add can be of the same type, or you can add a different type of file, such as a Sheet, Doc, Presentation, Whiteboard, Social Media template, Video, or Print Product.

Add a Page

Step 1: Pinch your fingers inward on the screen to zoom out.

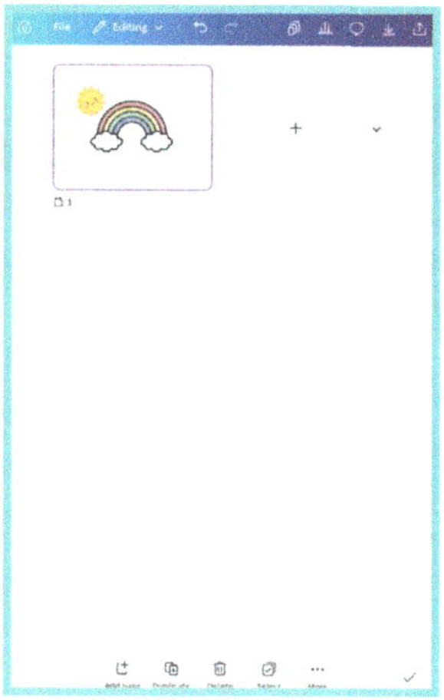

Step 2: Option A: To add a page of the same type, tap the **box with a + sign** or tap **Add page** at the bottom of the screen.

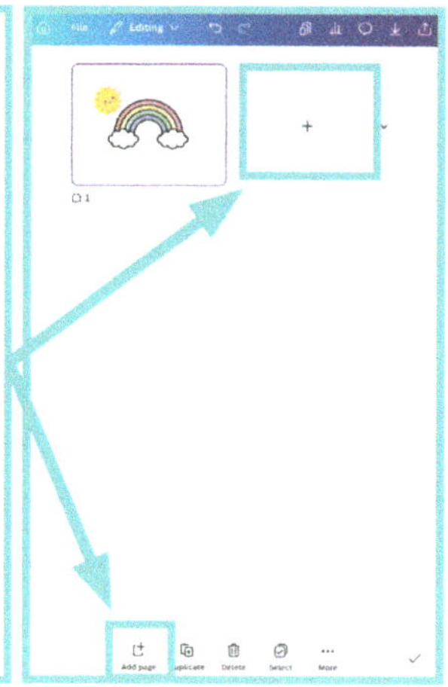

Step 2: Option B: To add a different type of page, tap the arrow by the **box with a + sign**, then choose your page type.

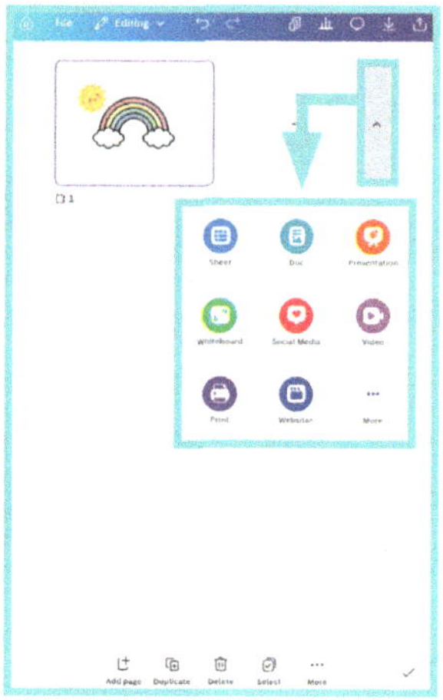

Duplicate a Page

Step 1: On the page you want to duplicate, tap on your canvas, then tap the **More** icon.

Step 2: Tap the **Duplicate** icon in the menu that appears below the canvas.

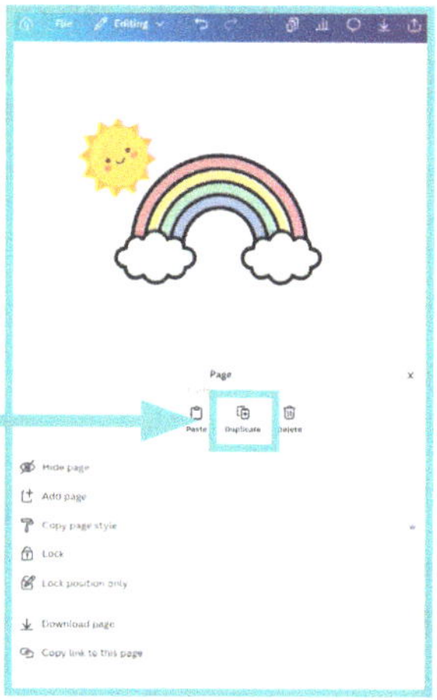

An identical project page will appear. Use two fingers to zoom out to see it. Tap on it to bring it up.

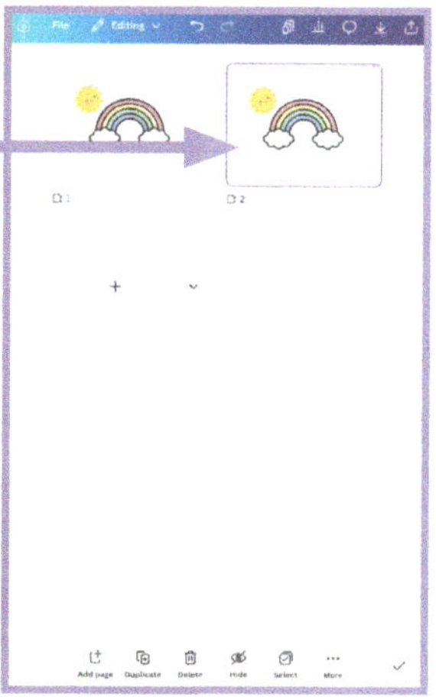

NOTE: Adding new pages to a design is a good way to keep all designs — even those of a different format — for a single project in one place. This is ideal for projects with multiple designs, such as a sublimated blanket, or a project that has a presentation that accompanies it.

HOW TO QUICKLY CHANGE THE LOOK OF YOUR DESIGN

The Templates tab is where you can find layout templates that fit your canvas, as well as curated color palettes, font sets, and recent design styles.

Step 1: Tap on the **Templates** tab, then see below to learn about templates and styles.

TIP: Templates and Styles are useful when you have an idea in mind and want to find something that matches. They are also good to look through if you need design inspiration.

Templates: Tap on **Templates** below the search bar to access all templates that fit your canvas size and shape.

Styles: Tap on **Styles** below the search bar to find preset color palettes, font combinations, and color/font combinations.

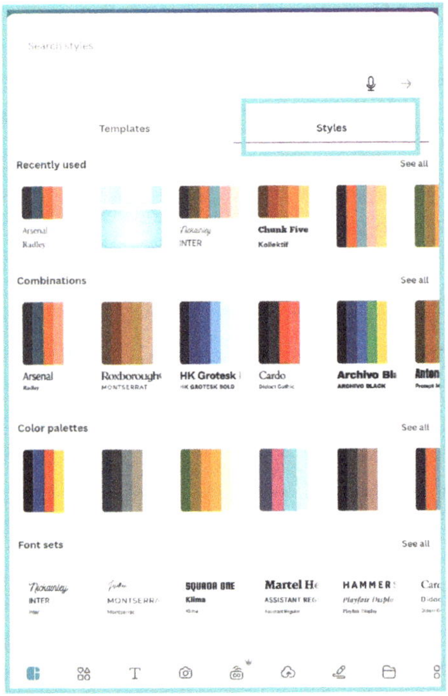

HOW TO MATCH COLORS AND FONTS WITH CANVA STYLES

Use the Styles section to search through and choose from curated collections of color palettes and font sets.

Step 1: Tap on the **Templates** tab, then tap **Styles** near the top of the screen. Optionally, type a word or two into the search box if you have a style in mind.

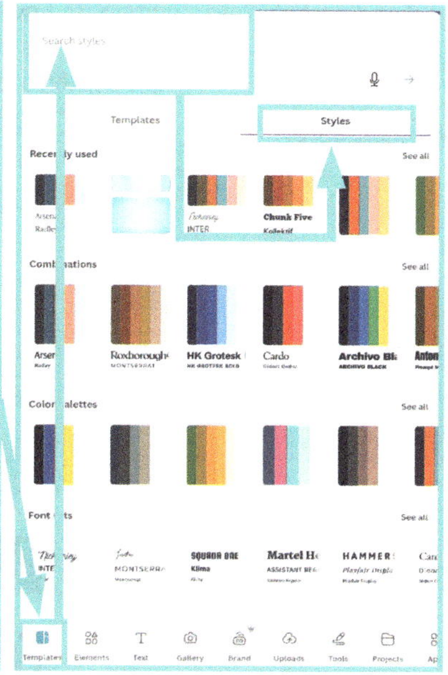

Step 2: Scroll through the results. Tap on one of the words below the search box to narrow the results.

Vibrant
Bold
Dynamic
Lively
Creative

Step 3: Tap on a style to add it to your canvas. One of the color options will appear, along with the font styles.

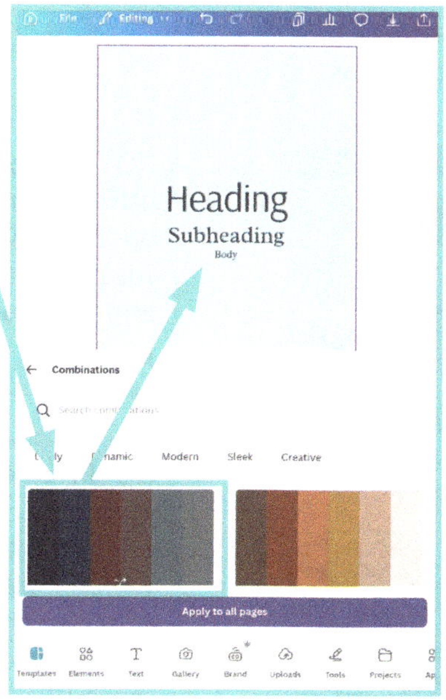

Step 4: Tap on the same style again to try one of the other colors in the style collection. Tap again to change the colors once more.

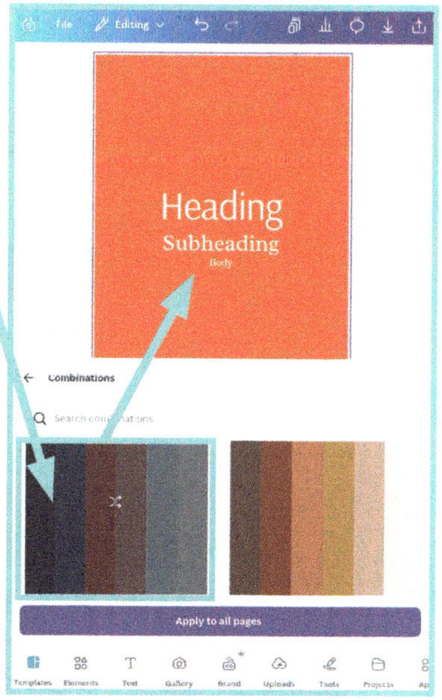

HOW TO APPLY A BACKGROUND TO YOUR CANVAS

The Background tab is a quick way to add a full-coverage background to your canvas. Canva has a large library of ready-to-use backgrounds.

Step 1: Click on the **Background** tab.

Background

Step 2 (Optional): Tap the palette to search for specific colors.

Step 3: Look through the categories and click **See all** next to one.

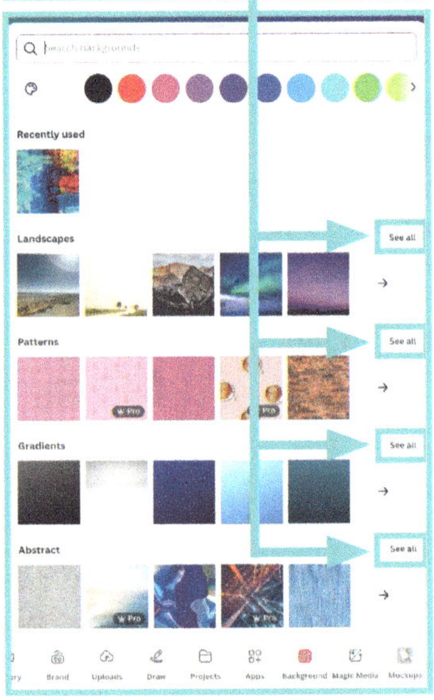

Step 4: Tap on a background to add it to your canvas.

The background will cover your entire canvas.

NOTE: You can use other elements as backgrounds. You will just have to resize and position them for yourself.

NOTE: Like other elements, you can change the transparency, which may be necessary to make the other elements on your canvas more visible.

HOW TO FIND AND USE DESIGN ELEMENTS

The Elements tab is where you'll find most of the resources you'll need for your projects: frames, graphics, photos, shapes, audio, video, mockups, charts, and more.

Step 1:
Tap on the **Elements** tab. Type in a word or short phrase into the search bar, then tap the **Enter/ Return** key on your device.

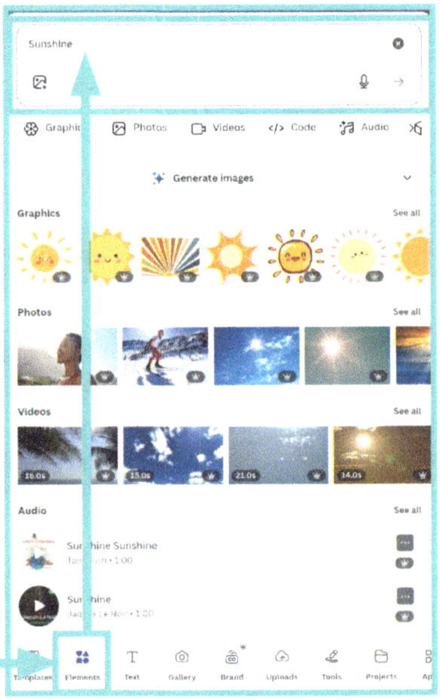

Step 2:
Tap on a category to see more results in that particular category. I chose "Graphics."

Step 3:
Scroll through the results to find one you want to use. Remember that elements with "Pro" on them are for Pro members only.

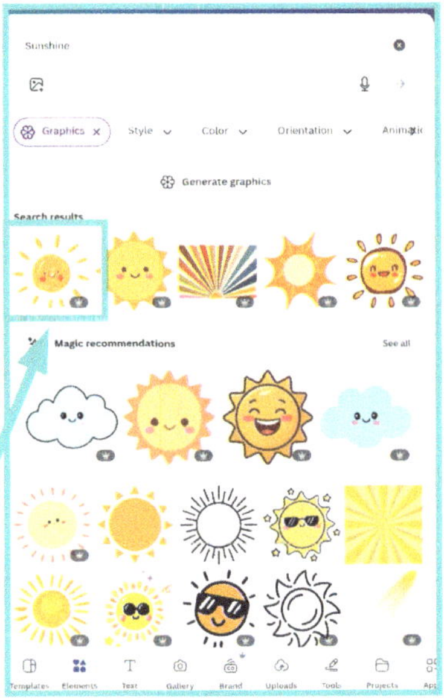

Step 4:
Tap on an **element** to add it to your canvas. You can add more elements the same way.

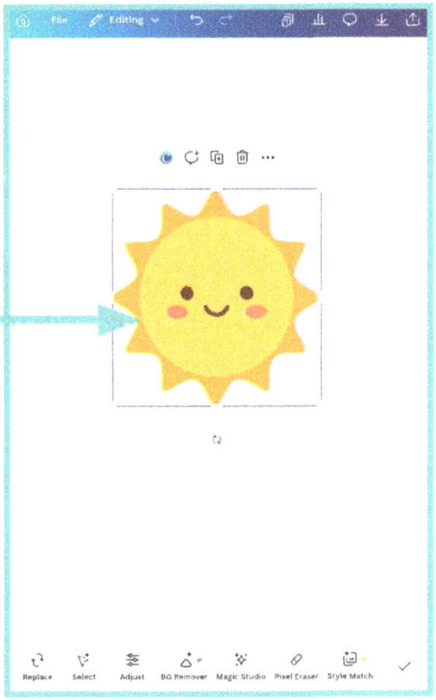

TIP: If you see a "Magic Recommendations" box within the search results, click on **See all** within the box to see elements with a similar style or feel to the element you added to your canvas.

HOW TO SEARCH SMARTER FOR GRAPHICS AND IMAGES

Search term suggestions can be very helpful for helping you find the exact element you're searching for, as well as related elements.

Step 1: Click on the Elements tab, then search on a specific term.

Step 2: Click on "See all" next to "Graphics," which will let you see all of the results that are graphics.

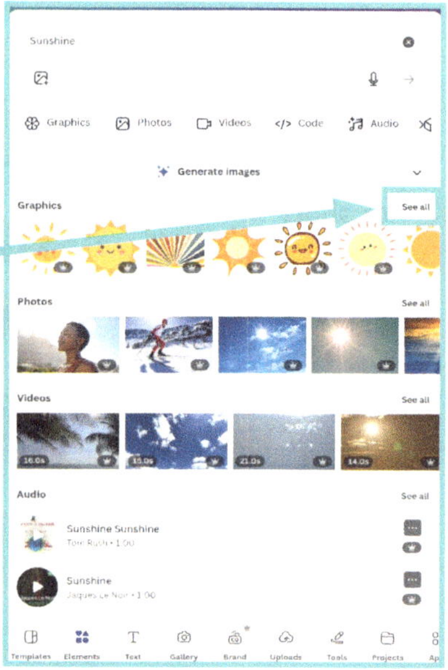

Step 3 (Optional): Click on an element, then click See all inside the Magic Recommendations box to see similar graphics.

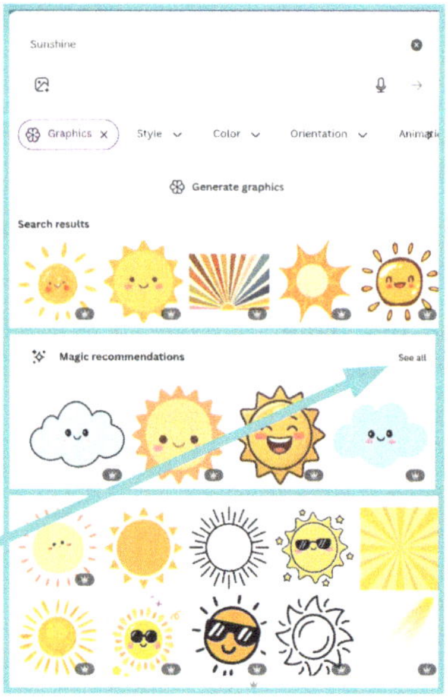

Once you find the element you want to use, click on it to add it to the canvas.

HOW TO EDIT PHOTOS

Canva's Photo Editor is part of their new Visual Suite 2.0 and allows you to customize your uploaded photos before opening or creating a new project.

Step 1: On the homepage, tap on the **Photo Editor** icon below the big search bar.

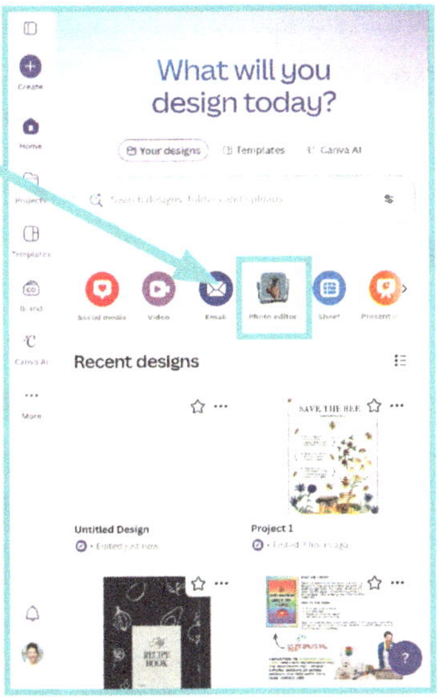

Step 2: In the pop-up menu, tap on the photo you want to edit, or upload a new image.

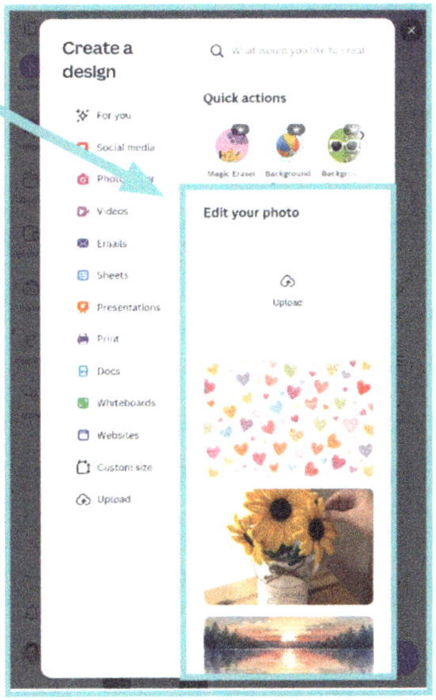

Step 3: Edit your photo using the **Crop**, **Adjust**, **Magic Studio**, **Filters**, **Pixel Eraser**, and **Effects** functions.

Step 4: Tap the purple check, then tap **+Create design** to open the image as part of a new project.

NOTE: You can also edit photos while you're working on a design. Just click on your image, then click **Edit** in the menu bar that appears above the canvas, then use the tools that appear on the left side of the screen.

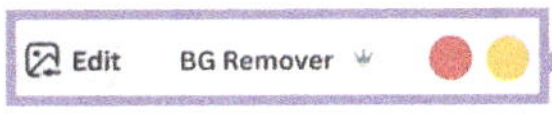

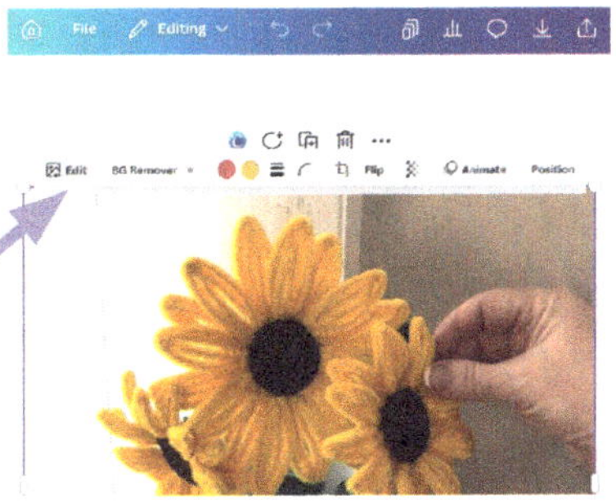

MOBILE

HOW TO SHAPE YOUR IMAGES WITH FRAMES

Frames are very useful elements that allow you to add any image inside. There are many shapes and styles of frames available within the Elements tab.

Step 1: Tap the **Elements** tab, find **Frames**, and tap to add one to your canvas.

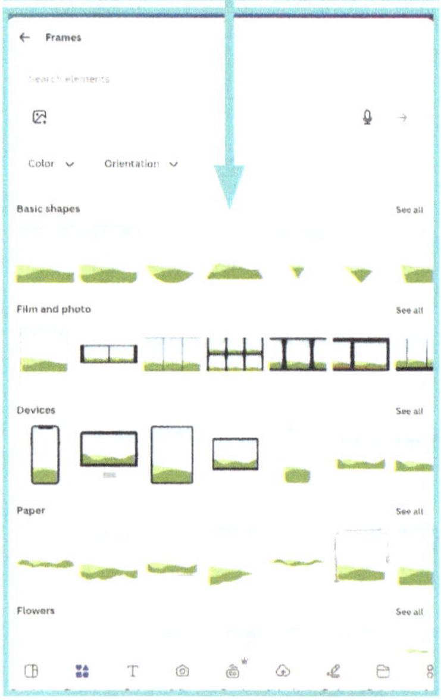

Step 2: Resize the frame to your desired size.

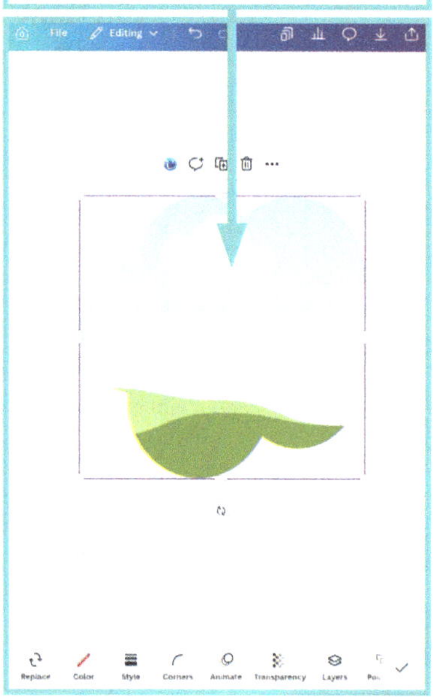

Step 3: Tap the **Elements** tab again and search for an image to add to the frame. Tap to add it to the canvas.

Step 4: Tap, hold, and drag the image on top of the frame until it snaps into the frame.

The image is fit into the frame. You can also do this with an uploaded image.

MOBILE

HOW TO ADD EYE-CATCHING GRAPHICS TO YOUR DESIGN

Graphics are useful in any projects that will be printed, as well as digital projects. Canva's library has a huge number of graphics available.

Step 1:
Tap on the **Elements** tab. Type in your search term(s) in the search bar and tap the **Enter/ Return** key on your device.
Tap on **See all** next to **Graphics** in the search results.

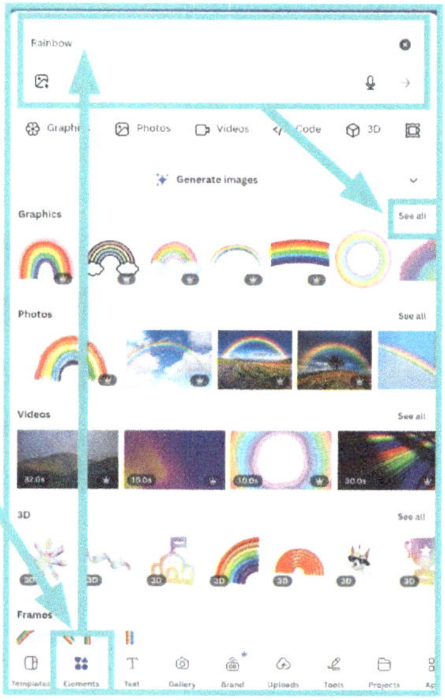

Step 2:
Scroll through the results to find a graphic you want. Remember that elements with "Pro" on them are for Pro members only.

Step 3:
Tap on the graphic of your choice. It will appear on your canvas.

Step 4: Add additional graphics as desired.

TIP: You can add additional graphics and other elements that are outside of your original search results. Just tap on the **Elements** tab again, type in a new search term, tap on **See all** next to the category you want to look under, and tap on the next element you want to add to your canvas. You can repeat this process as many times as desired.

HOW TO CHOOSE THE RIGHT PHOTOS FOR YOUR DESIGN

Photos are useful in any projects that will be printed, as well as digital projects. Canva's library has a huge number of photos available.

Step 1: Tap on the **Elements** tab. Type in your search term(s) in the search bar and tap the **Enter/ Return** key on your device. Tap on **See all** next to **Photos** in the search results.

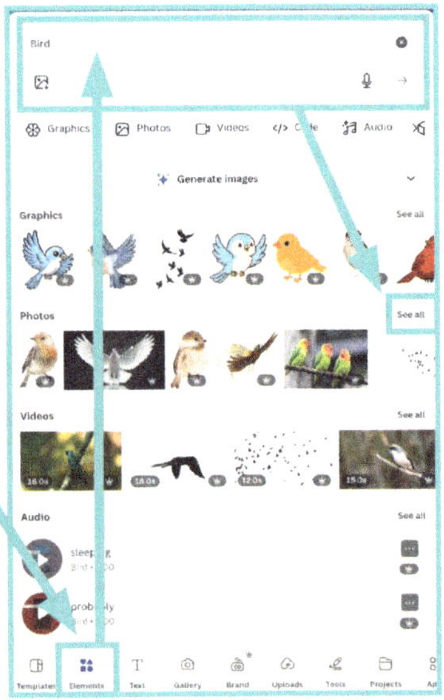

Step 2: Scroll through the results to find a photo you want. Remember that elements with "Pro" on them are for Pro members only.

Step 3: Tap on the photo of your choice. It will appear on your canvas.

Step 4: Add additional photos as desired.

TIP: You can add additional photos and other elements that are outside of your original search results. Just click on the **Elements** tab again, type in a new search term, click on **See all** next to the category you want to look under, and click on the next element you want to add to your canvas. You can repeat this process as many times as desired.

CANVA COACH PLAYBOOK

MOBILE

HOW TO USE SHAPES TO ENHANCE YOUR LAYOUTS

Shapes are a very versatile element available in the Canva library. They have a variety of purposes that you'll find useful in your projects.

Step 1: Tap the **Elements** tab, then tap **See all** next to "Shapes" to see available shapes.

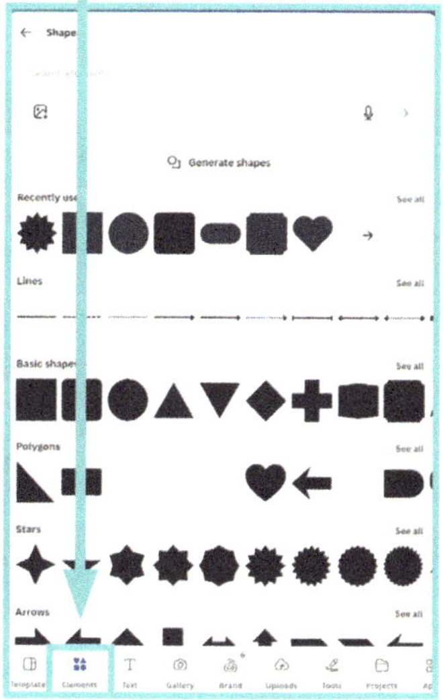

Step 2: Tap on a **shape** element to add it to your canvas.

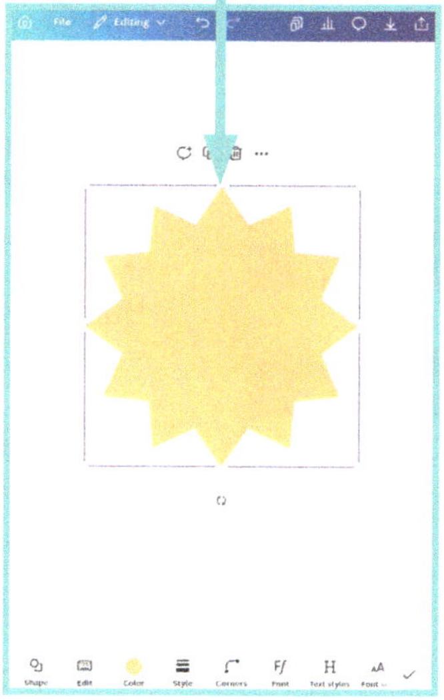

Step 3: Color – Tap on the **shape**. Tap the **Color Picker icon**, then choose a **color** or **gradient**.

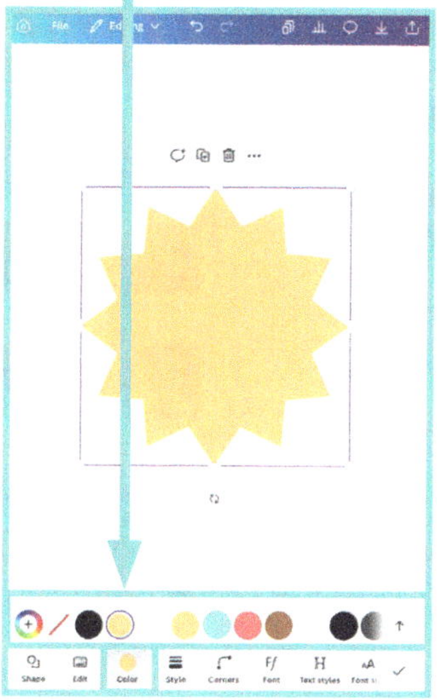

Step 4: Border – Tap the **shape**. Tap the **Style** icon. Choose a **border** and **weight**.

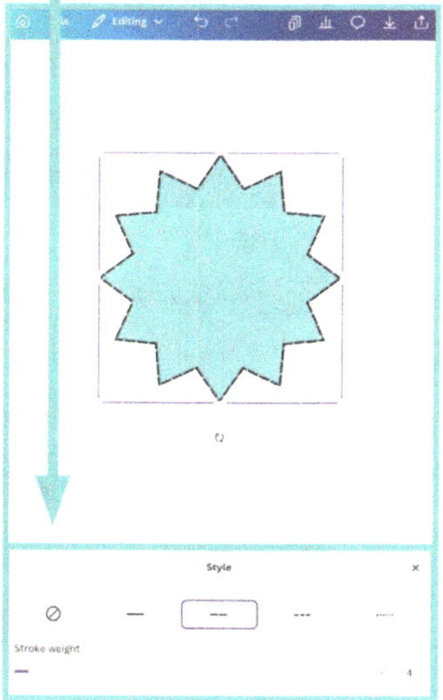

Step 5: Rounding – Tap the **shape**, tap the **Corner icon**, then choose **corner rounding**.

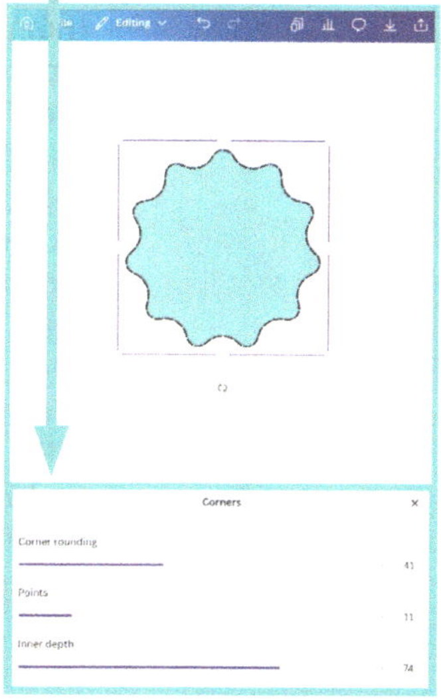

Step 6: Text – Tap the **shape**, then tap the **Font icon**. Choose **font size**, **color**, and **style**.

HOW TO
FIND AND USE VIDEOS

Videos can be great additions to any projects you plan to view, send, or present in digital format. Canva has a large library of videos to choose from.

Step 1:
Tap on the **Elements** tab. Type in your search term(s) and tap on your device's **Enter/Return** key.

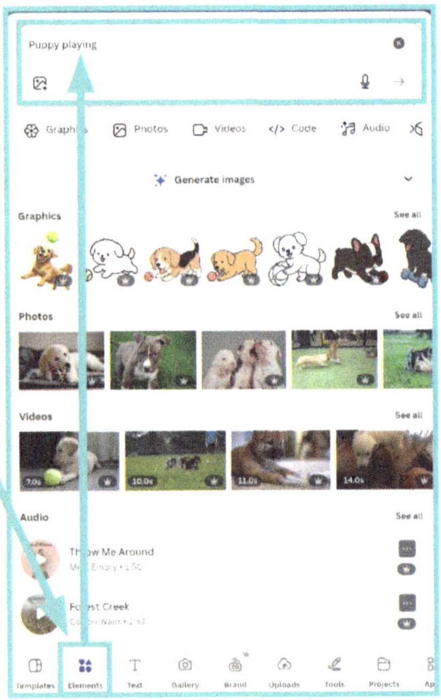

Step 2: Tap **See all** next to **"Videos"** in the search results. Scroll through the results to find a video, then tap on it to add it to the canvas.

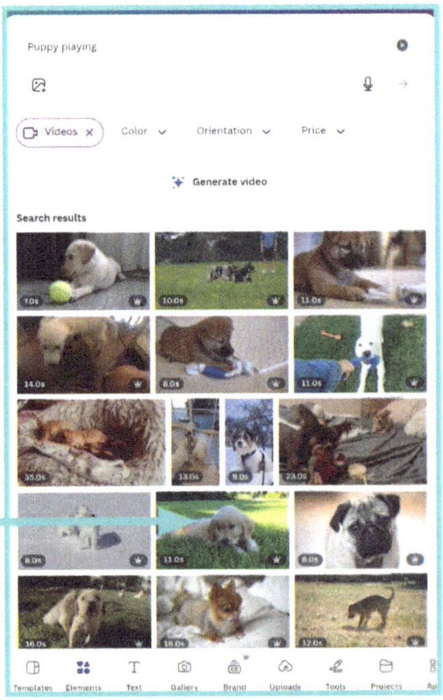

Step 3: Once the video is on your canvas, it will start playing. Tap on the video to see video options, which will appear below the canvas.

NOTE: You can see the length of each video in the bottom left corner of each thumbnail. The videos lengths are listed in minutes and seconds. For example, the videos to the right are 14.0 seconds, 29.0 seconds, and 30.0 seconds, and 24.0 seconds from top to bottom.

HOW TO
EDIT AND ENHANCE VIDEOS

You can make some changes to video clips in the Canva library through the **Edit** button and by trimming the video clip down in length.

Tap on the video on your canvas to make the **video editing menu** appear.

Magic Studio – Remove the background of the video.

Adjust – Change the white balance, light, color, and texture of the video.

Filters – Add a filter over the video to change its appearance.

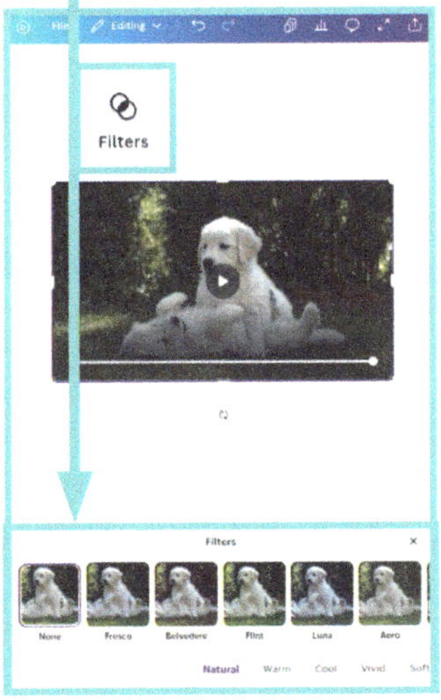

Trim – Tap the scissors to trim the video to just the part you want.

Use your finger to tap and drag the purple areas of the video bar to shorten the video. The length of the clip will appear on the right side of the video bar.

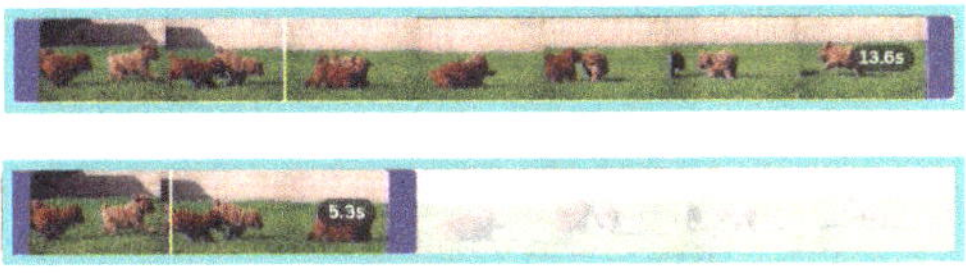

NOTE: Some options are only for Pro members. This includes **Auto-Trim**, which trims a video clip to the most essential part.

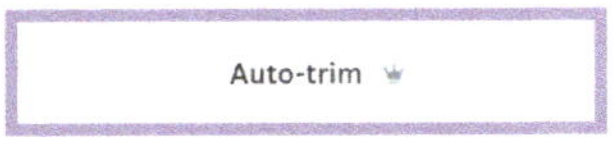

MOBILE

HOW TO ADD AUDIO TO YOUR PROJECTS

Audio clips can be great additions to any projects you plan to view, send, or present in digital format. Canva has a large library of audio clips to choose from.

Step 1: Tap on **Elements**. Type in your search term and tap on your device's **Enter/Return** key.

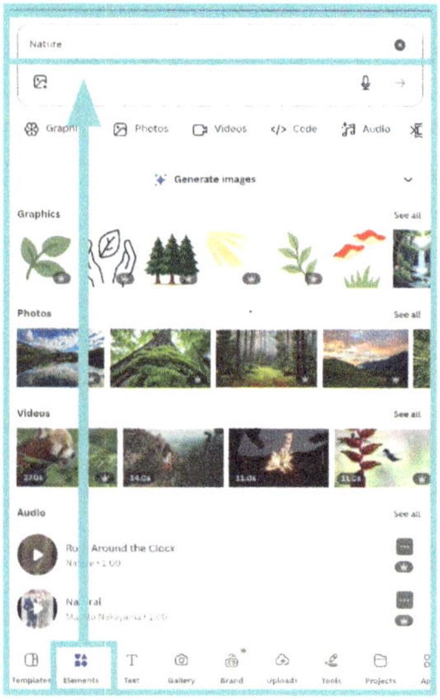

Step 2: Click **See all** next to "**Audio**" to see all audio results.

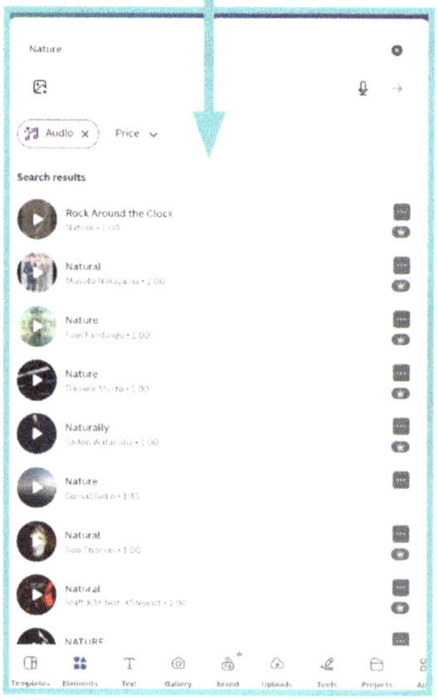

Tap 3: Tap an audio recording to add it below your canvas. Tap the audio to access options.

Beat Sync – Sync the beats of the music to your project. For Pro members only.

Adjust – Shorten the audio clip to only the section you want.

Fade – Use the sliding bars to toggle the level of fading in and fading out on the audio clip.

NOTE: Audio is only for digital finished projects.

HOW TO MAKE YOUR DESIGNS LOOK REAL WITH MOCKUPS

Mockups are a great way to demonstrate how a finished product you're making or selling will look with your image or logo on it.

Step 1: Tap on the **Elements** tab, then tap "**Mockups**."

Step 2: Tap **See all** on a Mockup category to see all of the available Mockups.

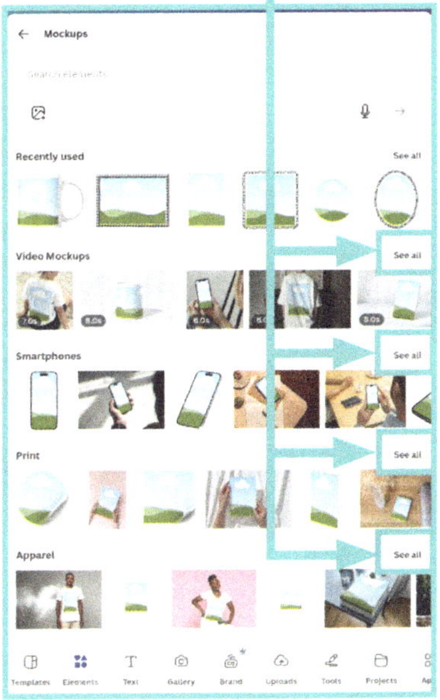

Step 3: Look through the Mockups and tap one to add it to the canvas.

Step 4: Tap the **Uploads** tab. Tap **Upload files.** Upload your image.

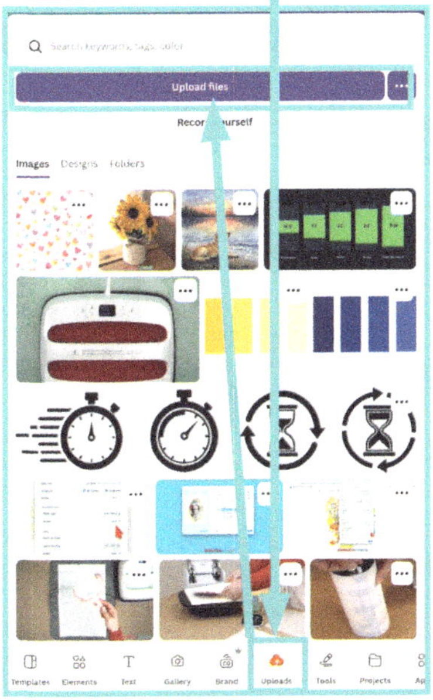

Step 5: Tap on your uploaded image. It will appear on your canvas.

Step 6: **Tap and hold** the image on the Mockup to combine them.

MOBILE

HOW TO CREATE CHARTS TO VISUALIZE DATA

Charts are a great way to show data in a presentation. Canva has a library of almost any chart you could need for your data.

Step 1: Tap the **Elements** tab, then tap **"Charts."**

Step 2: Tap **See all** next to the chart type you want to see.

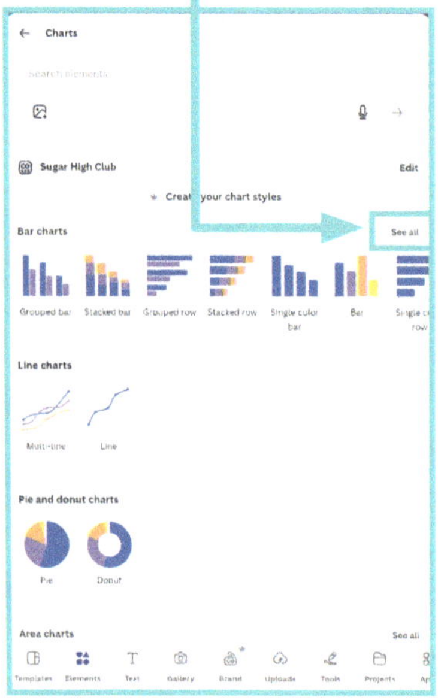

Step 3: Add a chart to your canvas by tapping on it.

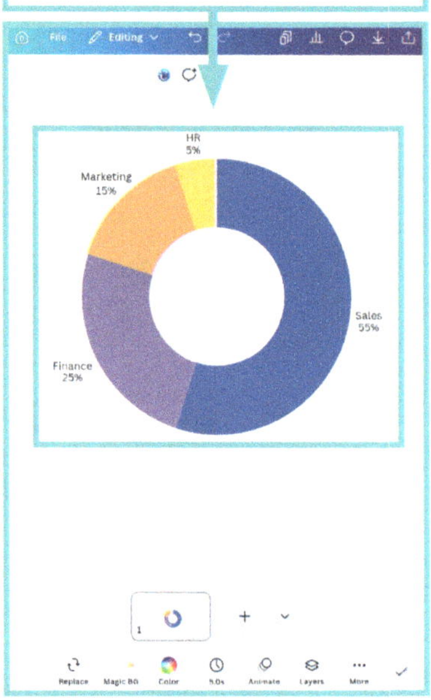

Step 4: Input your labels and numerical data into the chart.

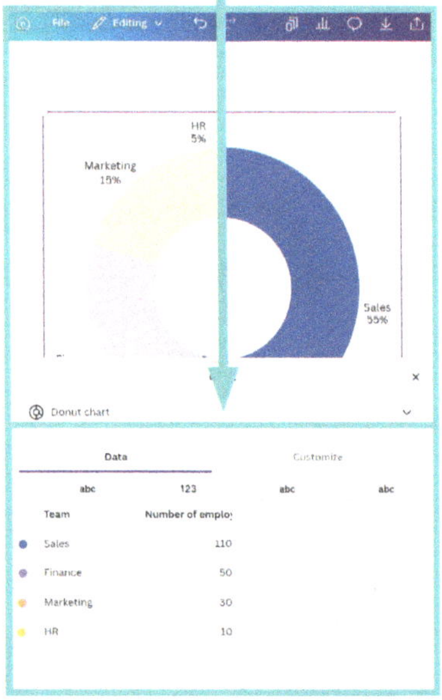

Step 5: Tap on the chart again.

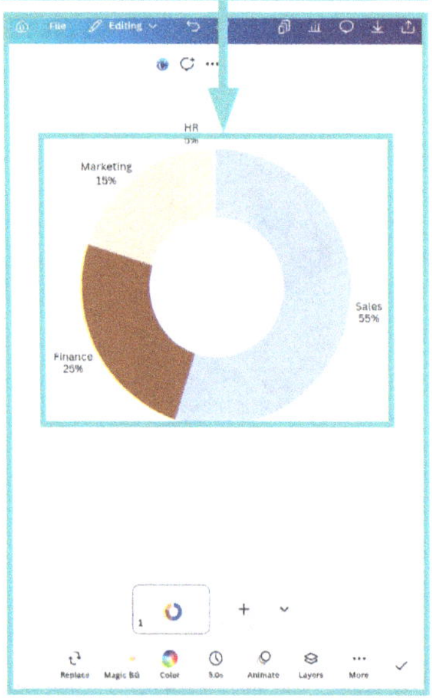

Step 6: Tap on one of the **"Color"** options below the canvas to change colors.

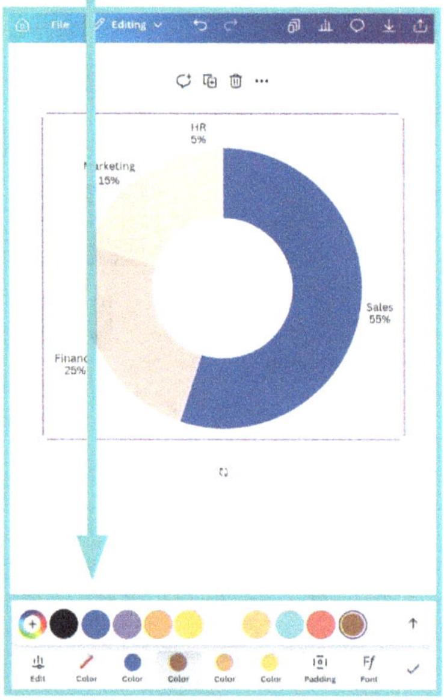

MOBILE

HOW TO ARRANGE PHOTOS AND ELEMENTS WITH GRIDS

Grids are organized collages for elements such as graphics, photos, stickers, and more. Canva has a library of grids available for you to use.

Step 1: Tap on Elements, then find and tap "Grids."

Step 2: Look through the library of Grids to find the one you want to use.

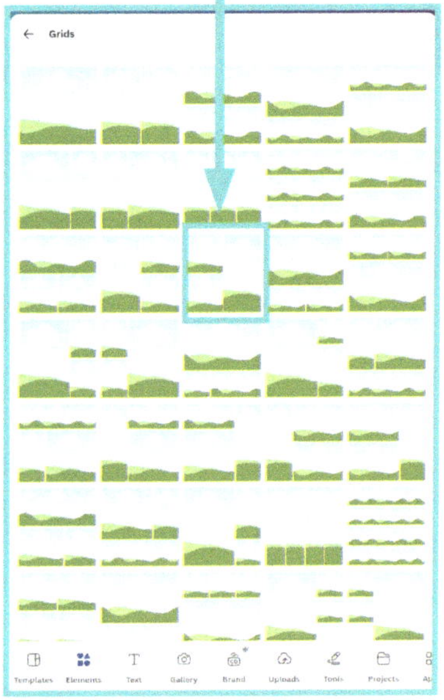

Step 3: Tap on a Grid to add it to your canvas.

Step 4: Tap on Elements again to find elements to add to your grid.

Step 5: Tap and drag elements into each Grid space.

NOTE: If you decide that you don't want a certain element in any given space on the grid, just tap on it, then tap the trash can icon that appears.

MOBILE

HOW TO FIND CURATED ELEMENT COLLECTIONS

Collections are curated groups of images. Each individual Collection is similar in style, tone, color, and subject.

Step 1: Tap on the **Elements** tab, then tap on **Graphics.**

Step 2: Scroll down until you find **Collections,** then find one that you want to look at.

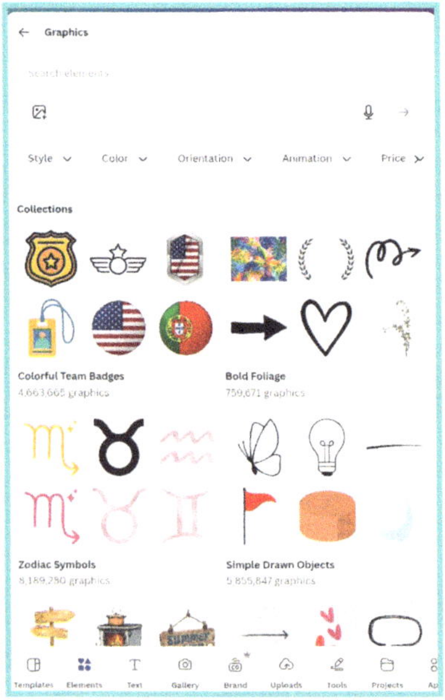

Step 3: Tap on the Collection to look through the images within the Collection.

Step 4: Tap on images within the collection to add them to the canvas.

NOTE: The number of Collections continues to grow. Expect it to expand over time.

MOBILE

HOW TO ADD STICKERS FOR FUN DESIGNS

Stickers are cute animated graphics that can be used to catch your eye on digital finished projects.

Step 1: Tap on the **Elements** tab, scroll down, and tap on the **Animations** icon (formerly called Stickers.)

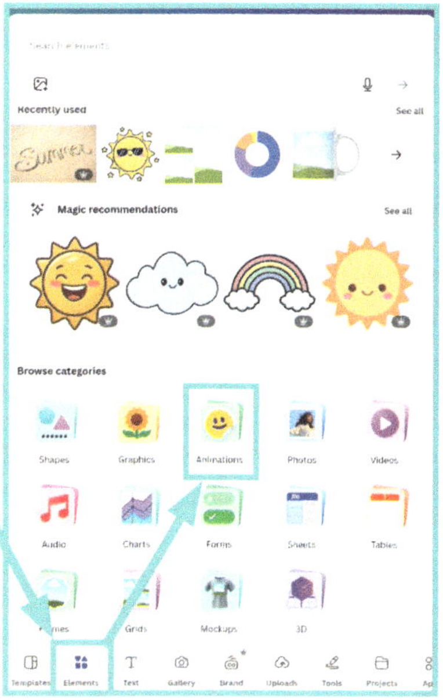

Step 2: Scroll through the Animations to find a category you want, then tap **See all**.

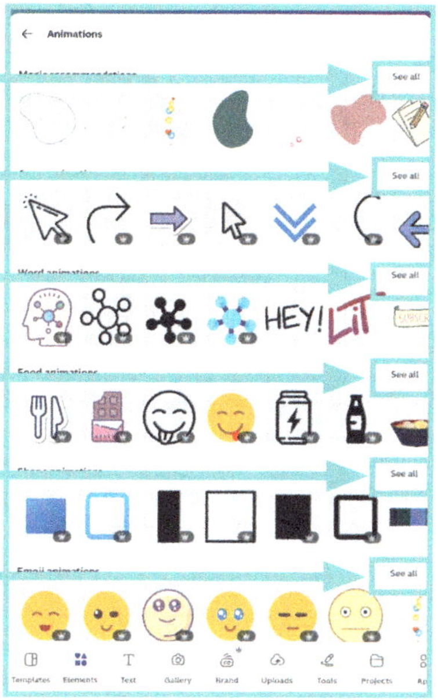

Step 3: Look through the stickers within the category.

Step 4: Tap on stickers to add them to the canvas. The animation will start as soon as you add it to the canvas.

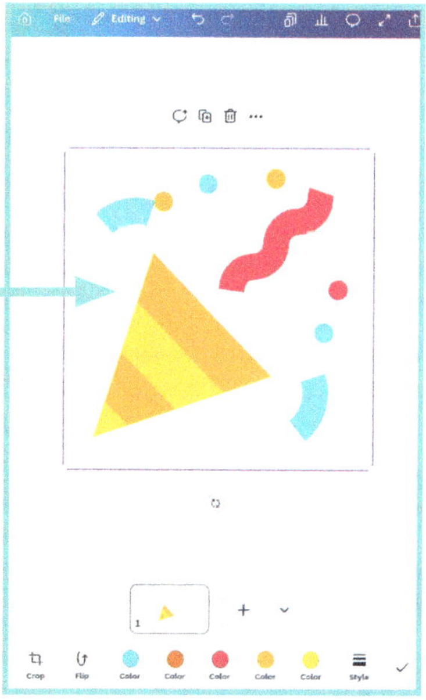

NOTE: Stickers are only for digital finished projects since they are animated.

MOBILE: PRECISION EDITING AND ENHANCEMENTS

- ✔ GROUP MULTIPLE ELEMENTS TOGETHER
- ✔ RESIZE ELEMENTS TO THE SIZE YOU NEED
- ✔ ROTATE ELEMENTS FOR THE PERFECT LOOK
- ✔ CROP IMAGES AND ELEMENTS TO FIT YOUR DESIGN
- ✔ ADJUST ELEMENT TRANSPARENCY FOR A COOL LOOK
- ✔ MAKE YOUR DESIGN STAND OUT WITH ANIMATION

HOW TO:

HOW TO GROUP MULTIPLE ELEMENTS TOGETHER

If you want to move elements together while keeping their arrangement and spacing, you can group them together so they move as one.

Step 1: Tap on one of the elements that you want to group, then tap on the three dots in the menu bar that appears, which will bring up a menu at the bottom of the screen.

Step 2: Tap Select multiple in the menu, then tap the rest of the elements you want to group together.

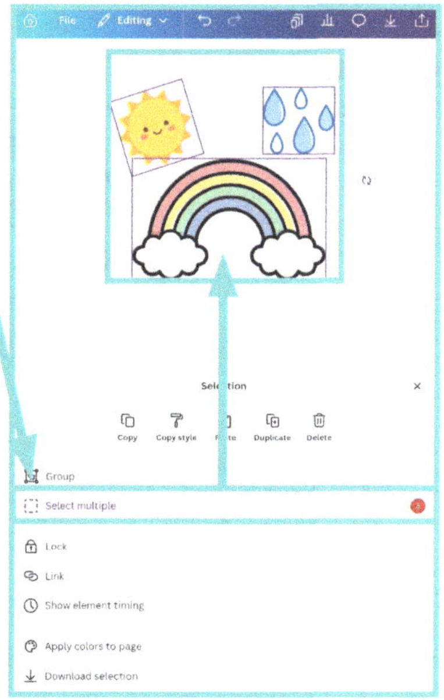

Step 3: Tap Group in the same menu.

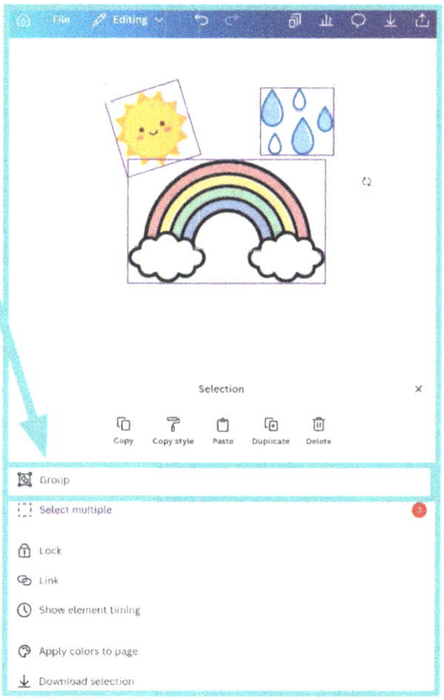

To Ungroup elements, tap on the group, then tap the word "Ungroup" in the menu that appears.

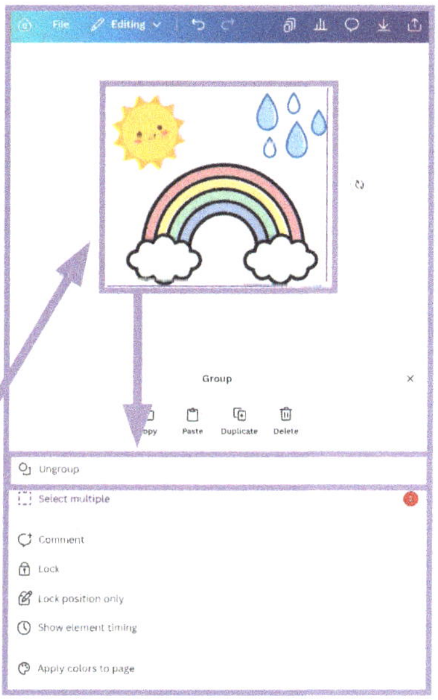

NOTE: Grouping is not permanent and can always be undone.

HOW TO RESIZE ELEMENTS TO THE SIZE YOU NEED

You will need to resize and reposition almost every element that you add to your canvas in order to create the projects you envision.

Step 1: Add an **element or text** to your canvas.

Step 2: Tap on the **element or text** on your canvas.

Step 3: Tap and hold one of the **circles** at each corner of the element.

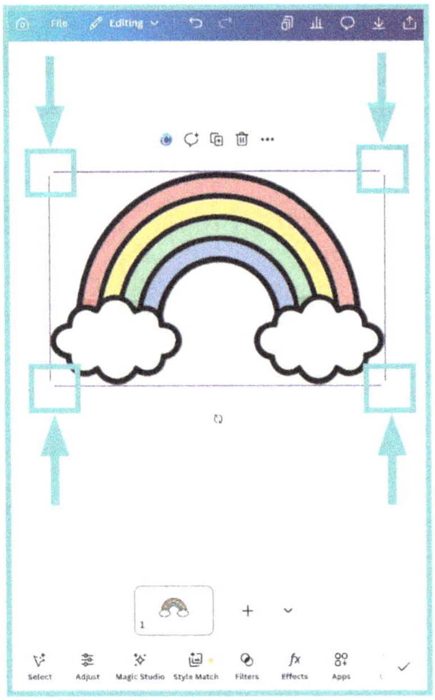

Step 4: Drag your finger outward and away from the element to enlarge it and inward towards the element to shrink it.

NOTE: You can resize an element as many times as needed.

NOTE: The dimensions of the element will appear as you are resizing the element. w: 4 h: 2.7

MOBILE

HOW TO ROTATE ELEMENTS FOR THE PERFECT LOOK

You can rotate elements and text to any angle on your canvas.

Step 1:
Add an **element or text** to your canvas.

Step 2:
Tap on the **element or text** on your canvas. The **Rotate** icon will appear below the element.

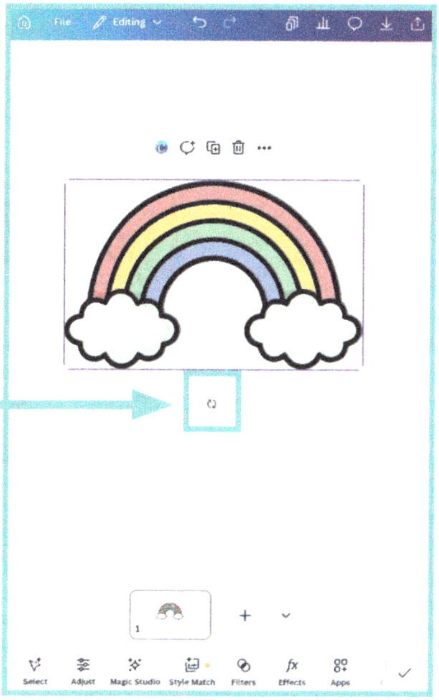

Step 3:
Tap and hold on the **Rotate** icon. Drag your finger right to rotate the element counter-clockwise or left to rotate the element clockwise.

Step 4:
If you want to lock the element in a specific place and angle, tap on the element, tap the three dots icon that appears, then tap **Lock** in the menu.

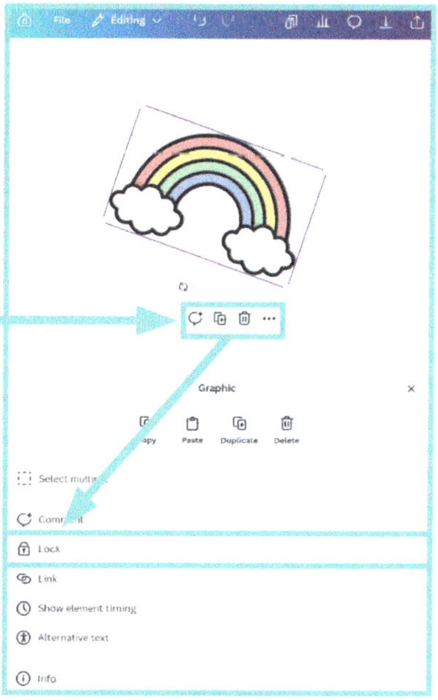

NOTE: The degree of the angle will appear as you rotate an element. -38°

HOW TO CROP IMAGES AND ELEMENTS TO FIT YOUR DESIGN

You may need to crop an element if you only want a part of it. You can uncrop an element you have cropped if you decide you want the whole image.

Step 1:
Add an **element or text** to your canvas. Tap on the **element or text**.

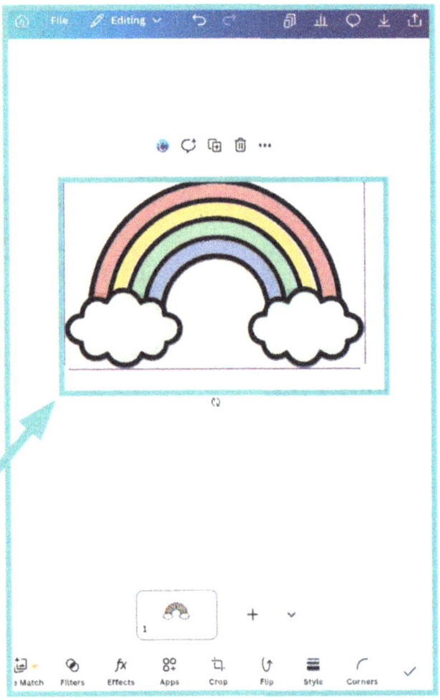

Step 2:
Tap **Crop** to bring up the menu, then tap **Freeform.**

Step 3:
Tap, hold, and drag one of the four **white edges** in the corner of each side of the element to crop.

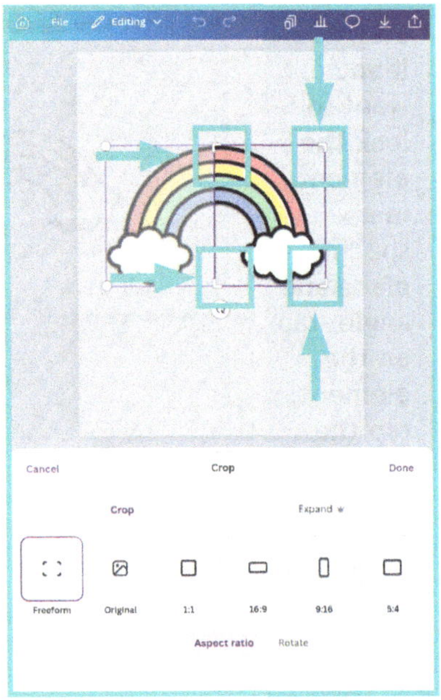

To **uncrop** an element, tap **Crop** again, then drag it back out using the bars.

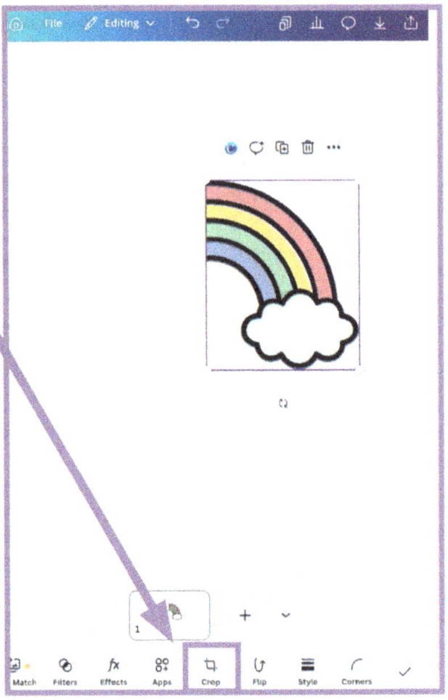

MOBILE

HOW TO ADJUST ELEMENT TRANSPARENCY FOR A COOL LOOK

You can adjust the transparency of any element or text. This is useful when you need a particular image to stand out or look faded.

Step 1:
Add an **element or text** to your canvas.

Step 2:
Tap on the **element or text** on your canvas.

Step 3:
Tap on the **Transparency icon** in the toolbar, which looks like a fading checkered square.

Step 4:
Move the **sliding bar** or type a number from 0-100 in the box to adjust the transparency: slide left to increase and right to lower transparency.

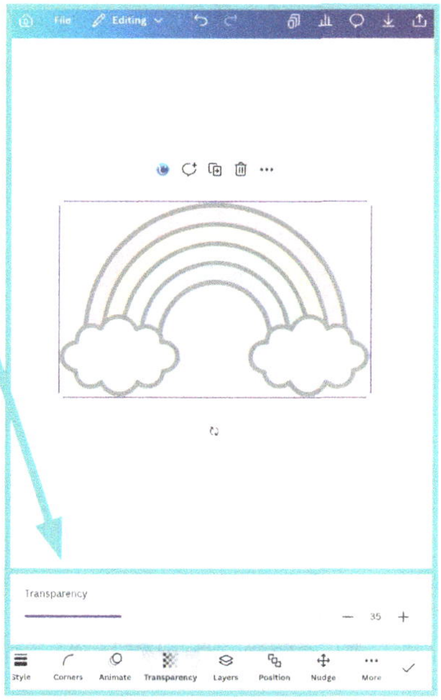

MOBILE

HOW TO MAKE YOUR DESIGN STAND OUT WITH ANIMATION

Bring your designs to life by animating elements in Canva! Follow these simple steps:

Step 1: Add an **element** to your canvas.

Step 2: Tap on the **element** you want to animate.

Step 3: Tap **Animate** in the bottom toolbar.

Animate

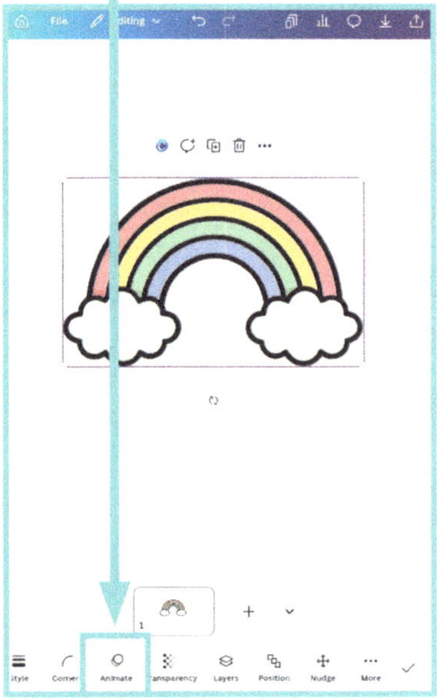

Step 4: Browse the animation effects in the menu that appears.

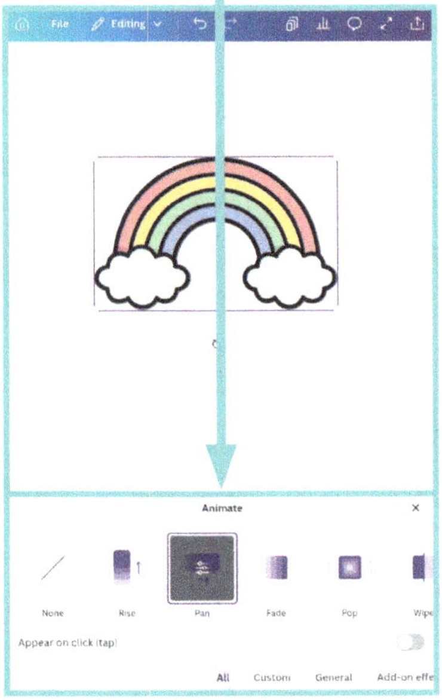

Step 4: Tap on an animation to see it. Tap it again to choose details.

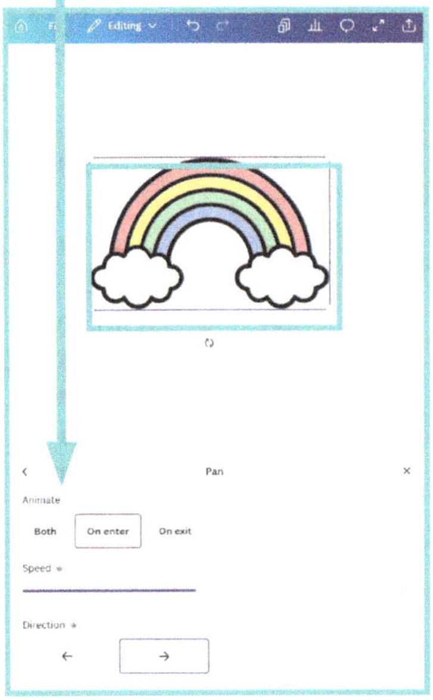

NOTE: To create your own animation, first tap **Custom** and **Create an Animation**. Then tap, hold, and drag your element around the canvas. Then choose when the animation should start and the style in which the animation should move.

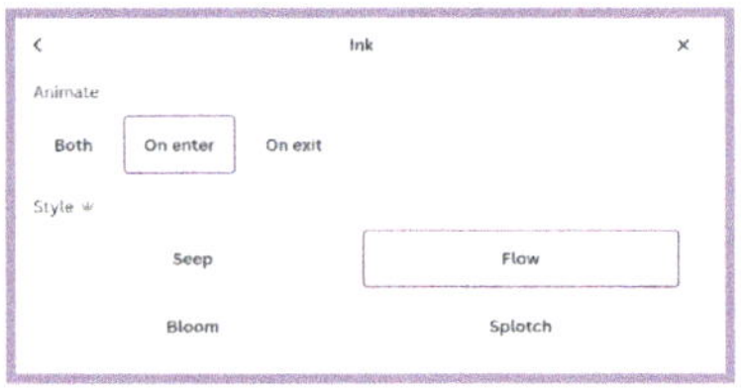

WARNING: Some animations are marked with a crown icon and require a Canva Pro subscription.

HOW TO:

MOBILE: MASTERING TEXT IN CANVA

- ✔ FIND AND USE TEXT TOOLS
- ✔ ADD AND RESIZE TEXT BOXES TO FIT YOUR TEXT
- ✔ PICK AND CHANGE FONTS FOR THE RIGHT LOOK
- ✔ ADJUST TEXT ALIGNMENT AND SPACING
- ✔ EASILY STYLE YOUR TEXT
- ✔ ADD PAGE NUMBERS THAT UPDATE FOR YOU
- ✔ PAIR FONTS LIKE A PRO
- ✔ FADE TEXT FOR A SUBTLE EFFECT
- ✔ MAKE YOUR TEXT POP WITH SPECIAL EFFECTS
- ✔ ADD MOVING TEXT TO CREATE ENGAGING DESIGNS

HOW TO
FIND AND USE TEXT TOOLS

The Text tab lets you add, format, and style text in your Canva designs. It provides pre-designed text templates to save time and inspire creativity.

Step 1: Tap on the **Text** tab in the bottom menu.

Step 2: Choose from pre-designed **Font Combinations** or click **Add a heading**, **Add a subheading**, or **Add a little bit of body text**.

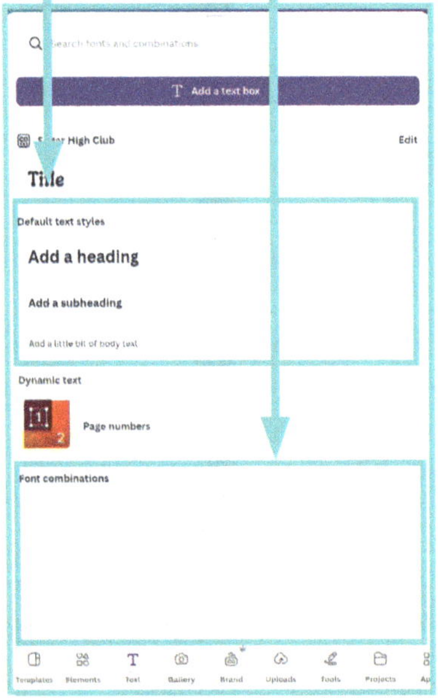

The text box will appear on your canvas. Start typing your text.

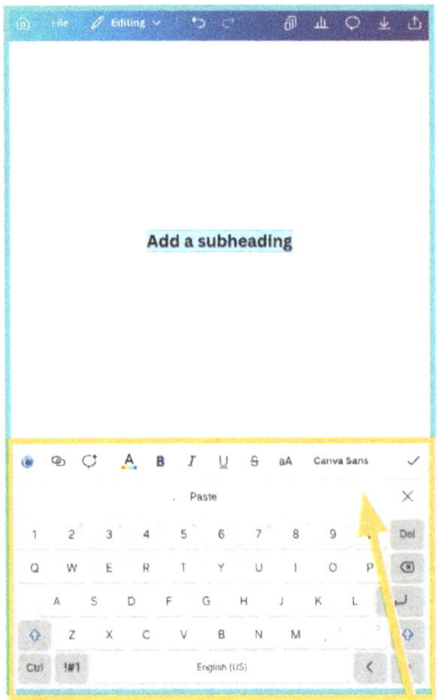

Customize the **font**, **size**, and **color** as needed.

TIP: With your text selected, use the bottom menu to customize your text font, styles, size, color, format, spacing, and more!

Click on a **Font combination** if you'd like to use one.

MOBILE

HOW TO ADD AND RESIZE TEXT BOXES TO FIT YOUR TEXT

Adding and resizing text boxes is essential for organizing text in your design.

Step 1: Tap on your Text on the canvas.

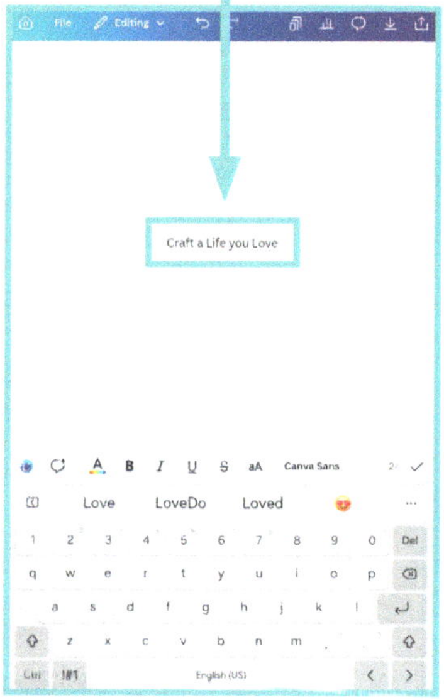

Step 2: Tap **Font Size** to change the size of your font. Use the slider to adjust the size to your preference.

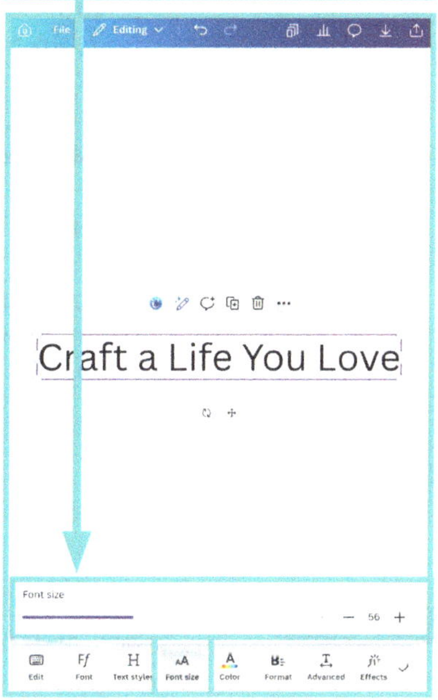

OR Tap, hold, and drag the **corners** of the text box to resize it.

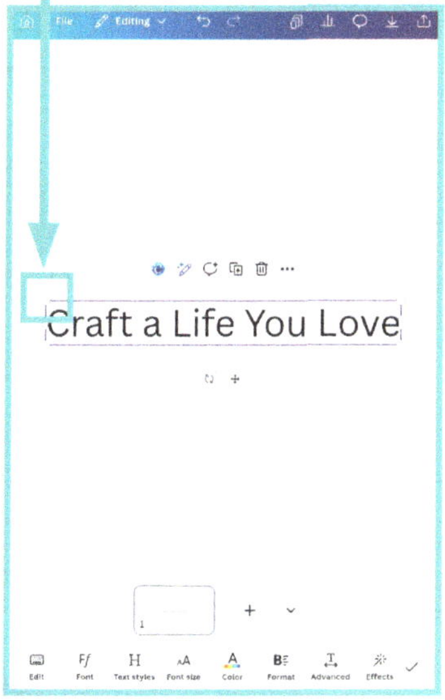

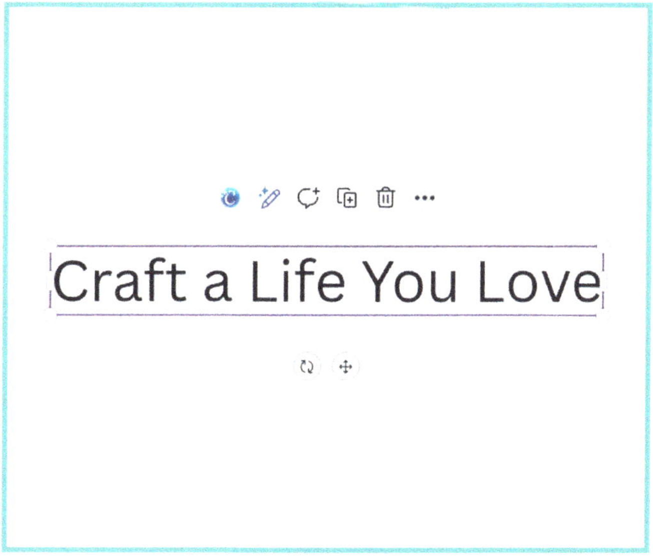

Your text is now resized to your desired preference!

HOW TO PICK AND CHANGE FONTS FOR THE RIGHT LOOK

Customizing fonts and styles enhances the readability and aesthetic of your text.

Step 1: Tap on the text box that you want to edit.

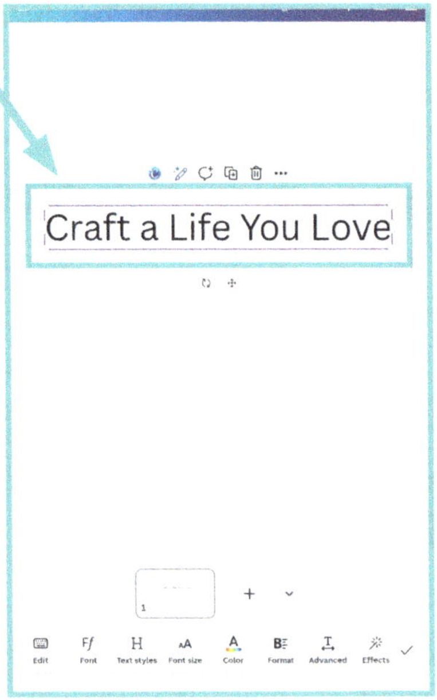

Step 2: Tap Font to change the font style of your text. From here, a new menu will appear with different font options you can choose from.

Step 3: Tap Font Size to change the size of your font. Use the slider to adjust the size to your preference.

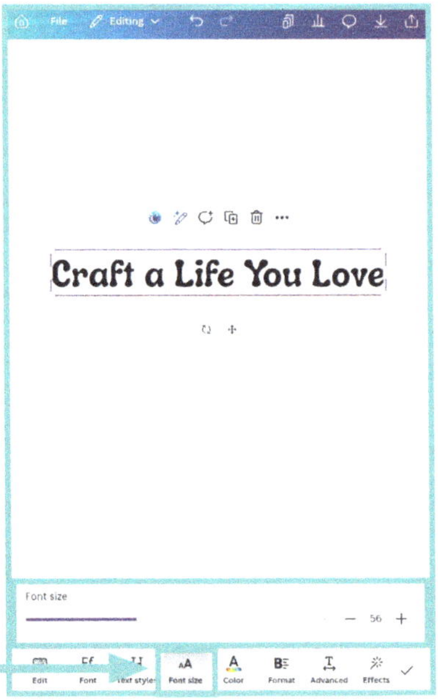

Step 4: Tap Color to change the color of your font. A new menu will appear with different colors you can choose from.

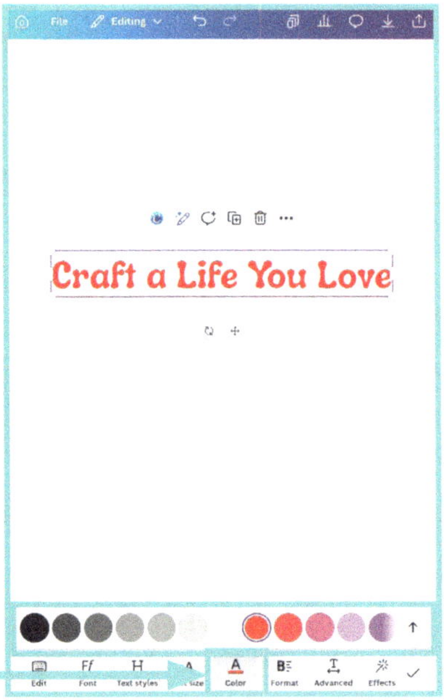

MOBILE

HOW TO ADJUST TEXT ALIGNMENT AND SPACING

Text alignment and spacing help structure your text for better readability.

Step 1: Tap on the text box you want to align and/or change spacing.

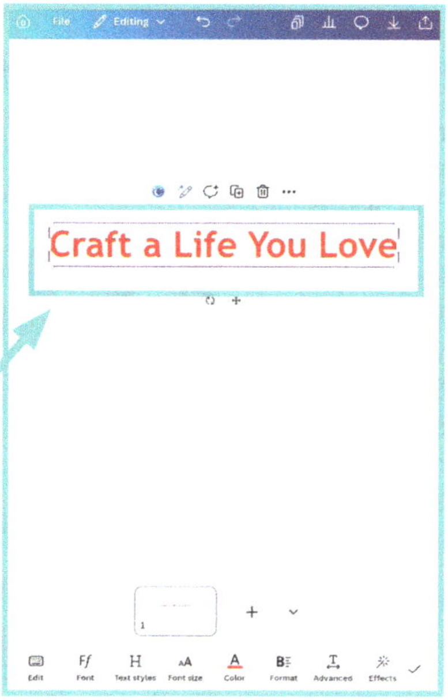

Step 2: Tap **Advanced** at the bottom of the screen.

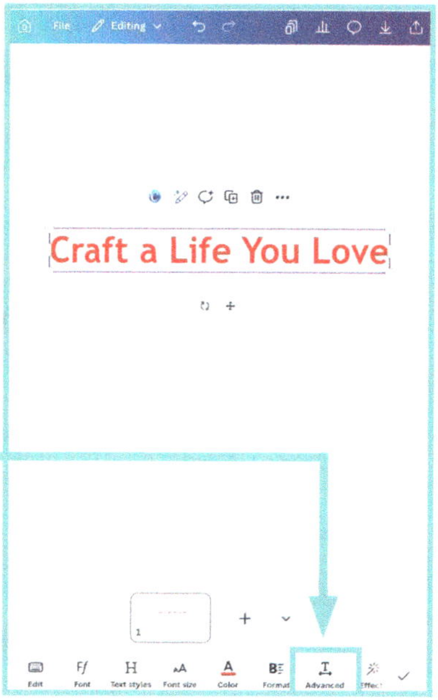

Step 3: To change the spacing, use the sliders to change the letter and/or line spacing of your text. Then use the slider to slide down to see the whole canvas again.

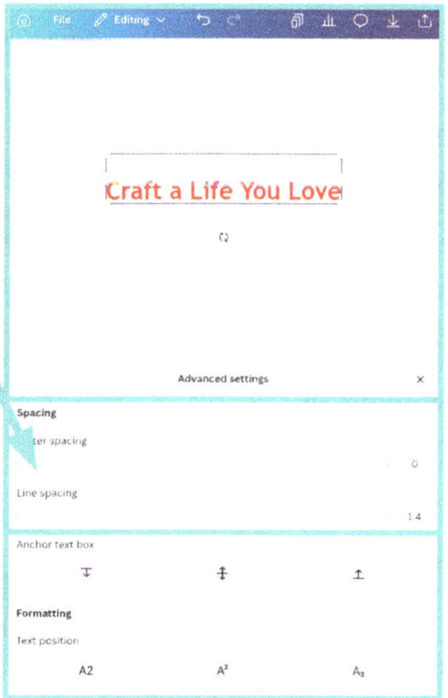

Step 4: To change the alignment, tap **Format**. You can then tap the icons for left-align, right-align, center-align, and justify your text.

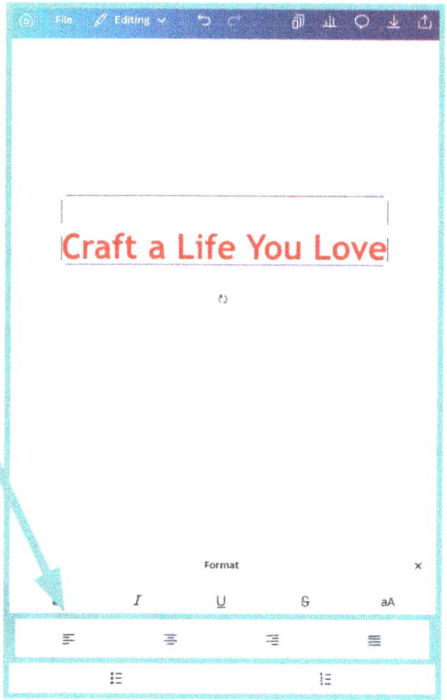

HOW TO
EASILY STYLE YOUR TEXT

Text styles in Canva allow you to quickly apply pre-designed font combinations, color palettes, and font sets to maintain consistency and save time in your designs. Perfect for creating cohesive visuals with minimal effort.

Step 1: With your design open, tap the **Templates** tab in the lower menu.

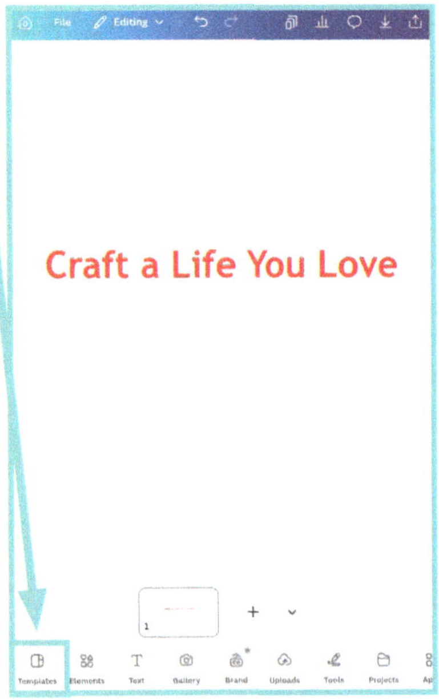

Step 2: A new menu will appear. Tap **Styles** and choose a style you'd like to go with. Tap **See all** to see even more text styles.

Step 3: Once you have chosen the style you'd like to go with, tap on the style again to change the style based on the style you chose.

TIP: There are lots of Text Styles you can choose from. Play around with them and see which one you prefer the best.

HOW TO ADD PAGE NUMBERS THAT UPDATE FOR YOU

Dynamic text in Canva allows you to automatically add page numbers for document features that update dynamically. This is perfect for multi-page documents, reports, and eBooks.

Step 1: Open your design and add another page by tapping the **+** sign.

Step 2 (optional): You can add more pages by continuing to tap **+** sign.

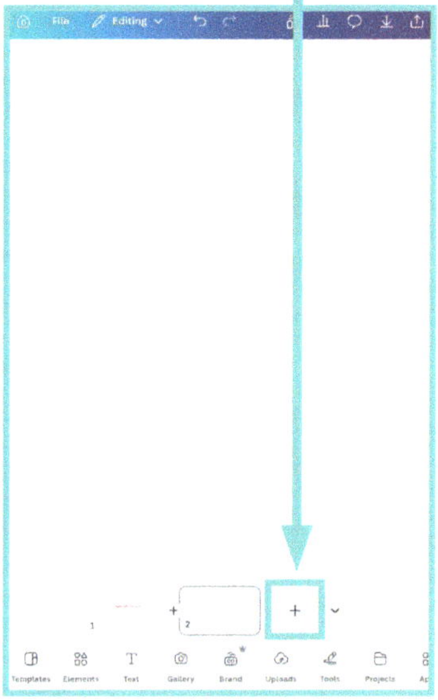

Step 3: Tap **Text** in the lower menu and click **Page numbers**.

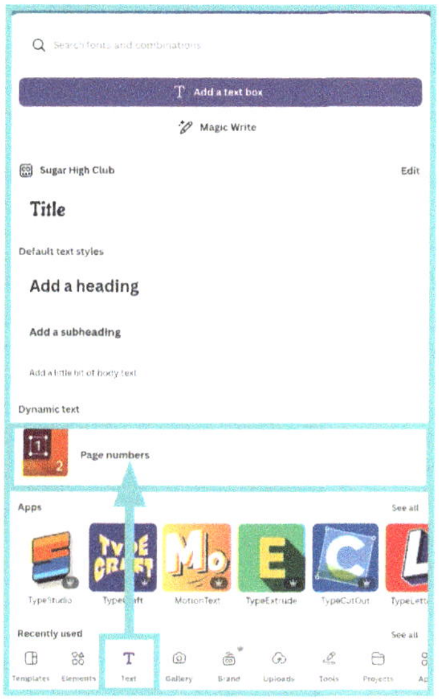

Step 4 (optional): Change the format of the page numbers under **Format**.

Step 5: Tap **Apply properties to all pages** to save your desired format.

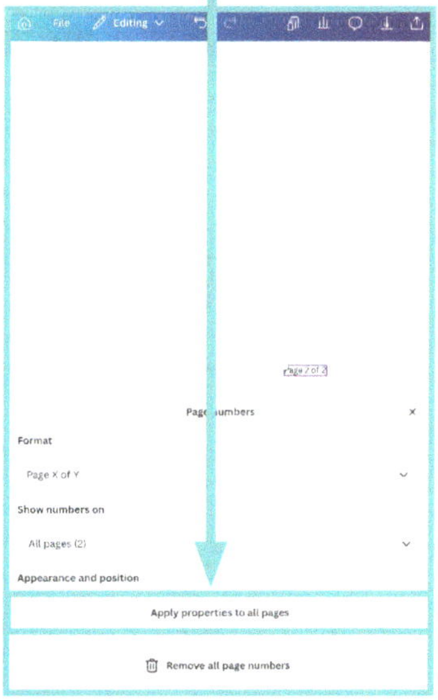

Step 6 (optional): Change the styling of the page numbers by tapping on it.

CANVA COACH PLAYBOOK

MOBILE

HOW TO
PAIR FONTS LIKE A PRO

Font combinations in Canva provide pre-paired fonts that work harmoniously together, saving you time and ensuring a visually appealing design. These are great for projects like posters, social media posts, and presentations.

Step 1: Tap the **Text** tab in the lower menu.

Step 2: Scroll down until you find the font combination you prefer.

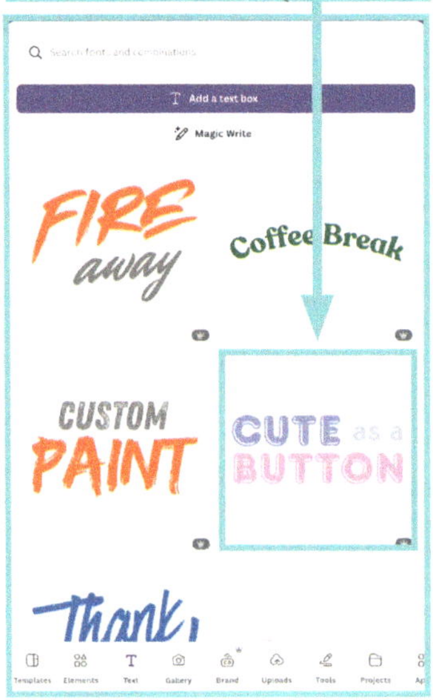

Step 3: Tap on the text and tap **Ungroup** to edit individually.

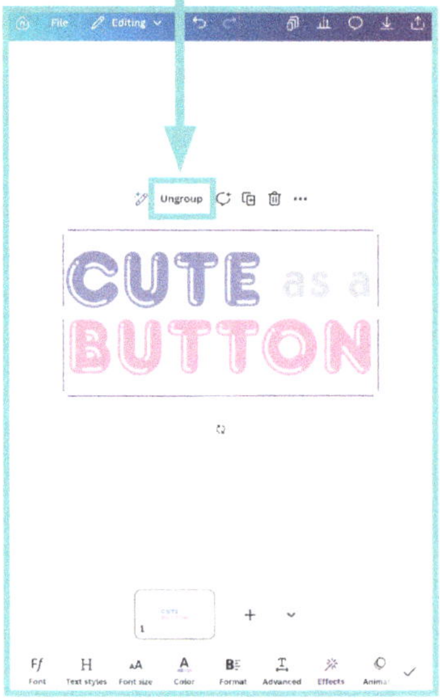

Step 4: Change the text to whatever you'd like it to say.

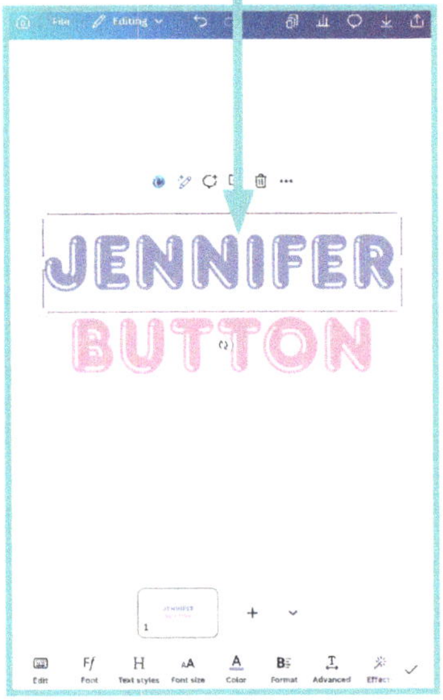

Congrats! You've used a font combination for your text!

TIP: Swap the colors in the font combination to match your project's aesthetic or palette.

WARNING: Some font combinations are marked with a crown icon and require a Canva Pro subscription.

MOBILE

HOW TO FADE TEXT FOR A SUBTLE EFFECT

Transparency allows you to tone down text for watermarks, overlays, or subtle effects.

Step 1: Click on the text box you want to edit.

Step 2: Click Transparency and a sliding bar will appear at the bottom of the screen.

Step 3: Slide the slider to the right to decrease transparency, slide it to the left to increase transparency.

WARNING: Too much transparency can make text unreadable; make sure your text is visible before finalizing.

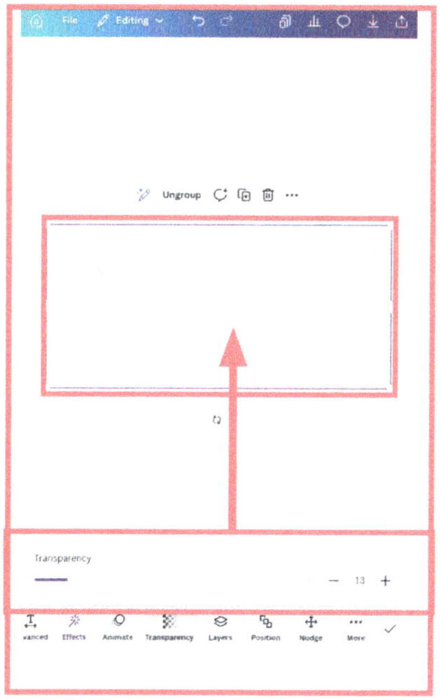

MOBILE

HOW TO MAKE YOUR TEXT POP WITH SPECIAL EFFECTS

Text effects in Canva allow you to add depth and creativity to your designs with features like shadows, glows, and outlines. These effects can make your text stand out and enhance the overall aesthetic of your design.

Step 1: Tap a text box to enhance, then tap the Effects tab.

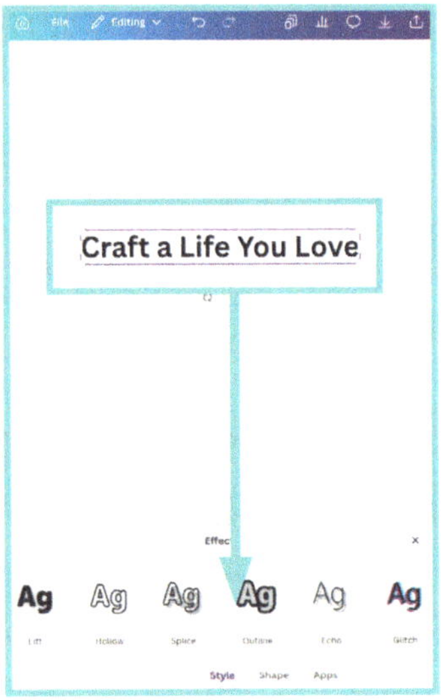

Step 2: In the Style menu, choose an effect you'd like to use.

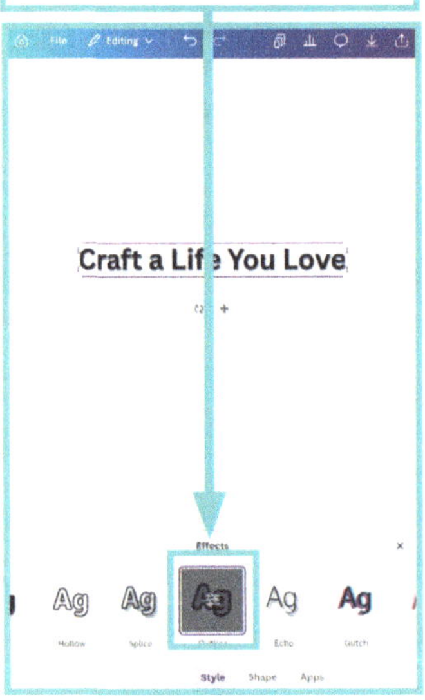

Step 3: Tap on the effect again to edit the effect settings. Settings will vary based on the effect you choose.

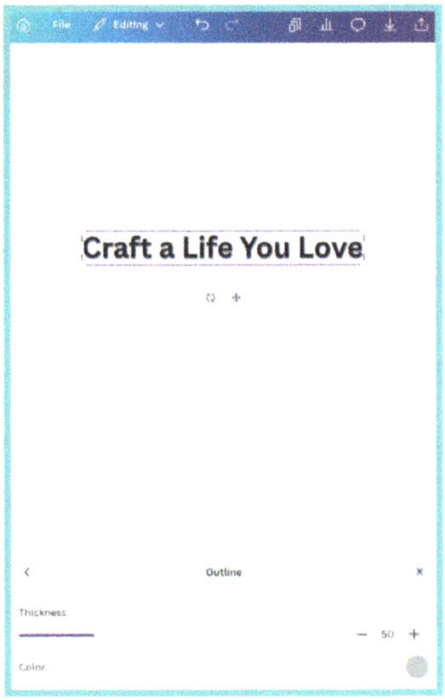

Step 4 (optional): Tap on Shape to change the shape of your text into a curve. Tap on the effect again to edit the Curve settings.

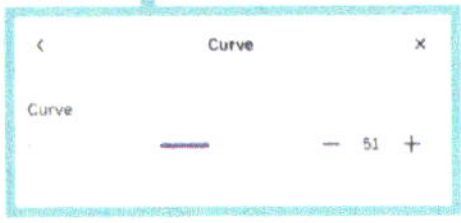

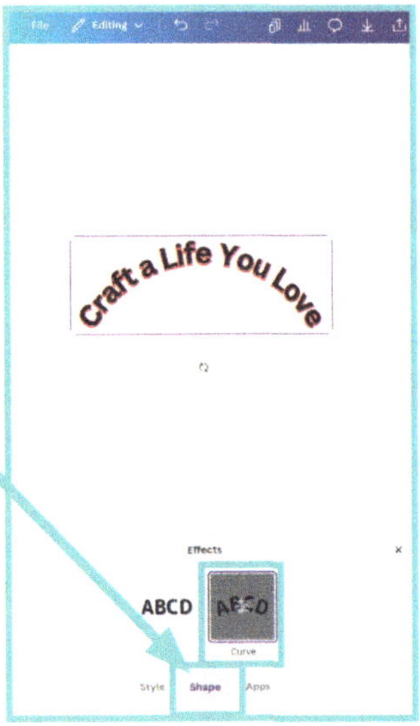

NOTE: There are several effects to choose from as well as the settings that go along with them. Take the time to look through them and get a feel for what looks best with the project you are working on creating.

MOBILE

HOW TO ADD MOVING TEXT TO CREATE ENGAGING DESIGNS

Animating text in Canva adds motion and energy to your designs, making them more engaging and dynamic. This feature is perfect for presentations, social media posts, and video content.

Step 1: Tap on the text box you want to animate and tap **Animate**.

Step 2: Browse through the categories and choose an animation style.

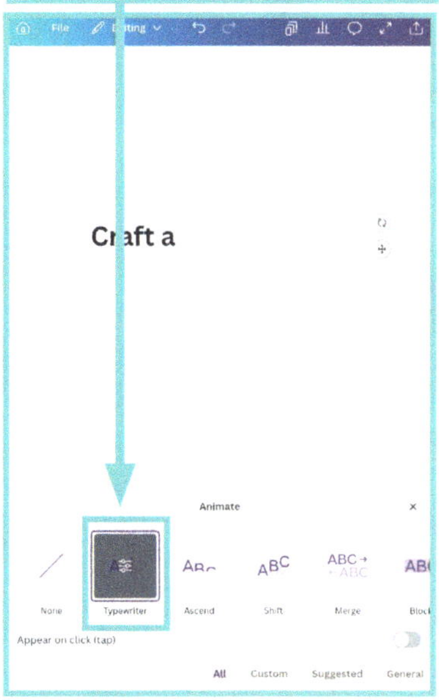

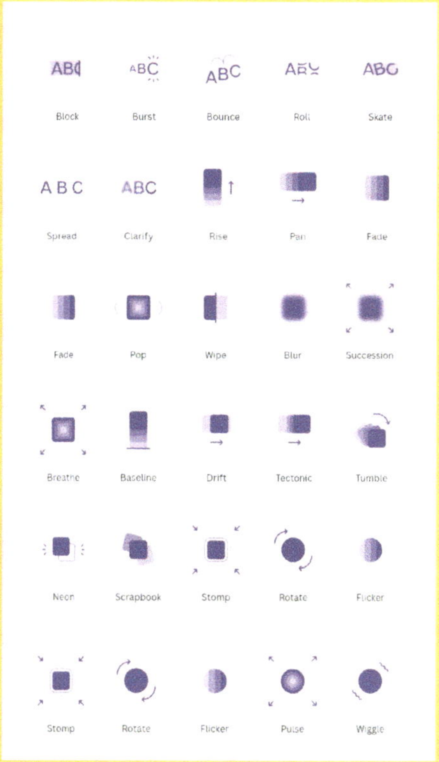

Step 3: Tap on the animation again to change its settings.

NOTE: You can create your own animation by tapping on **Custom**.

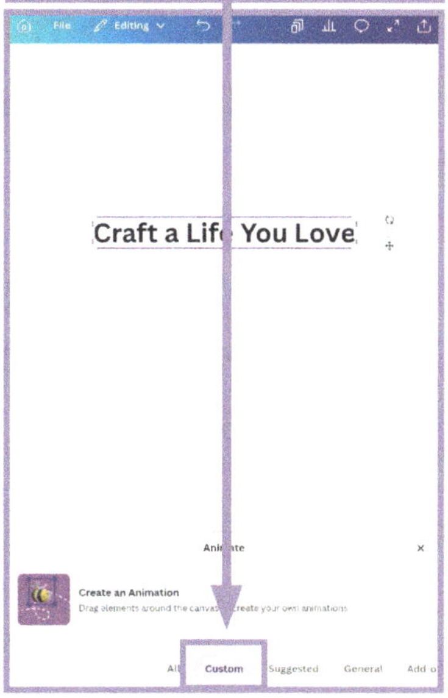

TIP: There are lots of animations to choose from. Browse through the categories to get a feel for them and which you like best for your project.

WARNING: Some animation settings are marked with a crown icon and require a Canva Pro subscription.

NOTE: Animations won't appear in static file formats like PNG or PDF; choose MP4 or GIF when exporting.

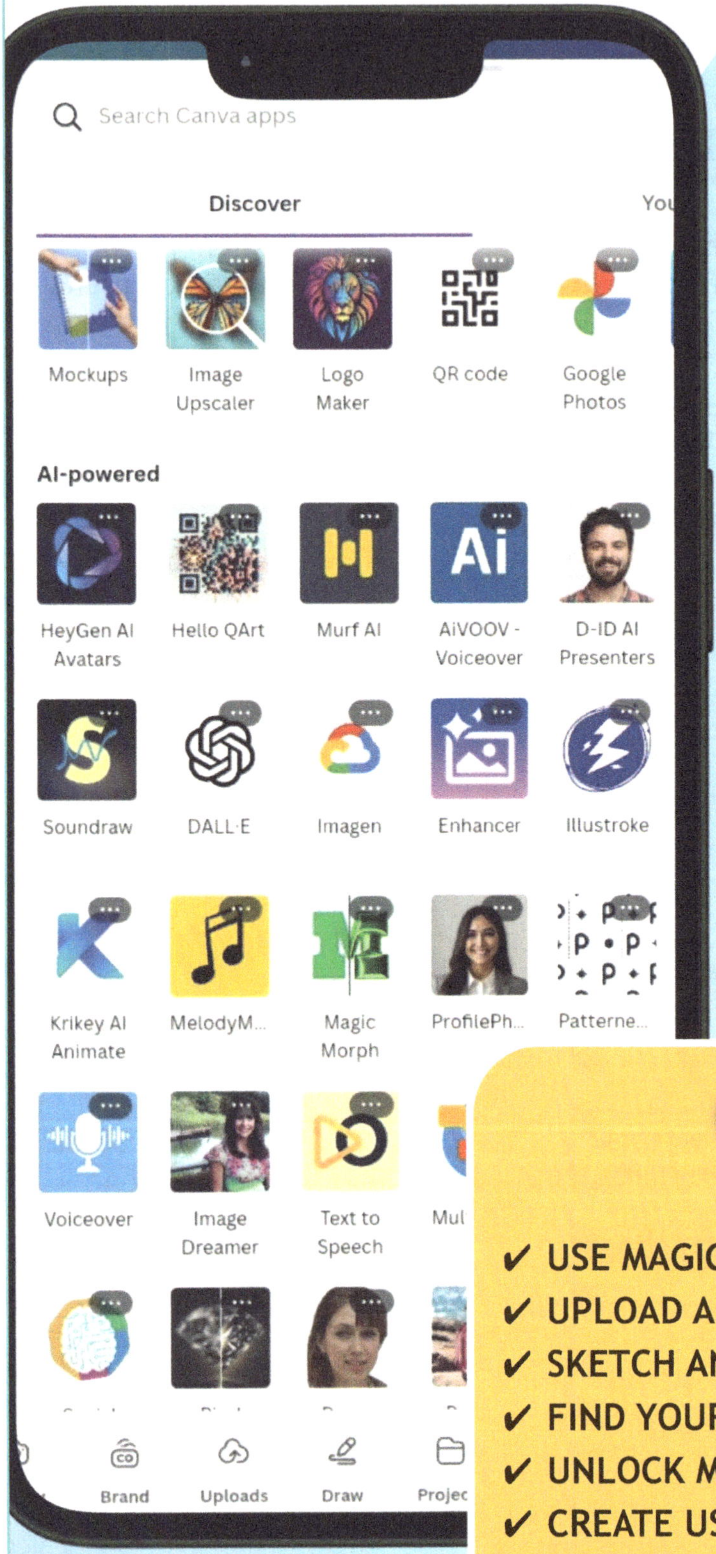

HOW TO:

MOBILE: ADVANCED CANVA FEATURES

- ✔ USE MAGIC WRITE™ TO GENERATE TEXT FOR YOU
- ✔ UPLOAD AND ORGANIZE YOUR FILES
- ✔ SKETCH AND DRAW DIRECTLY IN CANVA
- ✔ FIND YOUR SAVED PROJECTS
- ✔ UNLOCK MORE FEATURES WITH APPS
- ✔ CREATE USING CANVA AI
- ✔ CREATE AI-GENERATED IMAGES WITH MAGIC MEDIA™

MOBILE

HOW TO USE MAGIC WRITE™ TO GENERATE TEXT FOR YOU

Magic Write™ is Canva's AI-powered text generator, designed to help you brainstorm, create, and polish written content with ease. Whether you need captions or outlines, Magic Write™ saves time and boosts creativity.

Step 1: From the Canva homepage, tap on Doc.

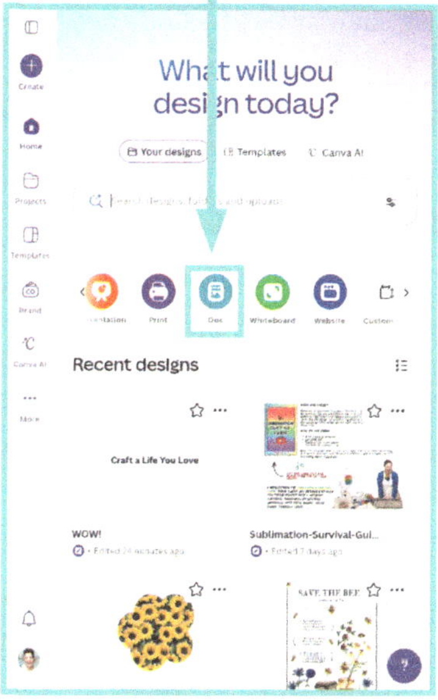

Step 2: Tap the sparkly pencil icon.

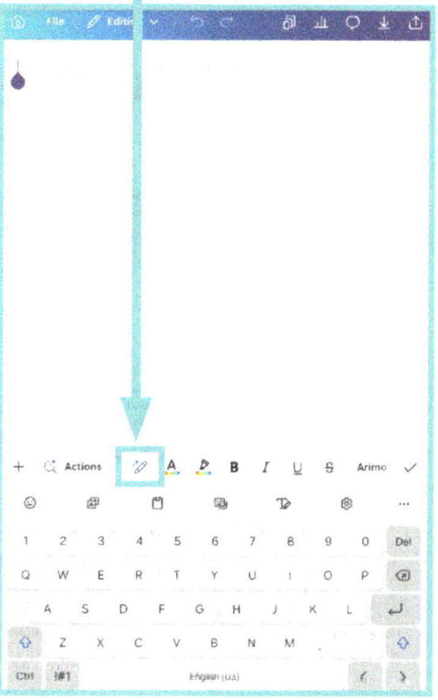

Suggestions will appear to spark new ideas.

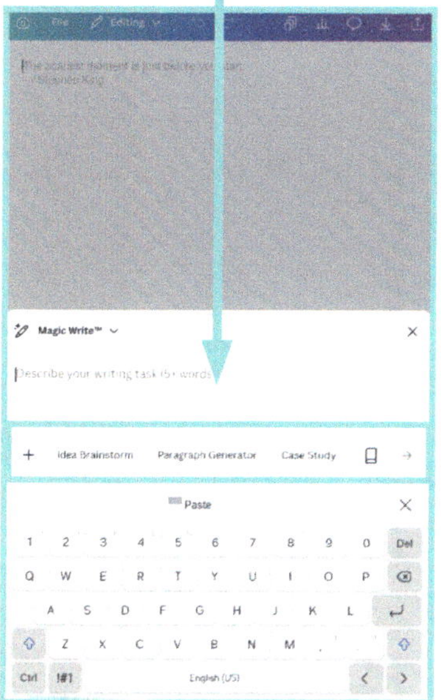

Step 3: Enter a clear and specific prompt.

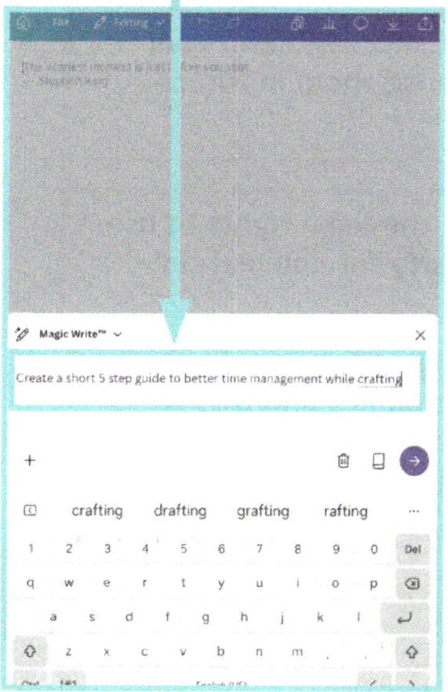

Step 4: Review and Edit - Magic Write™ will create content based on your prompt. Edit the results to align them with your voice or objectives. If you approve, click Insert to add it to your doc.

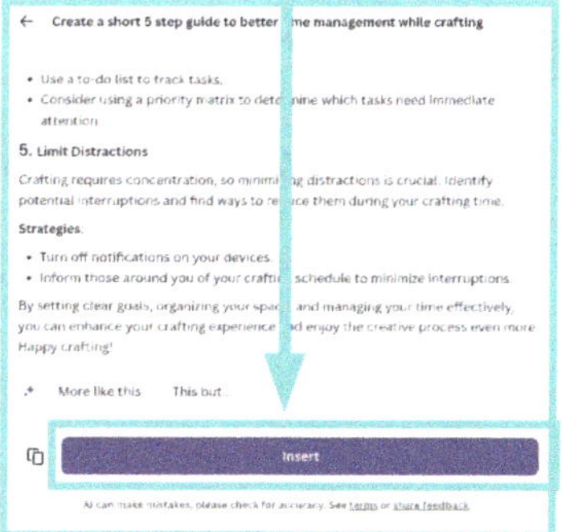

Step 5: Edit your text settings as needed.

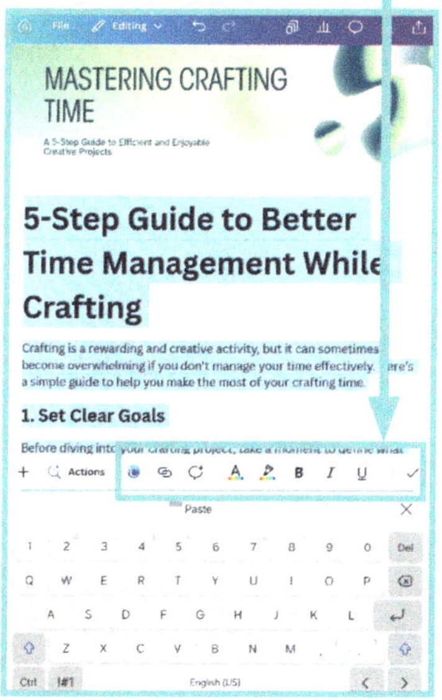

MOBILE

HOW TO UPLOAD AND ORGANIZE YOUR FILES

The Uploads tab in Canva allows you to add custom images, videos, audio, or other media to your designs, helping you personalize projects or incorporate external assets seamlessly.

Step 1: Tap **Uploads** from the lower menu.

Step 2: Tap on the purple **Upload Files** icon.

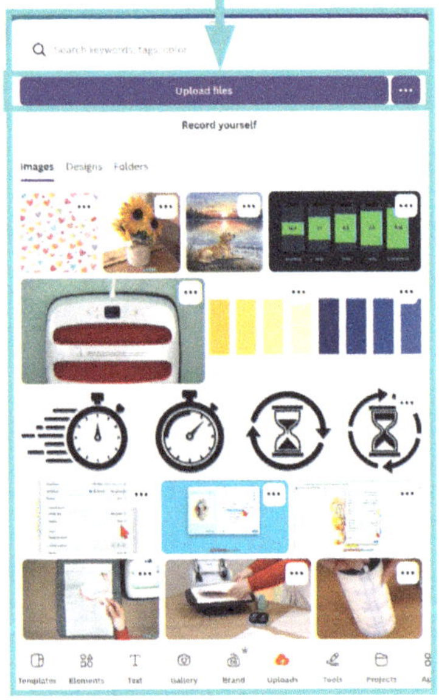

Step 3: Choose where you'd like to upload from.

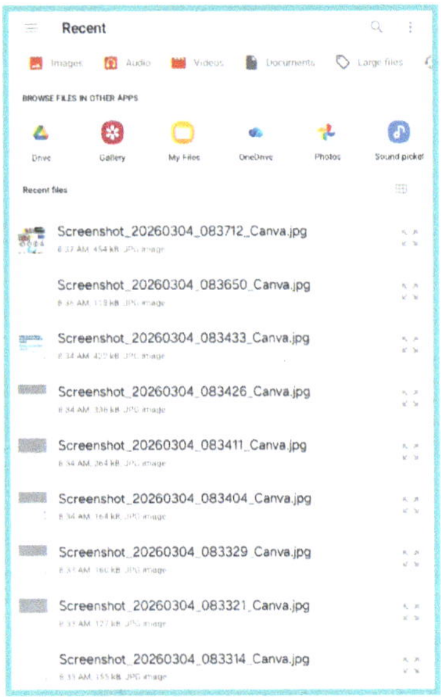

Step 4: Your image will appear on your canvas!

NOTE: Uploaded files remain accessible in your Canva library, so you can reuse them in future projects.

WARNING: Ensure you have the legal rights to use uploaded content, particularly for commercial projects.

TIP: Add relevant image file names and tags to your images so you can easily find them when searching for them in the future.

HOW TO SKETCH AND DRAW DIRECTLY IN CANVA

The Tools tab in Canva allows you to create custom freehand drawings directly on your design. It's a great tool for adding personal touches, sketches, or creative elements to any project.

Step 1: Tap Tools from the lower menu.

Step 2: Tap on the red marker.

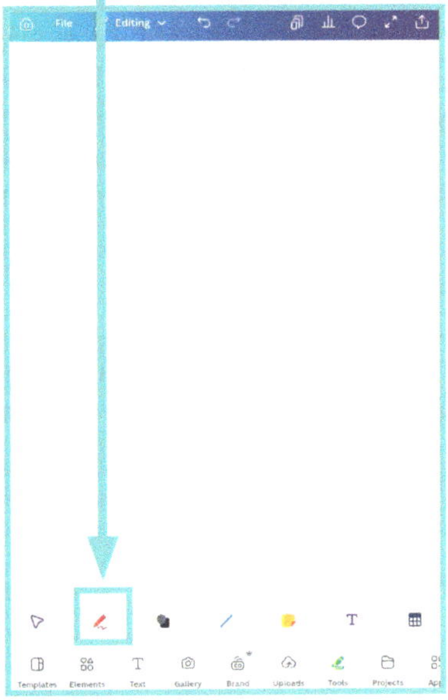

Step 3: Tap the brush you want to use.

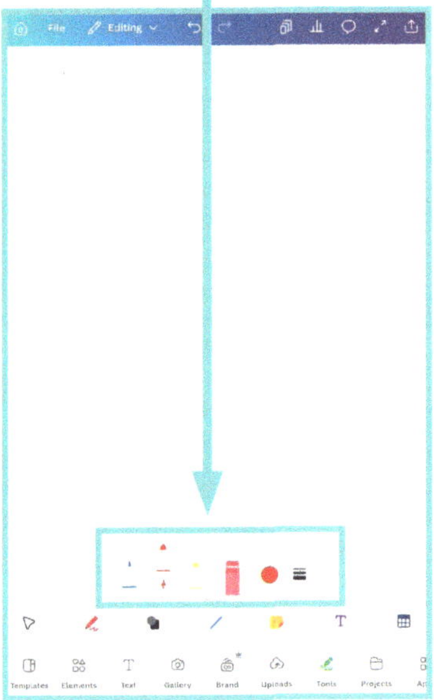

Step 4: Tap the red circle to choose a color.

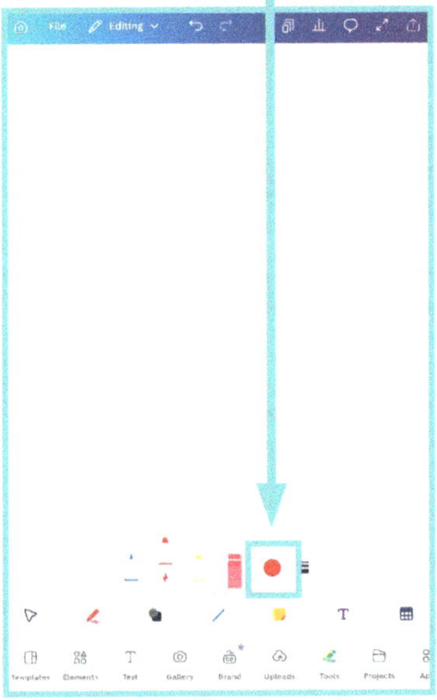

Step 5: Use your finger or stylus to draw.

Tip: Move individual strokes around if you need to by clicking on them.

WARNING: Freehand drawings cannot be edited like vector shapes, so undo any mistakes immediately or use the eraser to correct them.

MOBILE

HOW TO FIND YOUR SAVED PROJECTS

The Projects tab is where all your saved content is stored, including designs, folders, images, and videos. It provides easy access to organize and reuse your work efficiently.

Step 1: Tap **Projects** from the lower menu.

Step 2: The **All** section shows every file stored in your Projects tab, including designs, uploads, and folders, in one centralized view. Use the **Search Bar** to quickly find a specific design by name.

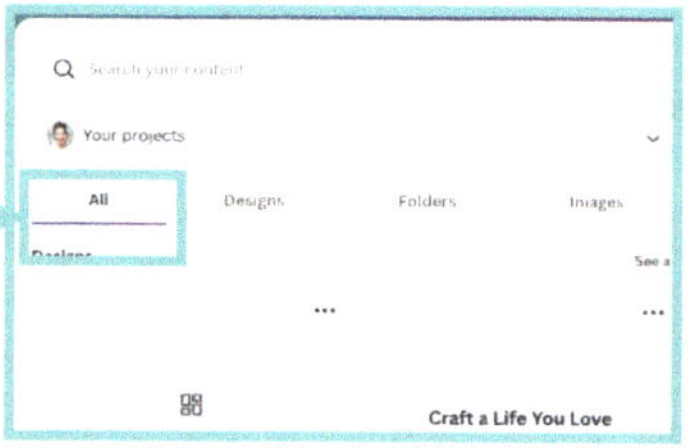

Step 3: The **Designs** section lists all the Canva designs you've created or saved.

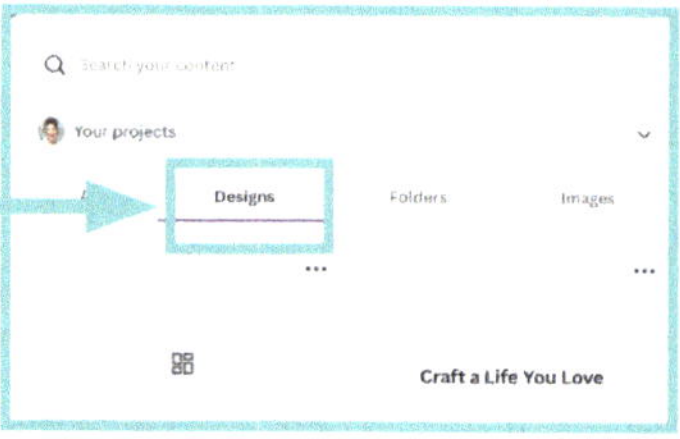

Step 4: The **Folders** section lets you organize your designs and files into labeled groups for better management. To create a new folder: Tap the **+ Create Folder** button. Enter a folder name and tap **Continue**.

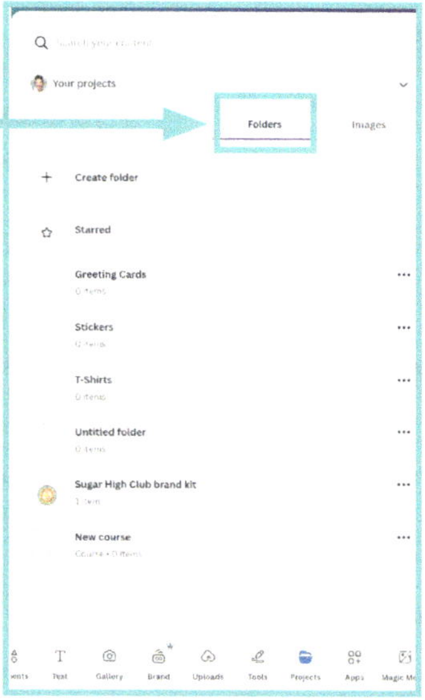

Step 5: The **Images** section displays all the photos or graphics you've uploaded to Canva.

MOBILE

HOW TO UNLOCK MORE FEATURES WITH APPS

The Apps tab in Canva lets you integrate third-party tools, access stock media, and unlock creative features like AI-powered tools or dynamic content. It's a hub for extending Canva's capabilities and streamlining your workflow.

Step 1: Tap on the Apps tab in the menu at the bottom of the screen.

Step 2: A new menu will appear. Scroll down until you see all the apps Canva has to offer.

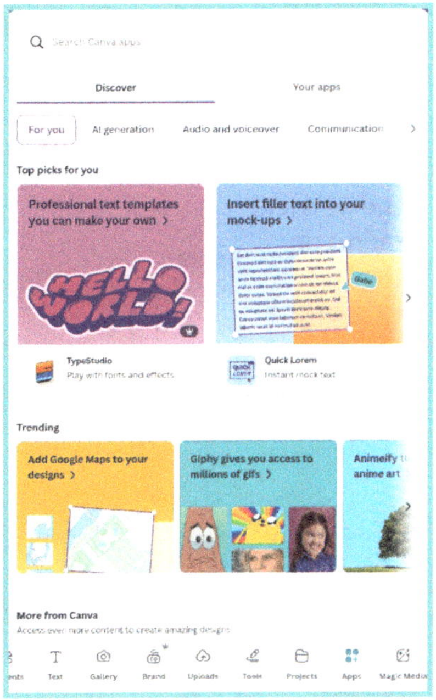

Step 3: Tap on the app of your choice.

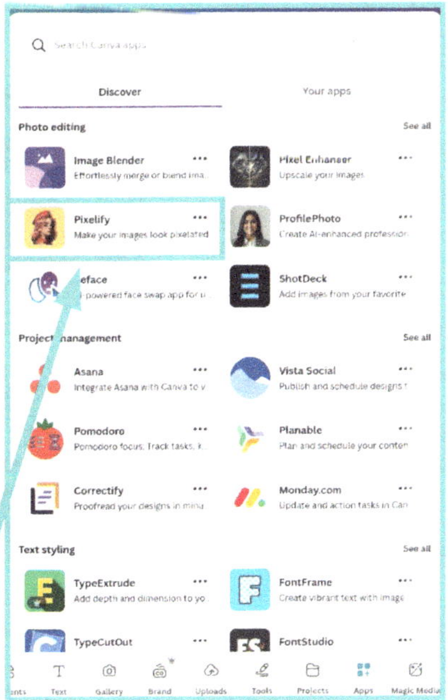

Step 4: Tap Open to open the app and start using it.

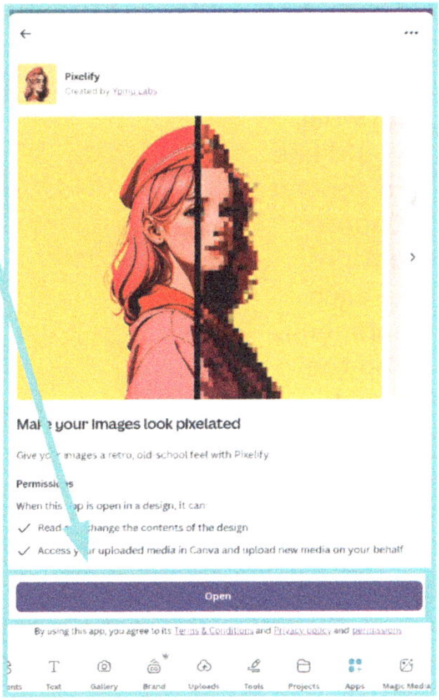

MOBILE

HOW TO CREATE USING CANVA AI

Canva AI is a great tool to use when you aren't quite sure what the idea in your head should look like, as well as create multiple options of a design for you to choose from.

Step 1: Tap on **Canva AI** above the search bar or tap on the **Canva AI** icon in the vertical menu on the left side of the screen.

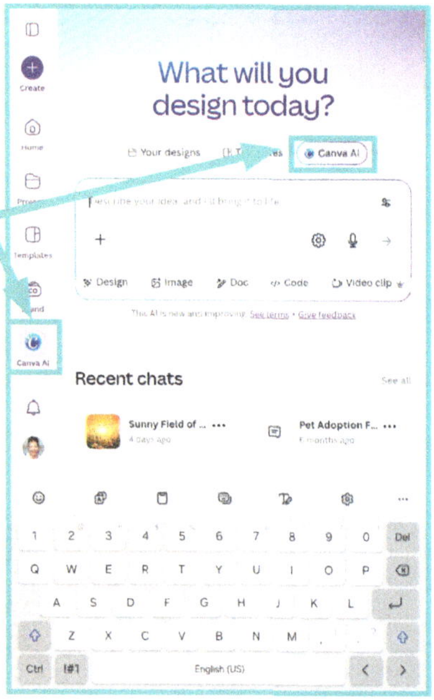

Step 2: Type what you'd like to create into the search bar. Don't tap the arrow icon yet.

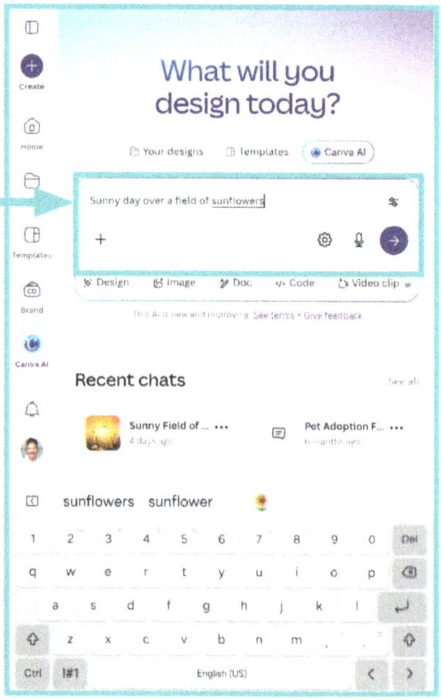

Step 3: Tap **Design**, **Image**, **Doc**, **Code**, or **Video Clip**, depending on what you'd like to generate. Choose options in each submenu. Tap the purple arrow button.

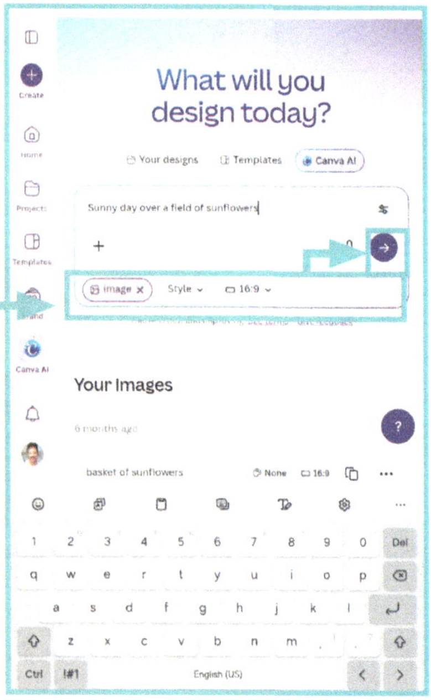

Step 4: Canva AI will generate four options for your design. You can further refine your design by typing desired changes into the **search bar**, or you can edit one by tapping "Edit."

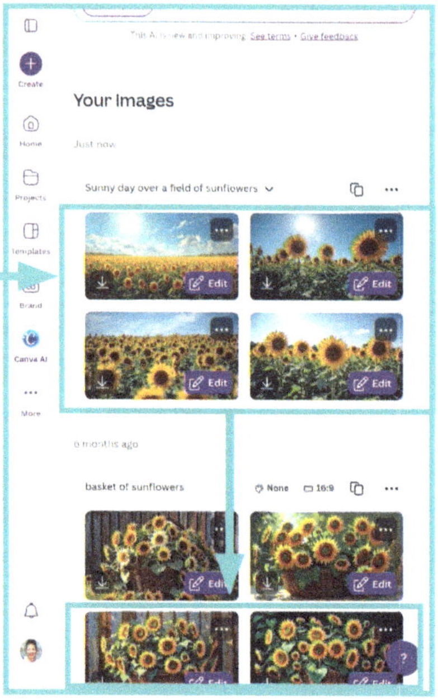

NOTE: There are the submenu options for each of the AI design choices.

MOBILE

HOW TO CREATE AI-GENERATED IMAGES WITH MAGIC MEDIA™

The Magic Media™ tab in Canva is an AI-powered tool that helps you discover or generate unique visuals for your designs. It's perfect for finding stock media or creating custom images based on text prompts, saving time and boosting creativity.

Step 1: Tap **Apps** from the lower menu.

Step 2: Search for and tap **Magic Media** to open the tool.

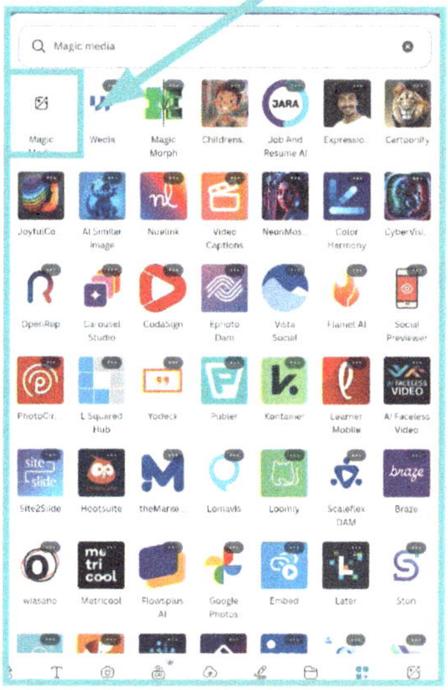

Step 3: **Enter keywords** in the search bar to find stock media like images, videos, or animations. Example: **Type** "Background of multicolored hearts." Tap **Generate images**.

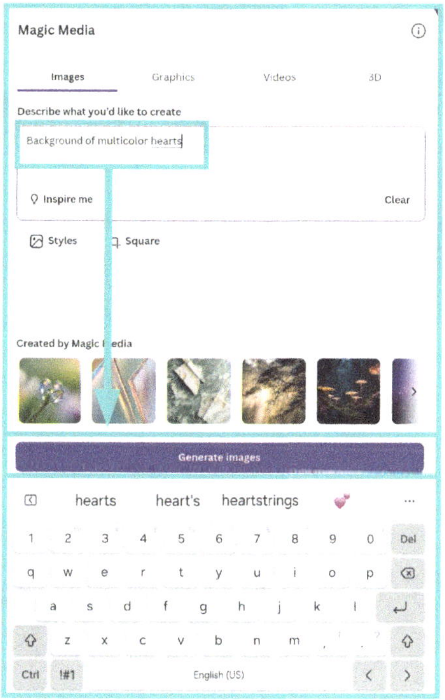

Step 4: Tap on the **stock photo** you want to use.

Step 5: Your photo is now added to your Canvas!

NOTES:

- Play around to get a feel of all the amazing capabilities that Magic Media has to offer.
- Some stock content may have usage limitations for commercial projects; review the licensing terms.

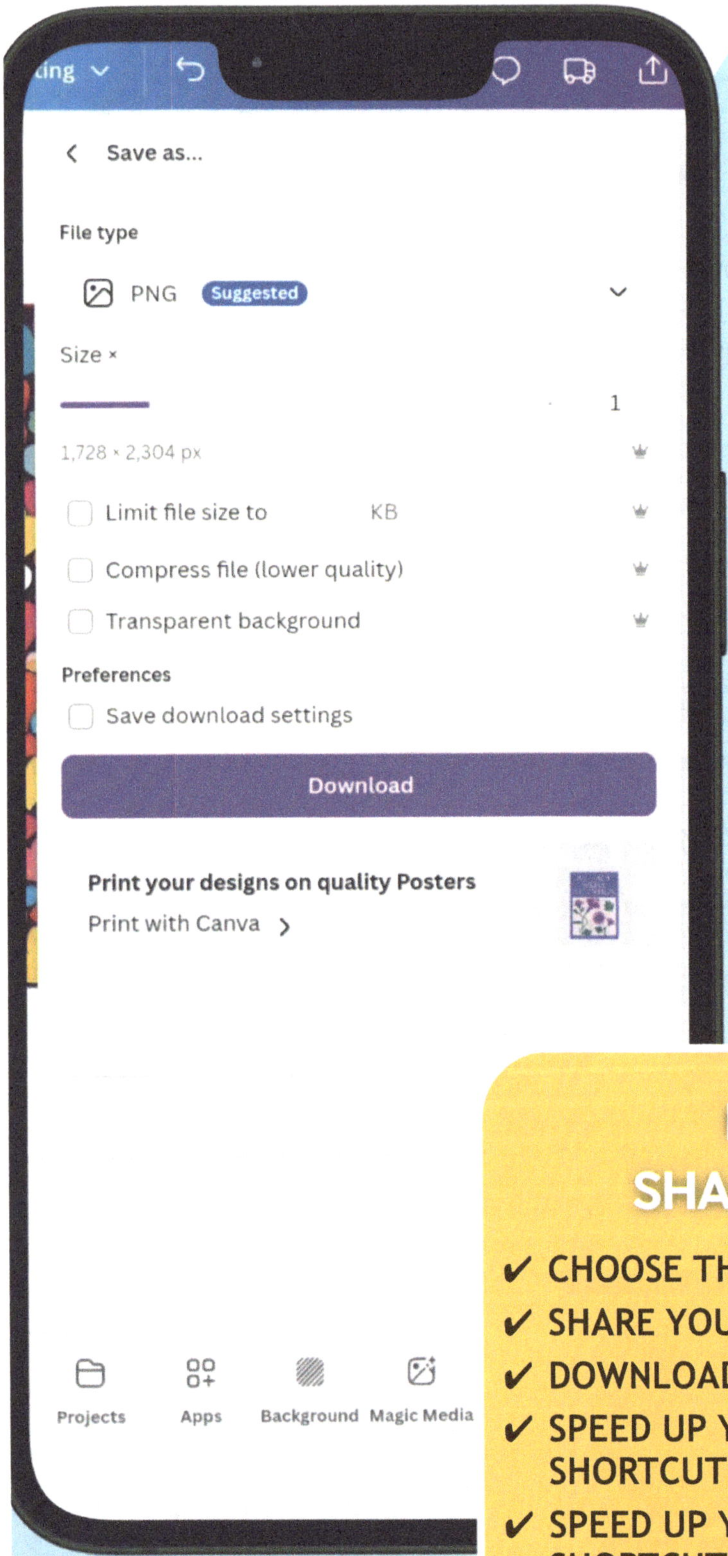

HOW TO:

MOBILE: EXPORTING, SHARING, AND SAVING TIME

- ✔ CHOOSE THE BEST FILE TYPE FOR YOUR DESIGN
- ✔ SHARE YOUR PROJECT WITH OTHERS
- ✔ DOWNLOAD YOUR PROJECT IN THE BEST FORMAT
- ✔ SPEED UP YOUR WORKFLOW WITH KEYBOARD SHORTCUTS FOR MAC
- ✔ SPEED UP YOUR WORKFLOW WITH KEYBOARD SHORTCUTS FOR WINDOWS

HOW TO CHOOSE THE BEST FILE TYPE FOR YOUR DESIGN

Choosing the right file type in Canva is essential for ensuring your design looks its best, whether for digital use, printing, or sharing. Each file type has unique qualities suited to different purposes.

PNG (Portable Network Graphics)
Best For: High-quality images and designs with transparency.
Key Features:
- Retains sharp details.
- Supports transparent backgrounds.

SVG (Scalable Vector Graphics)
Best For: Vector-based designs that need to scale without losing quality.
Key Features:
- Ideal for web and digital applications.
- Fully editable in vector design.

PDF (Portable Document Format)
PDF (Standard):
Best For: Lightweight, shareable documents.
Key Features: Optimized for on-screen viewing.
PDF (Print):
Best For: High-resolution designs for professional printing.
Key Features: Includes crop marks and bleed.

WARNING:
- Certain features like resizing and transparent backgrounds (PNG) are exclusive for Canva Pro users.
- Low-resolution settings can result in pixelation when printed; use PDF (Print) for high-quality results.

JPG (JPEG Image)
Best For: Compressed images with smaller file sizes.
Key Features:
- Quick to load.
- No transparency support.

GIF (Graphics Interchange Format)
Best For: Short, looping animations.
Key Features:
- Limited color palette.
- Small file size.

MP4 (Video Format)
Best For: Animated or video-based designs.
Key Features:
- Supports motion and audio.
- High-quality playback.

PPTX (PowerPoint Presentation)
Best For: Presentations created in Canva that you want to edit or present in PowerPoint.
Key Features:
- Compatible with Microsoft PowerPoint.
- Editable after export.

TIPS: For web use, opt for JPG when file size matters, or PNG for high-quality visuals.

MOBILE

HOW TO SHARE YOUR PROJECT WITH OTHERS

Sharing projects in Canva allows you to collaborate with others, present your designs, or share them with clients or team members. You can share as a link, email, or directly via presentation mode.

Step 1: Open the project you want to share and tap the **Share** button in the upper right corner.

Step 2: You can choose to either collaborate with someone by sharing a link, or see all other options for sharing.

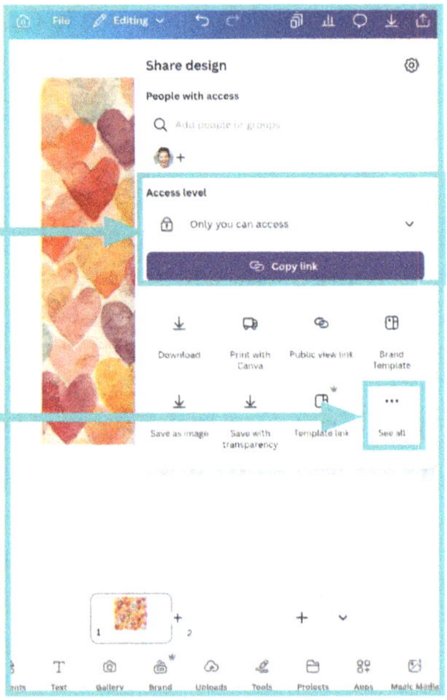

To share via collaboration link, tap on "**Only you can access**" and you will get more options on how you'd like to share the collaboration link.

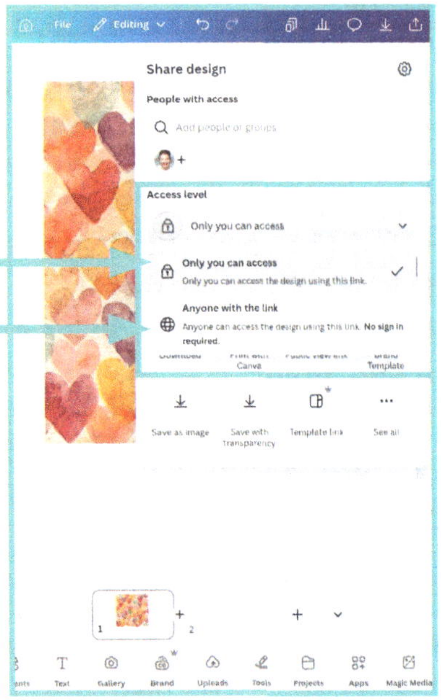

Otherwise, tap **See all** to see all the other sharing options you can choose from.

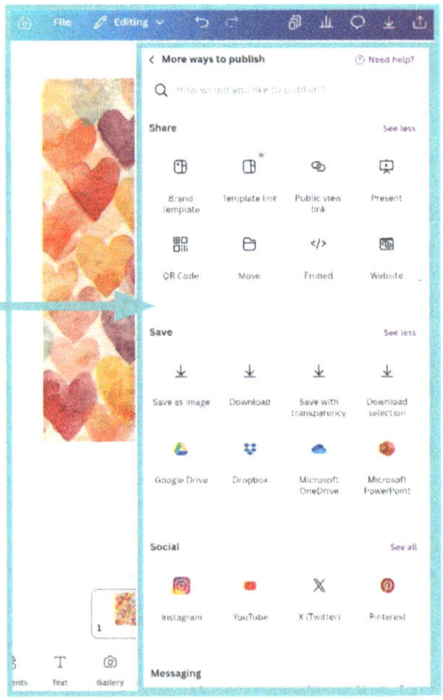

MOBILE

HOW TO DOWNLOAD YOUR PROJECT IN THE BEST FORMAT

Downloading your project in Canva allows you to save it in various formats for digital use, printing, or sharing. Canva offers several file types to match your specific needs, ensuring your design looks professional in any context.

Step 1: From your design Canvas, tap the **Share** button in the top-right corner.

Step 2: Tap **Download**.

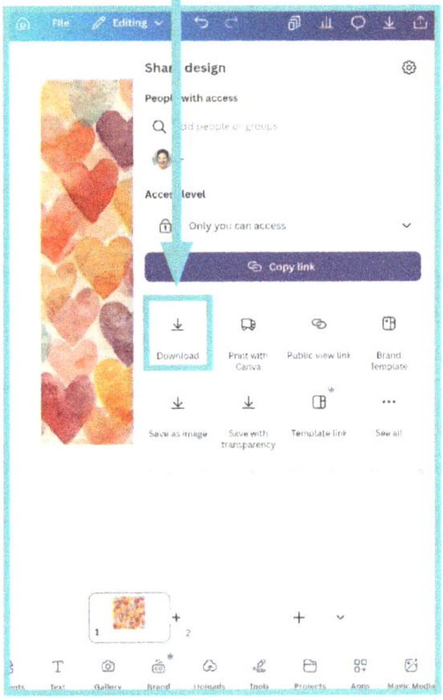

Step 3: Choose a file type such as JPG, PNG, PDF Standard, PDF Print, SVG, MP4 Video, GIF, or PPTX.

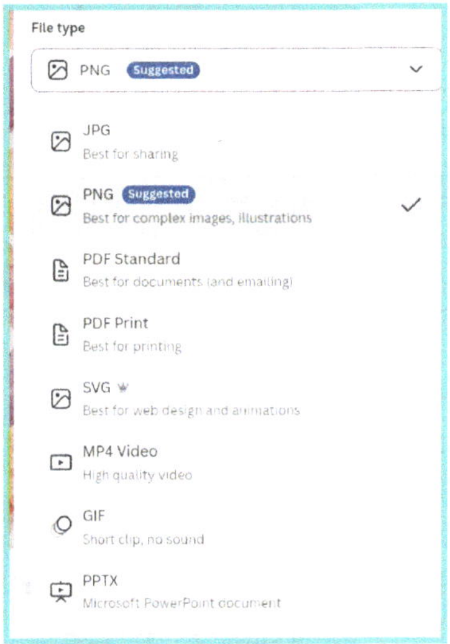

Step 4 (optional): Depending on the selected file type, you can adjust: size, quality, transparency, crop marks, and bleed.

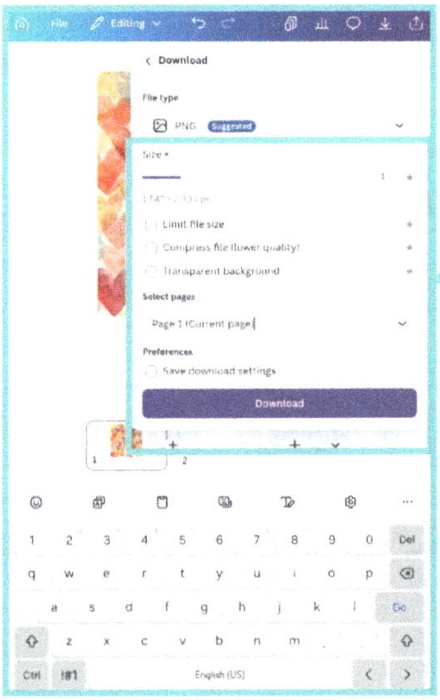

- **Size**: Resize your design dimensions (e.g., for social media or web use).
- **Quality**: Choose higher quality for sharper visuals (especially for PNG and JPG).
- **Transparent Background**: Available for PNG and SVG (Canva Pro required).
- **Crop Marks and Bleed**: Enable for PDF (Print) to prepare designs for professional printing.

Step 5: Once you've chosen your file type and settings, tap **Download** to save the file to your device.

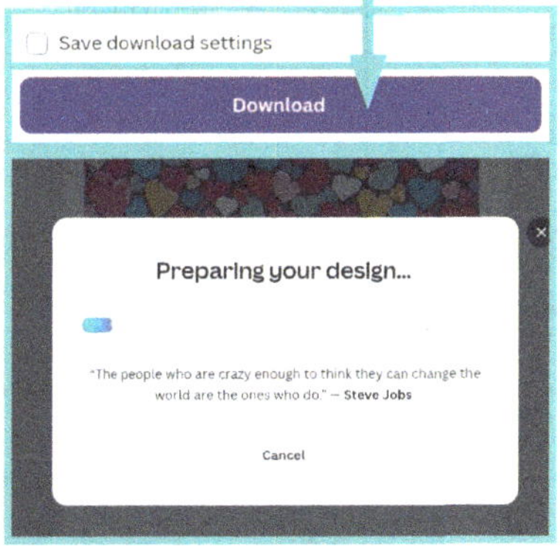

WARNING: You CANNOT print directly from Canva. You must first download your design, then print it from your device.

MOBILE

HOW TO SPEED UP YOUR WORKFLOW WITH KEYBOARD SHORTCUTS FOR MAC

You can do many tasks in Canva easier and faster using keyboard and mouse shortcuts. Here is a list of the most useful keyboard and mouse shortcuts on Mac:

Function	Mac
Undo	Command + Z
Redo	Command + Y
Save	Command + S
Select All	Command + A
Add Text	T
Add Empty Page	Command + RETURN
Delete Empty Page	Command + Delete
Navigate to Toolbar	Command + F1
Quick Actions	/
Delete Selected Elements	Delete
Group Elements	Command + G
Ungroup Elements	Command + Shift + G
Lock Element	Option + Shift + L
Arrange Element Forward	Command +]
Arrange Element Backward	Command + [
Arrange Element to Front	Option + Command +]
Arrange Element to Back	Option + Command + [
Zoom in	Command + +
Zoom Out	Command + -
Zoom to Actual Size	Command + 0
Zoom to Fit	Option + Command + 0
Zoom to Fill	Shift + Command + 0

Function	Mac
Open Font Menu	Shift + Command + F
Find and Replace	Command + F
Bold Text	Command + B
Italicize Text	Command + I
Underline Text	Command + U
Uppercase	Shift + Command + K
Left Align	Shift + Command + L
Center Align	Shift + Command + C
Right Align	Shift + Command + R
Justify Text	Shift + Command + J
Numbered List	Shift + Command + 7
Bulleted List	Shift + Command + 8
Copy Text Style	Option + Command + C
Paste Text Style	Option + Command + V
Play/Pause Video	Space
Mute/Unmute Video	M
Loop Video	Option + Command + L
Scrolling View	Option + Command + 1
Thumbnail View	Option + Command + 2
Grid View	Option + Command + 3
Presentation Mode	Option + Command + P

CANVA COACH PLAYBOOK

MOBILE

HOW TO SPEED UP YOUR WORKFLOW WITH KEYBOARD SHORTCUTS FOR WINDOWS

You can do many tasks in Canva easier and faster using keyboard and mouse shortcuts. Here is a list of the most useful keyboard and mouse shortcuts on Windows:

Function	Windows
Undo	Ctrl + Z
Redo	Ctrl + Y
Save	Ctrl + S
Select All	Ctrl + A
Add Text	T
Add Empty Page	Ctrl + E
Delete Empty Page	Ctrl + Backspace
Navigate to Toolbar	Ctrl + F4
Quick Actions	Ctrl + E
Delete Selected Elements	Backspace OR Delete
Group Elements	Ctrl + G
Ungroup Elements	Ctrl + Shift + G
Lock Element	Alt + Shift + L
Arrange Element Forward	Ctrl +]
Arrange Element Backward	Ctrl + [
Arrange Element to Front	Alt + Ctrl +]
Arrange Element to Back	Alt + Ctrl + [
Zoom in	Ctrl + -
Zoom Out	Alt + Ctrl + 0
Zoom to Actual Size	Ctrl + 0
Zoom to Fit	Alt + Ctrl + 0
Zoom to Fill	Shift + Ctrl + 0

Function	Windows
Open Font Menu	Shift + Ctrl + F
Find and Replace	Ctrl + F
Bold Text	Ctrl + B
Italicize Text	Ctrl + I
Underline Text	Ctrl + U
Uppercase	Shift + Ctrl + K
Left Align	Shift + Ctrl + L
Center Align	Shift + Ctrl + C
Right Align	Shift + Ctrl + R
Justify Text	Shift + Ctrl + J
Numbered List	Shift + Ctrl + 7
Bulleted List	Shift + Ctrl + 8
Copy Text Style	Alt + Ctrl + C
Paste Text Style	Alt + Ctrl + V
Play/Pause Video	Space
Mute/Unmute Video	M
Loop Video	Alt + Ctrl + L
Scrolling View	Alt + Ctrl + 1
Thumbnail View	Alt + Ctrl + 2
Grid View	Alt + Ctrl + 3
Presentation Mode	Alt + Ctrl + P

WANT THE ULTIMATE DESIGN EXPERIENCE?

WITH JENNIFERMAKER

ADVANCE

ADVANCE is a special program for ALL skill levels — I can help you advance from new to beginner or advanced to pro, and everything in between!

Do you love making things, but wish you could put your own unique spin on the design to create memorable, one-of-a-kind results? Are you tired of searching over and over for just the right design that fits your needs and spending all your money on files? Are you frustrated by your results when you try to customize something on your own?

I can help!

Find out more at jennifermaker.com/advance

LEARN HOW TO CREATE CUSTOM AI ART FOR PROJECTS

WITH THE

AI ART PLAYBOOK

Find out more at

makeracademy.com/ai-art-playbook

SUBLIMATION MADE SIMPLE

EVERYTHING YOU NEED TO KNOW ABOUT SUBLIMATION

From what materials you need and what programs you can use to create designs, to how to use "hacks" and solve common issues, everything you need to do in order to create sublimation projects can be found in this book!

Want to create vividly colorful personalized matching tote bags for a family vacation to the beach? Interested in creating colorful ornaments to decorate a Christmas tree? Thinking about making yourself a personalized tumbler decorated with images of your pets? With sublimation, you can!

Find out more at

jennifermaker.com/sublimation-made-simple

MASTER CRICUT DESIGN SPACE

WITH THE

CRICUT COACH PLAYBOOK

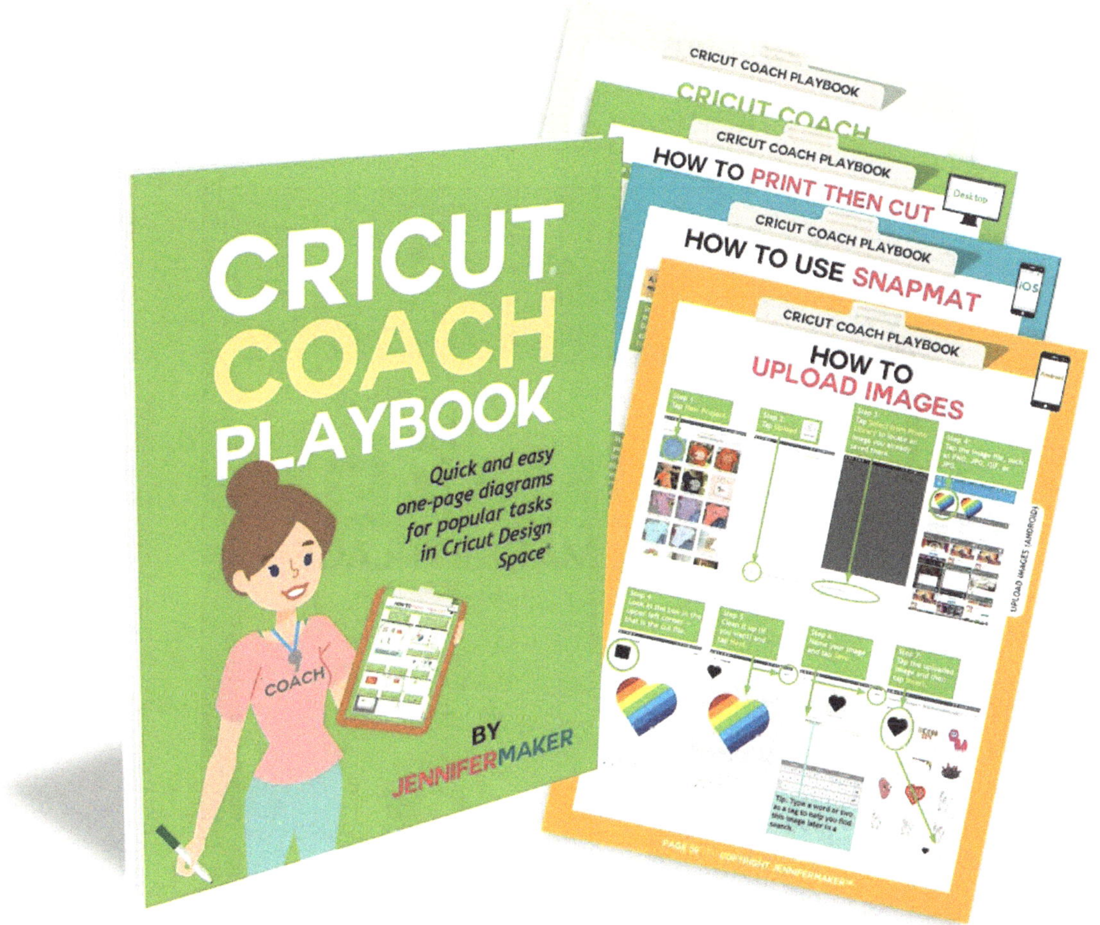

Struggling with your Cricut? Tired of looking up how to do things every time you want to make a project? Mystified by Print then Cut? Never fear, because the Cricut Coach Playbook is here! This Playbook contains 130+ full-color pages with easy step-by-step instructions for all the popular tasks you can do in Cricut Design Space.

Find out more at

jennifermaker.com/cricutcoach

BUILD A SOLID BUSINESS PLAN WITH THE MAKER MARKETPLACE

Have you heard people say, *"Wow! You could sell this!"* when they look at your crafts? Have you ever thought about selling your handiwork?

Have you been daunted by the prospect of what it takes to start a successful business selling your crafts?

It's no quick and easy task, but I'm here to help!

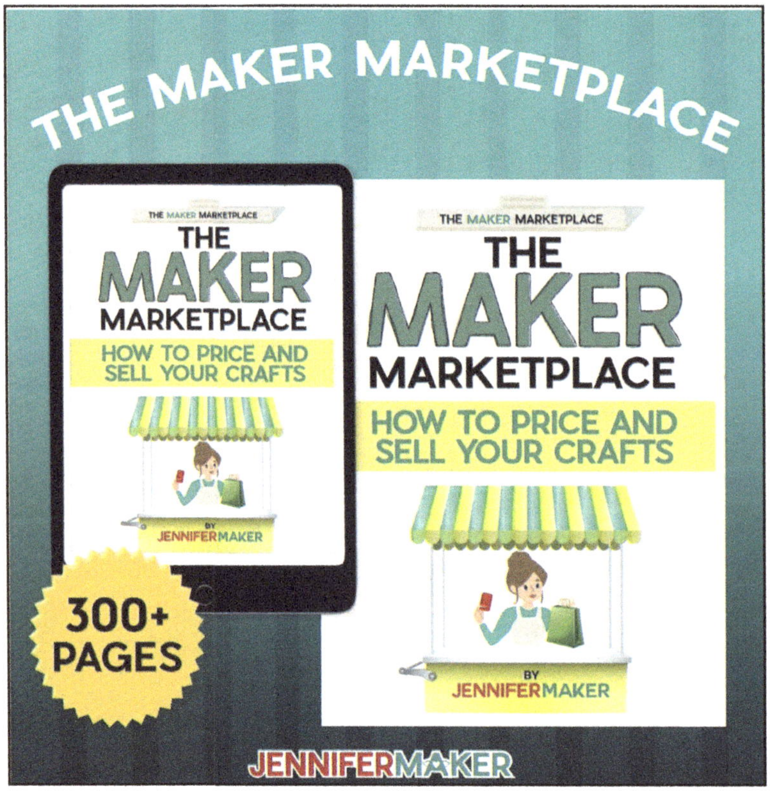

The Maker Marketplace handbook explores the many aspects of starting and running a handmade crafts business, **from the very beginning thoughts about why you'd like to start a business to evaluating your existing business.**

Find out more at jennifermaker.com/the-maker-marketplace

CRAFT A LIFE YOU LOVE

Visit me at jennifermaker.com regularly for inspiration, help, and projects!

Made in United States
Orlando, FL
04 November 2026

90202252R00085